ambridge
novation
pital

DEFINING THE FUTURE | GREATER CAMBRIDGE
GREATER PETERBOROUGH
ENTERPRISE PARTNERSHIP

MISSION
Therapeutics

PARKW
investing in in

ERSITY OF
BRIDGE
usiness School

GROSVENOR

Johnson&Johnson
INNOVATION

MONEY
MOVER

pwc

SYNDICATE
ROOM
Intelligent Equity Crowdfunding

ambridge
twork

horizon

Kleinwort Benson

Qatalyst
PARTNERS

ST JOHN'S INNOVATION CENTRE

CAMBRIDGE
WIRELESS

illumina®

kymab

mundi pharma

QUALCOMM®
QUALCOMM
TECHNOLOGIES
INTERNATIONAL, LTD.

TaylorWessing

NTAB
AL PARTNERS

Innovation
FORUM

Marshall

OAK
INVESTMENT
PARTNERS

REAL
VNC

ttpgroup

GENICA
SED MEDICINE

ipgroup

MedImmune
A member of the AstraZeneca Group

PA
CONSULTING
TECHNOLOGY
INNOVATION

Schlumberger

TWI

MINO

MILLS & REEVE

SQW

Virata

The Cambridge
PHENOMENON
GLOBAL IMPACT

The Cambridge
PHENOMENON
GLOBAL IMPACT

PREFACE BY DAVID SAINSBURY
FOREWORD BY MARTIN REES

KATE KIRK AND CHARLES COTTON

Third Millennium
Publishing

Right: *Kenneth Martin's sculpture* Construction in Aluminium, *which stands outside the Department of Engineering at Cambridge University.*

First published in Great Britain in 2016 by
Third Millennium Publishing, an imprint of Profile Books Ltd

3 Holford Yard
Bevin Way
London WC1X 9HD
United Kingdom
www.tmiltd.com

A CIP catalogue record for this book is available from The British Library.

ISBN: 978 1 908990 61 7

Writing and Editing: Kate Kirk
Design: Susan Pugsley and Matt Wilson
Picture research: Patrick Taylor and Neil Burkey
Production: Simon Shelmerdine

Reprographics by Studio Fasoli, Verona, Italy
Printed and bound by Gorenjski Tisk Storitve, Slovenia
on acid-free paper from sustainable forestry

CONTENTS

The Sainsbury Laboratory, a plant science research institute funded by the Gatsby Foundation, was opened in 2011.

PREFACE

When I was an undergraduate at Cambridge in the early 1960s, knowledge transfer was not seen as a major role of the University. But in the 55 years since then, the situation has been transformed by a group of outstanding entrepreneurs who have commercialized scientific and technological breakthroughs, founded and built companies, and developed the institutions and networks which are an essential feature of a growing and dynamic cluster.

As a result there are today 4,300 knowledge-intensive firms in the Cambridge cluster with a turnover of over £11 billion, and the University innovation ecosystem is rated the third most successful in the world, with only Stanford and MIT rated higher.

The growth of the Cambridge cluster is important because it demonstrates the key role that universities need to play in today's knowledge economy, the contribution that technology can make to improving the quality of people's lives and solving global problems, and the need for universities, government

and entrepreneurs to work together as part of what has been described as a 'triple helix'.

It is important that this story is told and celebrated for three reasons. Firstly, so it inspires more young people to acquire scientific and technological skills and become entrepreneurs. Secondly, to show how UK companies can compete in the global 'Race to the Top' against low-wage countries such as China by innovating and upgrading their products and services. And, thirdly, to make the case that governments need to support such clusters by funding basic research, by supporting the intermediate bodies which play a key role in translating scientific and technological breakthroughs into new products and services, and by providing the physical infrastructure for growing cities and regions.

The last 50 years have been an exciting time for the Cambridge cluster, and this book celebrates what it has achieved, and sets the stage for an even more exciting future.

David Sainsbury

Baron Sainsbury of Turville, FRS, HonFREng. is the Chancellor of the University of Cambridge and was formerly Minister of Science and Innovation in the UK Government, between 1998 and 2006.

Earth as seen from the International Space Station.

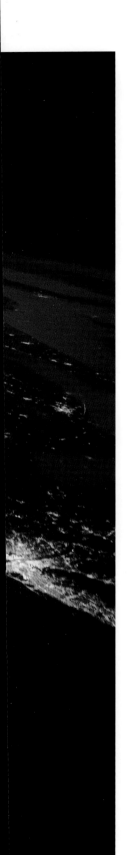

FOREWORD

In a world that is seeing dramatic changes every decade – if not every year – driven by advances in technology, it is quite remarkable to see how much of that life-changing technology originated in Cambridge. The spin-offs from discoveries and developments such as the structure of DNA, the isolation and humanization of monoclonal antibodies, and the design of low power, high efficiency computer chips, are profound not only for our generation, but for the generations to come.

These are just three areas where Cambridge technology has played a pivotal role – there are plenty more, including a long tradition of advances in telecommunications, going back over 100 years, and computer aided design, going back 50 years. My own field, astronomy, has been invigorated by the theories of Stephen Hawking, Fred Hoyle and many others based in Cambridge. Testing theorists' insights has needed novel instruments, like the radio interferometers that gained Martin Ryle a Nobel Prize, and led to the discovery of pulsars and cosmic evolution. And in other fields of science, the world is being changed by ideas that germinate in this small patch of Fenland – where there's a very special symbiosis between academia and industry.

I find it specially heartening that Cambridge's high-tech companies are not only benefiting those of us fortunate to live in advanced economies, but are also enhancing the lives of people living under challenging conditions around the world. The amazing progress in consumer electronics allows us to access information, to communicate, and to entertain ourselves – but it also enables farmers in remote areas to capture information about the impact of rainfall and soil conditions, gain access to wider markets and secure better prices for their crops. The same advances can bring better education and medical care to remote and impoverished places, and help in the fight to preserve important ecosystems and reduce poaching of endangered species.

What accounts for Cambridge's global impact – so disproportionately large for a small city? Its university has a record of scientific excellence stretching back to Isaac Newton – but never stronger and more diverse than it is today. So Cambridge is a magnet for the brightest minds from around the world. But more than that, there is a tradition of risk-taking – of entrepreneurship – nurtured in an atmosphere that is both competitive and also supportive. Indeed it is arguable that even the University's origin – when, in 1209, a few disaffected scholars from Oxford ventured to pastures new – manifested an entrepreneurial spirit.

The UK as a whole punches above its weight scientifically. Cambridge is home to one of the world's leading research universities. Its internationally renowned technology cluster leverages this scientific excellence into innovative 'high-value-added' products and services – the kind of activity crucial to this nation's economic success. With more than 4,300 knowledge-intensive companies, within 20 miles of Cambridge, 15 valued at over a billion dollars, and two at over 10 billion dollars, there is a virtuous circle encouraging the innovative to have a go and see what they can create.

No one has previously tried to describe the extent of Cambridge's contribution to global technological advancement, and perhaps a definitive list is an impossible task. The authors of this book, Kate Kirk and Charles Cotton, freely admit that they haven't captured everything. But in attempting to show the breadth and depth of Cambridge's impact on the world, they give us a snapshot of a unique technology cluster, embedded in a city where confidence and high morale drive creativity, innovation and risk-taking, whether in science, the arts, or entrepreneurial activity.

Martin Rees

Baron Rees of Ludlow, OM, FRS, FMedSci is the Astronomer Royal, and was formerly Master of Trinity College, Cambridge between 2004 and 2012, and President of the Royal Society between 2005 and 2010.

WE ARE GRATEFUL TO THE FOLLOWING FOR THEIR SUPPORT:

Professor Sir Leszek Borysiewicz
Lord Alec Broers
Sir Michael Marshall
Hermann Hauser KBE

ADVISORY BOARD

Chris Abell
Lily Bacon
Nigel Bond
Matthew Bullock
Chris Chapman
Charles Cotton
David Cleevely
Darrin Disley
Robert Driver
Warren East
Harriet Fear
David Gill
Hermann Hauser
Soraya Jones
Peter Keen
Kate Kirk
Christoph Loch
Chris Lowe
Robert Marshall
Ian Mather
Patrick McMahon
Tim Minshall
Jane Osbourn
Hugh Parnell
Jane Paterson-Todd
Hans Pung
Tony Raven
Andy Richards
Alan Richardson
Claire Ruskin
Peter Taylor
Shailendra Vyakarnam
Christoph Wiesner

Right: *Rooftops of Cambridge from Great St. Mary's, the University Church.*

A lecture theatre at the Cambridge Judge Business School.

INTRODUCTION: CAMBRIDGE IDEAS CHANGE THE WORLD

Bill Gates, in his Foreword to our earlier book, *The Cambridge Phenomenon: 50 Years of Innovation and Enterprise*, pointed to the fact that the impact of Cambridge 'reaches every corner of the globe'. In the Foreword to this book, Martin Rees comments that 'in a world that is seeing dramatic changes every decade – if not every year – driven by technology, it is quite remarkable to see how much of that life-changing technology originated in Cambridge'.

Until now, no one has tried to describe just how much 'life-changing technology' has emerged from this small but remarkable city. The Cambridge Phenomenon, a thriving technology cluster, is made up of approximately 4,300 knowledge-intensive businesses, the University of Cambridge, one of the world's leading research universities, and a number

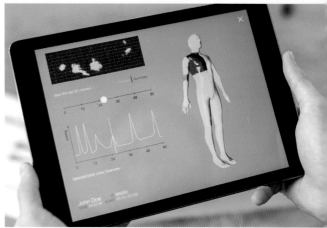

of specialized research institutions. The businesses alone employ some 58,000 people between them, and have a combined annual turnover of £11 billion. Over 90 Nobel Prize winners have done their pioneering research in Cambridge, and more than 30 of the world's largest and most important corporations have established operations in Cambridge to tap into this exciting and innovative ecosystem.

A number of books and studies have examined other aspects of the Cambridge Phenomenon, just as we did with our previous book charting the history of its growth, but no one has commented on what it means to the world. Yet the more we explored how Cambridge technologies are used every day around the planet, the more we found to surprise us.

From safety communications deep under the ground at the Large Hadron Collider to reducing traffic congestion in Moscow, from improving the survival chances for babies in Northern India to the most important new medical therapies, and from the way we purchase items using mobile phones

to the inner workings of the world's largest stock exchanges, Cambridge technologies are indeed global. And sometimes out of this world, too, with the Iridium satellite network and a pair of Raspberry Pi computers on the International Space Station being just two ways that innovations from the Cambridge Phenomenon have left the planet.

But how can the companies and organizations of the Cambridge Phenomenon be having a global impact when so few – if any – are household names? The simple answer is that most of them are focused on developing the technologies and innovations that help others to succeed, so while the technology is having an impact, those behind it remain obscure. A more complex answer hints at the impact of individuals, the entrepreneurs and innovators who have helped not only the Cambridge Phenomenon but also other technology clusters to succeed and grow. On top of that, we can say the impact extends to how Cambridge has attracted a roster of international companies that have come to the city

to grow their businesses, whether through acquiring companies, setting up research and development facilities, recruiting the best and the brightest as employees, or even to set up a global HQ.

Ultimately, we have to admit that impact is a multi-dimensional concept, and while it is easy to measure under some sets of criteria, it is much harder to quantify under others. Sometimes, the diverse nature of impact means simply that 'we know it when we see it', and we have certainly seen a lot of it as we have examined the Cambridge Phenomenon through this new lens.

From the bestselling drug in the world to the chips in the smartphone in your pocket, Cambridge is the origin of numerous examples of game-changing, disruptive technologies. In this book, we attempt to chart the impact of those

technologies across a number of different sectors, including life sciences and healthcare, computing, telecommunications and inkjet printing. We also look at the role the unique sub-cluster of technology consultancies has played, and highlight some of the research institutes that have grown up around Cambridge and make important contributions towards driving innovation.

Finally, we stick our necks out and highlight some companies, technologies and sectors that we believe have the potential to make a global impact in the future. Hostages to fortune, perhaps, but where there is potential there is possibility – and given the Cambridge Phenomenon's track record, possibility is a pretty good place to start.

"

So much of what comes out of Cambridge is hidden – the chips in your phone, the software that allows you to operate remotely, the technology behind the biggest-selling drug in the world – for anyone interested in entrepreneurship, it is crucial to understand the role of the Cambridge cluster in the global arena.

Frank Bonsal, co-founder of New Enterprise Associates and Red Abbey Venture Partners

LIFE SCIENCES AND HEALTHCARE

Cambridge companies and scientists have played key roles in some of the most important breakthroughs and innovations in life sciences and healthcare in the 20th and 21st centuries. The discovery of the structure of DNA and the method for sequencing it that underpinned the Human Genome Project (HGP) came from Cambridge. The isolation and subsequent humanization of monoclonal antibodies, now the foundation of more than half the bestselling drugs globally, and the world's first test-tube baby, Louise Brown, also owe their origins to Cambridge technology.

An embryologist extracts human embryonic eggs from amniotic fluid.

DNA Double Helix 1953
"The secret of life"
For decades the Eagle was the local
pub for scientists from the nearby
Cavendish Laboratory.
It was here on February 28th 1953 that
Francis Crick and James Watson first
announced their discovery of how
DNA carries genetic information.
Unveiled by James Watson
25th April 2003

"

I felt slightly queasy when at lunch Francis winged into The Eagle to tell everyone within hearing distance that we had found the secret of life.

James D Watson

Around these breakthroughs has grown a vibrant cluster of biotechnology and life sciences companies recognized worldwide for step-change innovations in drug discovery that save money, reduce the time to approval and produce more effective treatments for patients.

Cambridge was the source of the first pharmaceutical product produced by a UK biotechnology company to be approved in Europe and the US, is home to the company that created the first slow-release morphine tablets, and continues to host a number of companies developing better technologies for drug discovery, development and administration. One of the latest arrivals in the Cambridge life sciences sector is targeting rare and orphan diseases by combining deep analysis of trial data for already approved drugs and the great advances in genomic knowledge of the last decade.

And, since the arrival of Louise Brown in 1978, some five million babies have been born following successful in vitro fertilization.

Left: *James Watson and Francis Crick with the original model of DNA in 1953.*

Below: *The Wellcome Trust Sanger Institute.*

DECIPHERING THE CODE OF LIFE

One of the greatest scientific discoveries of the 20th century was announced in a pub in Cambridge one lunchtime in February 1953.

The Eagle public house was a few yards away from the Cavendish Laboratory, where the discovery of the double-helix structure of deoxyribonucleic acid, better known as DNA, was made. Although James Watson was afraid his colleague Francis Crick was rather premature in claiming that they had 'discovered the secret of life', the two young scientists' proposal would be published in *Nature* two months later and spark a revolution in biology and medicine.

Understanding the structure of DNA meant that answers to questions that researchers around the world had been puzzling about for years were now in reach. How does DNA replicate itself and get handed down from one generation to the next? How does DNA control and regulate the cellular processes responsible for life itself? What role does DNA play in disease? How can we use our knowledge about DNA and how it functions to better understand and treat diseases like cancer?

But first, although the components of DNA were known, the new knowledge about its structure suggested that genes could be 'read' if only the code were understood, and the race was on to find a way to sequence DNA and decipher what the sequence meant.

The Human Genome Project (HGP) was a multi-centre, multi-country project to sequence the entire human genome, and Cambridge's Wellcome Trust Sanger Institute would make the largest single contribution to the Project, using a sequencing technology originally developed by Cambridge scientist and double Nobel Laureate Fred Sanger.

Out of Cambridge University and the Wellcome Trust Sanger Institute would also come the next generation of sequencing technology, a method that was faster and more economic, but retained accuracy, and now has over 70% share of the world's $20 billion-plus gene sequencing market.

With the advances in sequencing and better understanding of the genetic and epigenetic components of diseases have also come new approaches to drug development and testing. Cambridge companies are responsible for novel therapies, including the first poly ADP ribose polymerase (PARP) inhibitor treatment on the market, and an innovative methodology that could turn the traditional drug discovery model from long, costly and frequently ineffective to quick, cheap and highly targeted.

A revolution in the way diseases are diagnosed and treated is on the way as personalized medicine becomes a reality, and Cambridge researchers and companies are deeply involved.

THE STRUCTURE OF DNA

The presence of DNA in the nuclei of cells had been known since it was first isolated by Swiss scientist Friedrich Miescher in 1869, and its components had been identified by 1919. It was also known to have a regular structure, and in 1952 was confirmed as responsible for carrying genetic information. But what eluded scientists was a proper understanding of how that genetic information was carried and transmitted from one cell to another, and then how it directed the formation of proteins to translate that information into cellular function. Watson and Crick's model for DNA would change all that.

"

We wish to suggest a structure for the salt of deoxyribonucleic acid (DNA). This structure has novel features which are of considerable biological interest.

Watson and Crick, *Nature*, 25 April 1953

"

It has not escaped our notice that the specific pairing we have postulated immediately suggests a possible copying mechanism for the genetic material.

Watson and Crick, *Nature*, 25 April 1953

F.H.C. CRICK
HONORARY FELLOW 1976

Opposite far left: *Rosalind Franklin's work in X-ray crystallography paved the way for the discovery of the DNA double helix.*

Left: *Stained-glass window of the molecular structure of DNA in the dining hall of Gonville and Caius College, Cambridge.*

Right: *At the 1962 Nobel Prize ceremony: (left to right) Maurice Wilkins, Max Perutz, Francis Crick, John Steinbeck, James Watson and John Kendrew. All but Steinbeck were closely connected to Cambridge.*

Below: *'Photograph 51', produced by a student of Rosalind Franklin, was key to the discovery of DNA.*

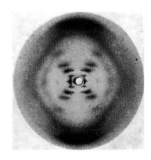

Crick and Watson were both working in the Medical Research Council Unit for the Study of the Molecular Structure of Biological Systems in Cambridge University's Cavendish Laboratory. Competition with other scientists, most notably Linus Pauling in California, was mounting as several groups attempted to work out the structure of DNA and unlock its secrets.

As has been well documented, Crick and Watson would not have reached their conclusions without the help of Maurice Wilkins, a physicist and molecular biologist working at King's College London, and his colleague, Rosalind Franklin, who specialized in X-ray crystallography, a technique for creating images of molecules. One of Franklin's PhD students, Ray Gosling, produced the image known simply as 'Photograph 51', which was key to Crick and Watson's discovery.

Crick and Watson subsequently shared the 1962 Nobel Prize in Physiology or Medicine with Wilkins. Franklin died in 1958, before the Prize was awarded. The Nobel Prize Committee cited the scientists 'for their discoveries concerning the molecular structure of nucleic acids and its significance for information transfer in living material'.

The two helices of DNA are made up of nucleotides. Each nucleotide consists of a base, adenine (A), cytosine (C), guanine (G) or thymine (T), a monosaccharide sugar, deoxyribose, and a phosphate group, which align themselves with the sugar-phosphate group on the outside and the base projecting towards the inside of the helix. The sequence of DNA is the order of the bases, for instance AGGCTAA, etc. Watson and Crick demonstrated that, in DNA, adenine pairs exclusively with thymine and cytosine with guanine, and these have come to be known as Watson–Crick base pairs. This exclusive pairing is the basis of DNA replication and how it codes for protein formation in the cell.

Crick and his colleagues subsequently demonstrated that the genetic code was carried in groups of three bases, referred to as codons, which defined the sequence of amino acids that made up proteins. A collection of codons made up a gene, which, when the codons were 'read' correctly, would produce a protein that had a defined role in cell regulation or function.

The challenge now was to sequence DNA itself. If an entire molecule of DNA could be sequenced, the genes it contained – and thus the proteins it coded for – could be identified.

> **"**
>
> *...just a chap who messed about in his lab...*

Fred Sanger describing himself, quoted in his obituary in *The Times*, 21 November 2013

THE RACE TO READ THE SEQUENCE OF DNA

Fred Sanger, working in the Biochemistry Department of Cambridge University, had already been awarded the Nobel Prize in Chemistry for identifying the amino acids that make up insulin and their sequence and arrangement – a major breakthrough in the understanding of proteins at the molecular level. Now he joined Max Perutz in the new Laboratory of Molecular Biology (LMB), being set up in Cambridge by the Medical Research Council (MRC), and turned his attention to ribonucleic acid, RNA. This molecule was known to be responsible for translating the code held in DNA into proteins, but was much smaller than DNA, and therefore an easier proposition to sequence.

Sanger wasn't first – that accolade went to a group in the US under Robert W Holley, who sequenced the 77 ribonucleotides that made up a yeast RNA – but he followed soon after with the sequence of the 120 nucleotides that make up ribosomal RNA in the bacterium *Escherichia coli*. However, the process for elucidating the sequence was very laborious and slow, and Sanger determined to find ways to improve the speed and accuracy of 'reading' the genetic code. By the early 1970s, Sanger and his team had developed a method based on radiolabelled nucleotides which could sequence 80 nucleotides at a time, and allowed them to map the 5,386 nucleotide sequence of a bacteriophage, ΦX174.

Further experimentation led to what became known as the 'Sanger Method', the universal method for sequencing DNA for the next quarter of a century. In 1980, this work led to Sanger being awarded his second Nobel Prize in Chemistry, making him only the fourth person to have won two Nobel Prizes, and the first to have won both prizes in the same category.

Above: *Robert W Holley (left) shared the 1968 Nobel Prize in Physiology or Medicine for his work sequencing the ribonucleotides that make up RNA.*

Top: *The Laboratory of Molecular Biology.*

Above left: *Fred Sanger won the Nobel Prize for Chemistry twice, first in 1958 for his work on the amino acids that make up insulin and then in 1980 (shared with Walter Gilbert) for 'contributions concerning the determination of base sequences in nucleic acids'.*

THE SANGER METHOD UNDERPINS THE HUMAN GENOME PROJECT

The HGP was a massively ambitious international collaboration set up in 1990 to map all the base pairs in the human genome – some 3.3 billion, coding for around 20,500 genes. Initially launched by the National Institutes of Health (NIH) and Department of Energy Office of Health and Environmental Research in the US, the UK joined the project in 1993, when the Wellcome Trust and MRC-funded Sanger Centre (now Sanger Institute) opened in Cambridge. The project grew to include more than 20 collaborators and institutions from around the globe, creating the International Human Genome Sequencing Consortium.

John Sulston, then head of the MRC LMB in Cambridge, had originally approached the Wellcome Trust to secure funding for the LMB's project to sequence the genome of the nematode worm (work for which Sulston would subsequently win the Nobel Prize), but the tie-up with the US-backed Human Genome Project was irresistible – not least because international researchers in the project were using the

sequencing technique developed by Fred Sanger and his team at the LMB. The Sanger Institute would go on to make the largest single contribution to the HGP.

In 1998, a commercial venture, Celera Genomics, under Craig Venter, entered the arena, intending to sequence the human genome and 'own' it, making their data available on a subscription basis. Celera also intended to patent any genes they identified that were clinically important, a situation that could have significant implications for future research into disease and the development of better drugs.

The HGP had by this time established its 'Bermuda Principles' of sharing data and making the sequences they identified freely available, without waiting for academic publication to assert their ownership of the data, or, more importantly, attempting to secure patents on the genes they sequenced. Only by releasing the complete human genome data before Celera Genomics did could this be achieved.

The first draft sequences of the human genome were announced in 2000. Both the independently funded HGP and the Celera Genomics project declared that they had complete draft sequences for the genome, and work then continued on refining the sequence and ironing out the many duplications. Both groups published their draft sequences in 2001 (HGP in *Nature*, Celera in *Science*, both in the February issues), but by this time, US President Clinton had mandated that the human genome sequence could not be patented, removing the commercial raison d'être for Celera Genomics (and consequently having a dramatic effect on the company's stock price).

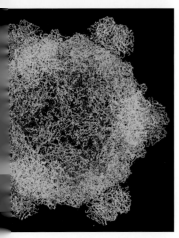

Above: *Bacteriophage ΦX174 was sequenced using radiolabelled nucleotides.*

Right: *John Sulston won the Nobel Prize in 2002.*

Far right: *Craig Venter (right) with President Clinton at the 2015 Clinton Global Initiative Annual Meeting.*

"

The Sanger Centre stood strong, accelerated and delivered a stunning genome for all human kind to view free of restrictions.

Kevin McKernan, Senior Director of Scientific Operations, Applied Biosystems
Life Technologies, in written evidence submitted to the UK Government's
Select Committee on Science & Technology, November 2008

Venter left Celera Genomics in 2002 and the company moved away from genomic research, leaving the HGP to publish what was referred to as the gold standard sequence in 2003. It is this sequence that is the reference for companies seeking to develop new, fast and accurate methods of sequencing genes.

At a cost of approximately $3 billion, sequencing the human genome was an expensive affair, and unless sequencing costs could be brought down exponentially, it was unclear how much individual patients might benefit from this knowledge.

James Watson was the first individual to have his entire genome published, a feat accomplished in 2007 by 454 Life Sciences, a US company founded by genomics entrepreneur Jonathan Rothberg. The sequence was estimated to have cost $1 million. In the same year, genome sequencing was offered to consumers by Knome, at a cost of $350,000.

Getting the cost of sequencing down was critical if the potential health benefits and commercial possibilities of understanding an individual's genetic make-up were to be realized. Affordable gene sequences would open up opportunities in a number of areas, from understanding diseases to personalized medicine. Commentators began to talk about the '$1,000 genome', but no one was sure if that was possible.

It would take another Cambridge group to come up with the technology to bring sequencing costs into the realm of affordability.

SOLEXA SEQUENCING SETS THE STANDARD

Another Cambridge pub was the scene for the next leap in the genome story. In 1997, the Panton Arms, located a few hundred yards from the Cambridge University Chemistry Department, was the setting for a 'beer summit' between two researchers, Shankar Balasubramanian and David Klenerman, and their colleagues Mark Osborne and Colin Barnes. The four got together to thrash out the possibilities of combining their knowledge of DNA polymerase (Balasubramanian) and laser spectroscopy (Klenerman) and applying it to genome sequencing.

The following year, **Solexa** was born. Funded initially by Abingworth, the aim of the company was to exploit Balasubramanian and Klenerman's idea for a method to improve DNA sequencing by several orders of magnitude, making it faster and over 100 times cheaper. By now, the

Above: *The Panton Arms, where Shankar Balasubramanian and David Klenerman (right) discussed genome sequencing.*

Illumina 3000 Sequencing System.

idea of a $1,000 genome had taken hold in the sequencing community, but so far it was a goal that no one was sure could be met. The Solexa method might just be the answer.

The Solexa team met with leaders of the HGP at the Sanger Centre, and opened their first lab nearby in 2001. The company's first CEO, Nick McCooke, began pushing the idea that Solexa could win the race to bring the cost of sequencing the human genome down to $1,000.

The acquisition of a novel technology to amplify DNA strands and some equipment from failing Swiss firm Manteia in 2005 gave Solexa a boost, allowing them to prove their concept and reassure investors. In February 2005, Solexa completed sequencing the genome of the same FX174 virus that Fred Sanger had sequenced in 1977. Sanger's sequence gave them a reference to measure the accuracy of their new process, and the success of this task, at 99.9% accuracy, heralded a breakthrough for the team.

New CEO John West, who had joined Solexa from US competitor Applied Biosystems Inc. (ABI), initiated a merger with California company Lynx Therapeutics in 2004 to give Solexa a US base, a marketing department and a stock market listing. Despite difficulties with the merger, not least the struggle to focus on Solexa's methodology rather than technology developed by the Lynx scientists, the new company began selling sequencing machines in 2006. Their customers were the major genome centres, institutions that could afford the still very high costs of the machines themselves and the sequencing operation.

West's initial claims that Solexa would bring the cost of sequencing a single genome down to $100,000 by the end of 2006 were not realized, but this did not put off US company Illumina, which bought Solexa for $650 million in November of that year. Now branded Illumina, the machines built on Solexa technology made genetic sequencing much more widely available and affordable. The Sanger Institute, which announced its one trillionth base in July 2008, was a major customer for Illumina.

In 2008, Illumina stated that the cost of sequencing a human genome had come down to $100,000. The same year, competitor ABI announced that they had brought the cost down to $60,000. In a race to the bottom, Helicos BioSciences made a claim for a $48,000 genome in 2009, and Complete Genomics knocked the price down to $5,000 – but only for bulk orders, and only for researchers.

> **"**
> *I remember going home feeling pretty excited, as I often did after a discussion at the Panton Arms. The acid test, of course, is how you feel when you wake up.*

Shankar Balasubramanian, quoted in *Bio-IT World*, 2010

27

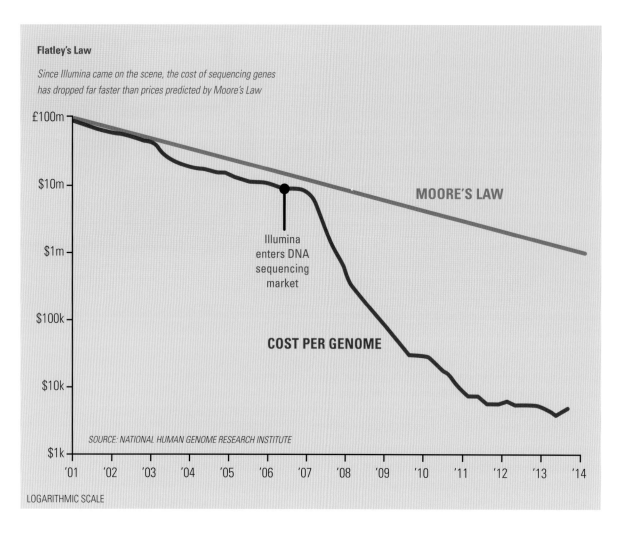

Flatley's Law

Since Illumina came on the scene, the cost of sequencing genes has dropped far faster than prices predicted by Moore's Law

MOORE'S LAW

Illumina enters DNA sequencing market

COST PER GENOME

SOURCE: NATIONAL HUMAN GENOME RESEARCH INSTITUTE

LOGARITHMIC SCALE

In 2010, Illumina announced that the cost per genome using their machines was now down to $50,000. The same year, John West (who had by now moved on to head up ViaCyte) told a Cambridge conference held to celebrate 50 years of the Cambridge Phenomenon that he, his wife and their two children were the first entire family to have their genomes sequenced.

It had taken 13 years for the HGP to sequence the human genome for the first time. Referencing the speed of the process for sequencing his own genome and that of his family barely seven years after the first genome was published, West pointed out that it had taken longer to write the press release announcing this 'first' and get it approved than to do the sequencing itself.

The goal was still the $1,000 genome, and Life Technologies, a descendant of ABI and another Jonathan Rothberg company, Ion Torrent, claimed that it would be able to meet this price by the end of 2012, but according to Erika Check Hayden, writing in *Nature* in January 2014, was yet to deliver. At the beginning of 2014, Illumina announced that their new machine, the HiSeq X Ten System, could sequence over 18,000 genomes per year at a cost of around $1,000 each. The verdict of Check Hayden was that Illumina's new machine 'probably will not be able to immediately sequence human genomes for under $1,000, but it will get close.'

Illumina currently has around 70% of the market in gene sequencing technology, with Goldman Sachs analysts predicting that this share will have risen to at least 75% in

Far left: Jay Flatley, CEO of Illumina.

Above: *MIT's Broad Institute.*

2015. Analysts at Credit Suisse described Illumina as 'best in class', and the company reached a market capitalization of over $27 billion in September 2015. While 2014 predictions for the gene sequencing market suggested an eventual value of $20 billion, this is now believed to be an underestimate, as expanding uses for DNA testing led to an even bigger demand for faster and more accurate sequencing technologies.

Having leapt ahead of competitors with the purchase of Solexa and its technology platform, Illumina has continued to develop its offering to keep at the forefront of gene sequencing. The new HiSeq X Ten machines are proving attractive, with the Broad Institute of MIT and Harvard purchasing 14, and Craig Venter's new company, Human Longevity, Inc., buying 20. Meanwhile BGI (the Beijing Genomics Institute), the largest sequencing operation in the world, now has around 30 Illumina machines. Illumina's commitment to Cambridge has recently been reinforced by a multimillion-pound investment in a new EMEA headquarters just outside the city.

> **"**
> *Almost every transformative advance in my field has come from using Illumina technology.*
>
> Daniel MacArthur, geneticist at Massachusetts General Hospital, US

NEW COMPANIES FOCUS ON NEXT-GENERATION SEQUENCING AND ANALYTICS

Cambridge Epigenetix continues the story for Shankar Balasubramanian, co-founder of Solexa. Research into DNA has revealed the existence of variants of the base cytosine in the genome. Of particular interest are the methylated and hydroxymethylated variants 5mC and 5hmC. However, the traditional method of bisulfite sequencing used to identify these variants is unable to distinguish between them, and yet each performs a very different function in the way genetic information is switched on or off in the cell. With his PhD student Michael Booth, Balasubramanian invented a new genome sequencing method, oxidative bisulphite sequencing, that is highly accurate and able to distinguish between the two variant bases. This is of major importance to the study of epigenetics, and Cambridge Epigenetix was founded by Balasubramanian and Bobby Yerramilli-Rao, a partner at Hermes Growth Partners, in 2012 to commercialize the discovery. With New Science Ventures joining original funders Syncona Partners and Cambridge Enterprise in a $5.5 million Series A round in late 2014 followed by a $21 million, B round led by Google Ventures and Silicon Valley thoroughbred Sequoia capital in March 2016 Cambridge Epigenetix is well positioned for future growth. Scientific papers are already citing the use of Cambridge Epigenetix's proprietary TrueMethyl technology to make significant discoveries in the field, a new avenue for understanding disease, drug discovery and personalized medicine is opening up.

Next-generation sequencing continues to be a goal, and companies in Cambridge continue to seek faster and more accurate methods. **Base4** is developing a microdroplet technology that provides long read-lengths of single molecules, which the company believes is the key to achieving cheap and near real-time results. Since 2013, Base4 has

been collaborating with manufacturing partner Hitachi High-Technologies Corporation, Tokyo.

But with faster and cheaper screening comes the challenge of analysing and understanding the vast amounts of data it produces. As a consequence, many teams focus on particular genes or sets of genes to keep the data manageable and target their efforts.

Paradigm Therapeutics was established in 1999 to focus on key gene families and use gene knock-out technology and in vivo pharmacology to identify and validate novel drug targets within those genes. A spin-out from Cambridge University and the Wellcome Trust CRC Institute, key areas of interest included pain, the central nervous system, breast and prostate cancer, obesity and diabetes. The company opened a subsidiary in Singapore in 2003, and entered an agreement with Takeda, Japan's largest pharmaceutical company, in 2005 to research and develop drugs for disorders of the central nervous system.

In 2007, Takeda acquired Paradigm Therapeutics outright, renaming its operations Takeda Cambridge and Takeda Singapore. The acquisition was part of Takeda's strategy to develop a global research base, adding Europe and Singapore to already established research operations in Japan and the US. The acquisition of Paradigm Therapeutics proved 'sticky', as Takeda went on to acquire and collaborate with other Cambridge companies and expand operations on the Cambridge Science Park.

The genomics story began as one of research and then drug discovery, but now it is also moving into clinical practice, and new companies are looking for ways that genomics can benefit patients directly.

One of these is Cambridge University spin-out **BlueGnome**, which has had a global impact that could be measured in babies. By the time the company was acquired by Illumina in 2012, it had customers in over 40 countries, had won a Queen's Award for Enterprise, had offices in the US and Singapore, and been listed twice as the fastest growing biotechnology company in the UK. Founded by Cambridge graduate Nick Haan and Graham Snudden, the embryonic company was supported by Cambridge Enterprise to develop its novel methodology for screening single cells for genetic abnormalities. Particularly applicable to IVF, where non-invasive preimplantation screening is so important, the company's technology platform 24sure was

Far left: Base4 focuses on developing technologies for single-molecule analysis.

reported in the journal *Molecular Cytogenetics* to improve IVF success rates by 65%.

Congenica, a spin-out from the Wellcome Trust Sanger Institute, was co-founded in 2014 by Matthew Hurles and Richard Durbin, both Senior Group Leaders at the Institute. Matthew Hurles is also joint leader of the Deciphering Developmental Disorders (DDD) study, funded by the Wellcome Trust Sanger Institute and the Health Innovation Challenge Fund and supported by the NHS National Institute for Health Research.

Congenica is focusing on genomic sequencing for the clinical diagnosis of genetic disease, and its flagship product, Sapienta, was developed based on insights from the DDD study. Congenica's technology speeds up the analysis of whole genomes, and has already been adopted by the Manchester Centre for Genomics Medicine (NHS), which is taking part in the Genomics England 100,000 Genomes Project. This project is the largest national genome sequencing project in the world, and plans to sequence 100,000 genomes from patients with rare diseases, their families, and patients with cancer.

Endorsement from Genomics England, a £2 million award from the UK's Small Business Research Initiative and a partnership with the world-famous Great Ormond Street Hospital indicate that the prospects for Congenica look promising.

Inivata is another new company targeting cancer genomics, in this case diagnosis via the detection and measurement of circulating tumour DNA (ctDNA) in the blood. Many cancers are diagnosed through invasive biopsy procedures, and for some patients biopsy is not possible at all, but Inivata's method requires a standard blood sample, making it much more accessible and immediate. Three of the four founders, Nitzan Rosenfeld, James Brenton and Davina Gale, are part of the Cancer Research UK Cambridge Institute, with the fourth, Tim Forshew, from the University College London Cancer Institute. Inivata

> *Genomics technology and analysis is moving rapidly from the research environment to the clinical environment and is now changing the lives of patients in the NHS and in healthcare systems around the world. The insights gained from matching the genomes of thousands of patients with their phenotype and in the case of cancer the genetic signature of their tumour will transform clinical diagnosis and practice. Initially this will be in rare monogenetic diseases and cancer, but will migrate into all disease areas.*
>
> Andy Richards, Chair, Congenica Ltd.

has a subsidiary in the US and has established a number of collaborations with institutions and companies in the UK and US to help develop clinical applications for its technology, including in non-small cell lung cancer. Inivata raised £31.5 million from Cambridge Innovation Capital, Imperial Innovations, Johnson & Johnson and Woodford Patient Capital Trust in January 2016.

The analysis of circulating tumour DNA and circulating tumour cells has been termed 'liquid biopsy' and is seen as a major transformative approach in cancer diagnosis with an addressable market estimated by JPMorgan to reach $22 billion by 2020.

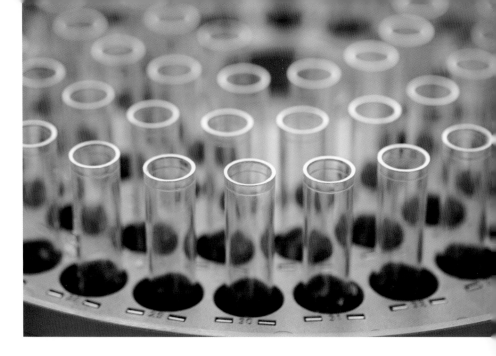

LATERAL THINKING AND THE BRCA GENES: KUDOS TAKES A NOVEL APPROACH TO TARGETS FOR TREATING CANCER

Lynparza (olaparib) is the first PARP inhibitor drug marketed anywhere in the world, and the first that targets an inherited mutation in the patient that leads to a specific defect in cancer cells. AstraZeneca was the first big pharma company to get into DNA repair, via its acquisition of KuDOS, and this approach is now a growing field in the search for new drugs against cancer.

Steve Jackson

In 1991, Steve Jackson returned to the UK from California to work as a Junior Group Leader at the new Wellcome/CRC Institute, which was just being set up Cambridge. For his PhD and postdoctoral work, Jackson had studied RNA splicing and the regulation of transcription, part of the process by which the DNA code contained in genes is turned into proteins that direct functions in the cell. He wasn't planning to be in Cambridge for very long as he could see numerous opportunities in his field around the world, but in 1995 he became the youngest person to be elected Professor in Cambridge University since Isaac Newton became Lucasian Professor of Mathematics in 1669, and has stayed in Cambridge ever since.

Jackson and his team started working on protein kinases, enzymes that modify and regulate proteins in the cell, and, in 1993, discovered that one, DNA-PK (later christened DNA-

PKcs/Ku), was involved in DNA repair. DNA repair is a crucial cellular function because our DNA is constantly being damaged by the environment and normal metabolic activities. Cancer therapies typically damage DNA in both cancerous and healthy cells, and this damage often leads to unpleasant side effects.

Healthy cells are very good at repairing DNA, but some cancer cells are not, so we thought that developing drugs to inhibit certain forms of DNA repair might give us a way to kill cancer cells without damaging healthy cells, DNA repair might be 'druggable'.

Steve Jackson

KuDOS, the first company to focus on DNA repair processes as drug targets to selectively kill cancer cells, was set up by Jackson as a 'soft start' in 1997 as he and his colleagues continued to work on the science behind his idea. Raising funds was tricky because genomics companies were flavour of the month and KuDOS looked like an old-fashioned drug discovery company. Another factor was the notion that DNA repair was a good thing, so why attempt to inhibit or stop it?

Nevertheless, with help from the University of Cambridge, Jackson persuaded the technology transfer arm of the forerunner of Cancer Research UK (CRUK) to provide seed funding. Then, after around 18 months of intensive effort, he persuaded the venture capital organizations Advent, 3i and SV Life Sciences to invest in his ideas, allowing KuDOS to grow and move out of the lab and onto the Cambridge Science Park. Jackson and the KuDOS investors brought in Barrie Ward, an experienced biotech manager, who promptly recruited a bright team from academia and industry. A further two rounds of venture capital funding brought in investors from the US, Germany, the Netherlands and Switzerland, and eventually the company raised about £42.5 million in total.

Above: *KuDOS Pharmaceuticals, founded in 1997 by Steve Jackson (below left), develops drugs that help save lives.*

By 2002, KuDOS had demonstrated that its strategy of targeting the DNA repair function could work, and by early 2004 the company was in discussions with several big pharma companies about partnering to progress the potential KuDOS drugs they had identified into the all-important, but extremely expensive, clinical trials. Some of these drugs had been developed to inhibit the functions of kinases such as DNA-PK, while others targeted other DNA repair proteins, including the enzyme poly ADP ribose polymerase (PARP).

At the same time that Jackson's group was working on protein kinases, much was becoming known about some of the mutations associated with breast, ovarian and other cancers, and in particular the genes BRCA1 and BRCA2. While BRCA1 was first isolated and sequenced by US company Myriad Genetics and researchers at the University of Utah, it was a collaboration between The Institute of Cancer Research in London and Cambridge's Wellcome Trust Sanger Institute that discovered BRCA2 and isolated it for the first time, something that would later prove pivotal for KuDOS.

Below: *The actress Angelina Jolie had a preventative double mastectomy after finding that she had a BRCA1 mutation.*

The protein products of the BRCA genes were found to play important roles in DNA repair and became known as 'tumour suppressors' as it was found that, by repairing mutations, they prevented cells from becoming cancerous.

When the BRCA1 or BRCA 2 genes are disabled, the benefits of BRCA1 and 2 mediated DNA repair are lost.

> **"**
> *It was a eureka moment – the KuDOS PARP inhibitor was very effective at killing cells that carried BRCA mutations. We were surprised to find that it even worked at very low concentrations that had almost no effect on normal cells.*
>
> Steve Jackson

An individual with mutations in the BRCA genes and a family history of breast or ovarian cancer has a much higher chance of developing one or both of these diseases than normal. The actress Angelina Jolie, for example, had a preventative double mastectomy after finding that she had a BRCA1 mutation. Since her mother, grandmother and aunt had all died of cancer, doctors calculated that she had an 87% risk of developing breast cancer and a 50% chance of developing ovarian cancer.

As BRCA genes were linked to a number of DNA repair mechanisms, this suggested to Jackson and others that they might be more reliant than normal cells on certain other DNA repair pathways, meaning that drugs inhibiting these pathways might selectively kill BRCA-deficient cancer cells.

The key to unlocking this potential was a meeting Jackson had with Alan Ashworth, at The Institute of Cancer Research in London. Ashworth had isolated and characterized cell lines with BRCA1 and BRCA2 mutations, and so he and Jackson agreed to enter into a collaboration to test KuDOS drugs for their ability to kill such cells. The drugs that were tested included compounds that inhibited PARP, forerunners of olaparib.

The results looked very good. They confirmed what Jackson and his team had hoped, and they also made KuDOS more attractive as an acquisition target. In 2006, AstraZeneca acquired KuDOS for £120 million.

As can be seen in the case of Lemtrada (see page 43), a change of ownership does not always mean a smooth path through the various stages of clinical trials and on to regulatory approval. AstraZeneca ran KuDOS as a subsidiary in Cambridge for a few years, but then changed strategy and took the KuDOS assets, drugs and programmes from Cambridge to Macclesfield.

Strikingly, even in the Phase I clinical trials in 2006 (the first in human patients), some patients showed dramatic responses to the PARP inhibitor, olaparib, with these patients invariably having BRCA1 or BRCA2 mutations. With this promising start, AstraZeneca continued to invest in the development of the novel therapy. However, Phase II results a few years later suggested that the drug did not extend the lives of patients (although this interpretation was tempered by the fact that trials had been expanded to all ovarian cancers, not just those connected to BRCA1 and BRCA2 mutations). In 2012, as a consequence of these results, AstraZeneca terminated the olaparib programme, at a charge to the annual accounts of £285 million.

But members of the AstraZeneca team working on the olaparib trials, including several who were originally KuDOS employees who had gone with AstraZeneca when it closed operations in Cambridge, wouldn't give up. Collectively they persuaded the new AstraZeneca CEO, Pascal Soriot, to review the data. He recognized that there was an opportunity, reactivated the programme in 2013 and requested that the data from the Phase II trials be re-examined and analysed anew.

This proved to be a remarkably worthwhile turnaround. It led to the results of the Phase II trials for the PARP inhibitor olaparib, now known as Lynparza, being submitted for regulatory assessment, and in late December 2014, the drug gained Food and Drug Administration (FDA) and European Medicines Agency approval for treating ovarian cancer patients who have BRCA gene mutations. It is now being tested in other cancers known to be associated with BRCA defects, including prostate, breast, pancreatic and gastric cancers. AstraZeneca predicts that annual sales may reach $2 billion.

MISSION THERAPEUTICS TACKLES THE DEUBIQUITYLATING ENZYMES

In 2010, when KuDOS in Cambridge was being closed, its founder, Steve Jackson realized that there were other opportunities in the DNA repair work still going on in his laboratory that could be exploited. Another potential drug target which various companies had explored but largely given up on were the deubiquitylating enzymes (DUBs), some of which regulate DNA repair processes in cells and play roles in cancer, inflammation, neurodegeneration and a number of other diseases.

Jackson thought that a bit of persistence could pay off, and brought back together Niall Martin (who had headed the PARP programme previously and taken the CEO position at KuDOS), Xavier Jacq and Keith Menear to start a new company, *MISSION* Therapeutics based on the Babraham Research Campus near Cambridge.

Their track record made it slightly easier to get funding second time around, and, with Cancer Research Technology, the technology transfer arm of CRUK, and support from Cambridge Enterprise, they raised £6 million from a group of investors led by Sofinnova and including Imperial Innovations, Roche and SR One. *MISSION* was the first investment for Imperial Innovations after their terms changed and they were permitted to invest outside Imperial College itself. The second round of funding brought in Pfizer Venture Investments to join the original investors.

It is early days yet for *MISSION*, but with a number of patents already filed on the chemistry, new technology platforms and methodologies – and by ensuring that biomarkers that will help identify the patients most likely to benefit from a particular new drug are identified as early as possible – it's not surprising that the company already has the attention of three big pharma companies, Roche, GlaxoSmithKline (through SR One), and now Pfizer.

Above: *AstraZeneca develops medicines used by millions of patients worldwide.*

HORIZON DISCOVERY IS GETTING US EVER CLOSER TO PERSONALIZED MEDICINE

The first bottleneck on the path to personalized medicine — choosing the best treatment for an individual based on their genetic profile — was sequencing the genome itself. Now that problem has been largely solved and sequencing is becoming much more widely accessible, the new bottleneck is identifying which genetic variations — of which there are thousands — actually play a role in disease progression and can be targeted by molecular, cell and gene therapies.

Chris Torrance and Alberto Bardelli were working on methods of gene editing with Bert Vogelstein at Johns Hopkins in the early 2000s, getting frustrated at how long it took to get results — up to 18 months — and the high likelihood of failure. At around the same time, David Russell at the University of Washington was developing a new way to edit genes that used recombinant adeno-associated virus vectors (rAAV) to make accurate and repeatable changes at specific points. Torrance and Bardelli identified the method as something around which they might form a company if they could secure ownership of the technology.

> *The new gene editing method was a potential game-changer, but Chris was back in the UK, Alberto was in Italy, and the intellectual property was in Washington State. The Cambridge ecosystem swung into action to introduce myself to the founders, fund the company and make things happen.*
>
> Darrin Disley

Seeing the potential, Cambridge Enterprise offered a loan to purchase the rights to the method and tasked serial entrepreneur Darrin Disley with clearing the way to funding the company and driving it forward alongside Torrance. They used their seminal IP position to track down other scientists who were using the same methodology so that they could be licensed to carry on using it. Horizon Discovery was set up in July 2007 and seed-funded in March 2008.

The goal was to set up a company that would develop the rAAV gene-editing technology further and use it to create normal and mutated genetically defined cell lines in the laboratory. Although this could already be done using other methods, they were slow, laborious, and success was not guaranteed. The founders of Horizon Discovery were convinced

> **"**
>
> *The most pressing need in translational genomics was to develop a 'patient in a test tube', and that's what Horizon Discovery set out to do.*
>
> Darrin Disley, CEO, Horizon Discovery

> **"**
> *I saw that the cost of gene sequencing was going to come down dramatically – this meant that the traditional pharma model was going to have to change.*

Darrin Disley, CEO, Horizon Discovery

that their technology would be more efficient, more accurate, more precise and faster than existing methods.

It wasn't long before their confidence was rewarded and X-MAN was 'born', a genetically defined pair of cell lines, differing only in the genetic changes of interest, that could be used in a number of ways to identify or improve treatments for diseases, particularly cancer. Early X-MAN lines took three to six months to produce, as opposed to up to 24 months via older methods, and could be tailor-made for particular projects. By improving their technology and the in-license of additional gene-editing techniques such as Zinc Finger Nucleases and CRISPR/Cas9, Horizon Discovery can now make such cell lines per month at ten times throughput and at ten times less cost, meaning it now has over 22,000 X-MAN lines and derived

products available to researchers off the shelf, and many more that have been 'made-to-measure' for partners.

All these gene-editing approaches have advantages and disadvantages and deliver subtly different outcomes. Horizon Discovery uses whichever approach is most appropriate, and, importantly, unlike some of its competitors, has access to, and the IP for, all the most relevant tools to edit genes.

Cambridge has played a pivotal part in the development of gene editing through the work of two Nobel Laureates: Martin Evans, who focused on understanding how genes could be modulated using a cell's natural DNA repair mechanisms, and Aaron Klug, who identified that the zinc finger proteins could be used to precisely cut sequences of DNA to stimulate these mechanisms to edit a host cell's genome.

Diseases like cancer may involve a very large number of genetic variations – lung cancer, for instance, is not a single disease. X-MAN helps researchers and pharmaceutical companies understand how to treat these diseases more effectively because it allows them to test against many possible genetic combinations and design better clinical trials. One result is what Horizon Discovery CEO Darrin Disley calls the 'democratization' of genomics research, because Horizon's technology has now made genome editing much more widely accessible, whereas before it was restricted to large companies and organizations, just as sequencing itself has become more affordable.

One of the biggest scientific impacts of Horizon Discovery to date has been the proof of a new model for clinical trials based on their gene-editing technologies. The COLTHERES trial was a pioneering approach to the treatment of colon cancer. Four hundred patients being treated with epidermal growth factor receptor (EGFR)-targeted therapy (Erbitux) were 'deep sequenced' – both their genomes and exomes were sequenced – and biomarkers for the disease identified. These were then introduced into genetically defined X-MAN cell lines in vitro, which were tested using therapies, and combinations of therapies, to find which therapies made the cells more responsive to treatment or overcame resistance. At the same time, avatars of the living patient were created in humanized mice along with the key mutations associated with the disease. Where in vitro trials appeared promising, the same treatment was tested in the mice as a Phase I trial. If successful in mice, it was then tested in the human patients with that particular genetic profile.

The speed at which optimal treatment regimes were identified was remarkable – from laboratory experiments starting in May 2011, animal experiments to validate the laboratory results began just three months later, in August 2011. The first publication on this study appeared in *Nature* in March 2012, and the first clinical trial in a patient began in November 2012. The first clinical responses were recorded in April 2013, barely two years after the first laboratory

Far right: Horizon X-MAN® Cell Lines growing in an incubator.

Below: Stained Horizon HDxTM Reference Standard being reviewed by microscopy.

experiments. The COLTHERES example showed that the traditional drug discovery model could indeed be disrupted and become more adaptive to patient need.

There is already evidence that this model for drug discovery brings a higher return on investment, removes a lot of the risk and is more beneficial to patients because they receive better targeted treatment. For instance, Crizotinib (trade name Xalkori) is a lung cancer drug from Pfizer that was developed for patients with a particular genetic feature found in only 5% of cases. In 2011, it was approved by the FDA for that group. It had taken eight years to develop, as opposed to the usual 12 to 15, and clinical trials had been highly targeted because the genetics were understood.

Since its very successful IPO in March 2014, the highest yet for a life sciences company from the Cambridge cluster and on AIM, Horizon Discovery has been building a portfolio of products and services all designed to further impact translational genomics and personalized medicine.

Horizon now has a variety of technologies that it commercializes in its product, service and R&D/licensing businesses: a series of gene-editing tools which it uses to engineer cell lines and in vivo models and derived reagent products. These products are then sold on, or utilized in-house within contract research services for its clients, or used to develop drug candidates in its leveraged R&D business.

With over 1,200 customers in 50 countries, Horizon Discovery works with more than 30 of the top 50 pharma companies, has numerous partners in academic research, ten research grants of its own, and pursues a model of 'open innovation' to further the impact of its products wherever possible.

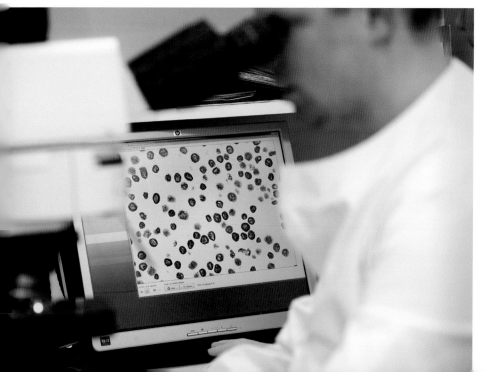

THE FIRST MONOCLONAL ANTIBODIES ARE ISOLATED IN THE MRC LABORATORY OF MOLECULAR BIOLOGY

A technology developed in Cambridge lies behind five of the top ten bestselling drugs of 2014 according to *Genetic Engineering & Biotechnology News*. The five are therapeutics based on humanized monoclonal antibodies, and include rheumatoid arthritis treatment Humira, the top-selling drug worldwide. It retained the number one spot from 2013 with a sales increase of over 17% on the previous year. Of the total $82.61 billion in sales that the top ten represented, over half was down to monoclonal antibody drugs, and Humira alone accounted for 15% of the total.

The development of immortal lines of monoclonal antibodies, the humanization process that made it possible to begin to realize their potential as therapeutics, and the early evolution of global top-seller Humira all started in the Medical Research Council-funded Laboratory of Molecular Biology in Cambridge and various departments of Cambridge University.

Today, several new companies in Cambridge are exploring next-generation platforms for producing fully human monoclonal antibodies and new ways of developing small proteins that mimic the activity of antibodies. Domantis (part of GSK since 2006) is developing therapeutic antibody fragments, while Kymab, one of 'Europe's 100 hottest startups' of 2015 according to *Wired* magazine, is working with transgenic mice to perfect a method of producing fully human monoclonal antibodies that should be cheaper and more efficient than

current methods. Crescendo Biologics works in the new area of antibody fragments, and Bicycle Therapeutics, co-founded by one of the 'fathers' of antibody engineering, is looking at smaller molecules that may be as effective as antibodies themselves, while virtual drug discovery company XO1 believes it has made such a profound discovery that it has named its new antibody after Ichor, 'the blood of the gods'.

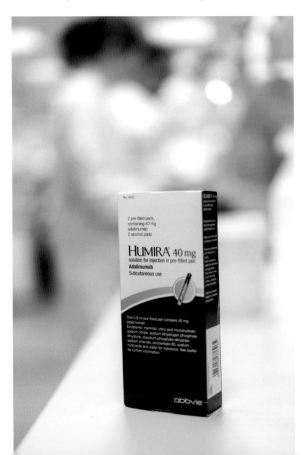

"

…it is certainly difficult for us to identify any immediate practical applications which could be pursued as a commercial venture…

National Research Development Corporation writing to the Medical Research Council about monoclonal antibodies, October 1976

Above: *Laboratory of Molecular Biology.*

Far right: *César Milstein (left) and Georges Köhler with their joint award (with Niels Jerne) of the Nobel Prize for Medicine.*

A CAMBRIDGE BREAKTHROUGH IN THE HUNT FOR MEDICINE'S 'MAGIC BULLET'

The 1984 Nobel Prize in Physiology or Medicine was awarded for theories concerning 'the specificity in development and control of the immune system' and the discovery of 'the principle for production of monoclonal antibodies'. The three recipients were Niels K Jerne, of the Basel Institute for Immunology in Switzerland, and Georges Köhler and César Milstein, of Cambridge's LMB.

Köhler and Milstein were being recognized by the Nobel Prize Committee for finally cracking the problem of isolating specific, or monoclonal, antibodies from cell cultures that contained a heterogenous mixture of antibodies and other proteins, something that scientists in a number of countries had been working on for many years. The critical characteristic of antibodies was that each antibody targeted only a particular antigen – or 'foreign' cell (which could be a bacterium from outside the body, or a cancer cell) – and this specificity, termed the 'magic bullet' effect, had huge potential for research and possibly therapeutic applications. But without being able to separate mixtures of antibodies, this potential could not be realized.

Köhler and Milstein had first announced the successful production of 'immortal' monoclonal lines of antibodies to myeloma in a letter to *Nature* in 1975. The antibodies were made by exposing mouse spleen cells to sheep blood cells and then fusing the spleen cells with human myeloma cells. Clonal antibodies to sheep blood cells were then isolated from the fused cells.

The members of the UK's National Research Development Corporation (NRDC) who saw no 'immediate practical applications' in what was going on at the LMB in the 1970s were right in one way – it would take many years for the practical applications of the new technology to start to be realized. But they were wrong about the lack of commercial possibilities, and there were several points along the way where opportunities to secure patents were missed, an issue that caused some political controversy in the late 1970s and early 1980s.

Despite this controversy over the failure to patent the monoclonal antibody technology, two prominent members of the team who worked on it, Geoff Hale and Herman Waldmann, believe that this omission 'probably did more than anything else to facilitate the widespread use of monoclonal antibodies'. The prevailing culture at the time was one that favoured scientific advance over commercial gain – indeed, many researchers gave no thought to the commercial possibilities of their work. In this climate, LMB shared their new technique, and cell lines, with scientist colleagues in a number of other laboratories around the world, multiplying its potential impact in research and medicine.

The less-than-enthusiastic response of what was then the NRDC was perhaps not surprising. Although they did acknowledge the possibility of 'long term potential rather than immediate application', it was hard to see how things might develop when they felt 'the general field of genetic engineering is a particularly difficult area from the patent point of view'.

According to medical science historian Lara Marks, the editors of *Nature* were equally circumspect, as they 'asked for the article to be shortened and failed to include it in the section reserved for findings considered to be of leading significance'. It would take a group of determined and entrepreneurial individuals to see these new substances out of the laboratory, into the clinic and into healthcare.

> *Transforming Mabs [monoclonal antibodies], which had started life as a laboratory tool, into something that could be of use to the outside world was neither straightforward nor inevitable.*
>
> Lara Marks

The first antibody isolated, dubbed Campath-1 ('Campath' from Cambridge Pathology, the University department where some of the initial research was done) was originally intended as a tool to help study the body's immune system. By the early 1980s, researchers were also looking for therapeutic applications in autoimmune diseases, where the body destroys its own cells. One possible target was lupus, and in particular the associated condition of vasculitis.

The new antibodies were tested on patients under the 'named patient' trial regime, but did not demonstrate a sufficiently strong response and the project faded, as did a second attempt at using the antibodies for patients with rheumatoid arthritis.

An overarching problem was that the patients developed their own immune response to the antibodies they were given. Despite benefits from the initial treatment, the human body eventually rejected the antibodies because they were derived from rats, and rendered them ineffective. Clearly, producing antibodies from human cells rather than rat cells would get round this problem, but repeating the methodology required to do this – for instance, vaccinating people with cancer so that their bodies produced antibodies to the cancer cells – was out of the question.

It was recognized that only a small part of the monoclonal antibody molecules being produced was responsible for its activity, the 'V-region'. The rest, the 'C-region', was redundant, but caused the problems. If the researchers could isolate the active portion and 'hide' or remove the rest, the antibody might fool the body and bypass its natural defences. If the C-region were human rather than rat, so much the better.

THE WORLD'S FIRST HUMANIZED MONOCLONAL ANTIBODIES ARE MADE IN CAMBRIDGE, AND OPEN UP THE POSSIBILITY OF THERAPEUTIC USES

Michael Neuberger, an early pioneer of antibody engineering, had joined the LMB to work on cloning the genes responsible for the V-region of antibodies. When Mike Clark, also at the LMB, moved to Waldmann's lab at the Department of Pathology, he realized that Neuberger's techniques could help efforts to make monoclonal antibodies that were closer to human antibodies, and staff from the two laboratories collaborated to develop a method that combined genetic engineering with the cloning techniques the LMB had already perfected. With this method, dubbed 'humanization', it was possible to create hybrid molecules that married the V-region from rat antibodies with a human C-region.

The first humanized monoclonal antibody with therapeutic potential was produced using Campath-1 in 1988, and named Campath-1H. Having missed patenting opportunities in the past, the method of humanizing antibodies developed by Greg Winter, Neuberger and the team was patented, and went on to generate significant revenues for the MRC and impact on patient treatment and healthcare around the globe.

Greg Winter.

> **"**
>
> *We estimate that more than 2,000 scientists, physicians, nurses and lawyers have been involved in the characterisation and development of Campath-1 antibodies, and…over 3,000 patients…have volunteered for clinical trials.*

Geoff Hale and Herman Waldmann, *From laboratory to clinic: the story of CAMPATH-1*, 1998

Above: *(left to right) Herman Waldmann, Mike Clark and Geoff Hale.*

Far right: *Michael Neuberger, an early pioneer of antibody engineering.*

Humanized monoclonal antibodies were much less likely to be rejected by the body, so they opened once more the therapeutic possibilities of these compounds. Work began in earnest to identify disease targets based on the antibody's property of binding to CD52, a protein found on the surface of mature lymphocytes, white blood cells that are pivotal to the body's immune response.

Attention also turned to leukaemia, and in particular chronic lymphocytic leukaemia (CLL). This time, the antibodies were effective enough to secure a licence for clinical use, and were marketed as MabCampath. Another use that was postulated was that these antibodies might suppress the immune response in kidney and bone marrow transplants. Again, the antibodies were helpful, but progress was slow.

Continuing Milstein's generosity in sharing his monoclonal antibodies with other laboratories, Campath-1H was provided to clinicians and researchers working in relevant areas, and gradually a Campath Users Network evolved that shared results and helped build a growing set of data on different diseases and patient responses in the absence of any formal clinical trials.

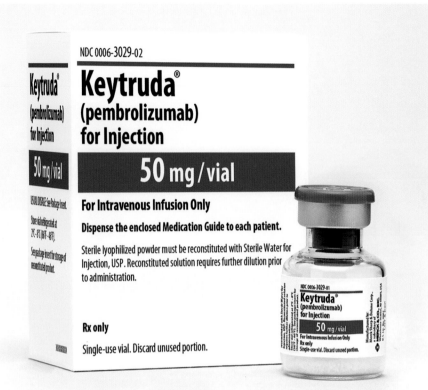

The LMB estimates that around a third of all new therapeutic treatments today are based on humanized monoclonal antibodies. Some of the better known ones include Avastin (bevacizumab), used for bowel, lung, kidney, ovarian, cervical and metastasizing cancers; Herceptin, used to treat HER2-positive cancers such as breast, stomach and gastro-oesophageal; and Mabthera (rituximab), used in chronic lymphocytic leukaemia and non-Hodgkin's lymphoma. Former US President Jimmy Carter, diagnosed with advanced melanoma in the summer of 2015, received novel immunotherapy treatment with recently licensed Keytruda, another monoclonal antibody also known as pembrolizumab.

Monoclonal antibodies are also used for further research into multiple other areas, including the immune system, for tissue typing (for instance to identify transplant matches) and for diagnostics, including detecting proteins in tissue samples using techniques such as the Western blot method.

Researchers and entrepreneurs in Cambridge and elsewhere continue to work to find ways to improve monoclonal antibody production and specificity, and also to create fully human antibodies, such as Humira, to eliminate the last residual effects of mouse and rat proteins.

HUMIRA, THE WORLD'S BESTSELLING DRUG, STARTS LIFE IN CAMBRIDGE

Recognizing the commercial potential of monoclonal antibodies if fully human forms could be isolated, Greg Winter and David Chiswell took the bold step of setting up a new company, Cambridge Antibody Technology (CAT), in 1990. The company was formed to develop a phage display technology that Winter and his colleagues had high hopes would enable them to produce fully human monoclonal antibodies in quantity.

Once the technology was established, it was intended to be used to create a pipeline of potentially therapeutic human antibodies. The world's first fully human antibody that showed such therapeutic promise, originally known as D2E7, subsequently became the subject of a collaboration between CAT and BASF Bioresearch Corporation, which resulted in a clinical candidate derived from D2E7, christened adalimumab.

Adalimumab was expected to have anti-inflammatory properties, as it bound to tumour necrosis factor-alpha receptors (TNFa) in place of TNFa itself, thus reducing the inflammatory response – an important element of autoimmune diseases.

Further clinical development was undertaken by BASF Knoll and then Abbott Laboratories, following their acquisition of

Above: Jimmy Carter (far left) was diagnosed with advanced melanoma in the summer of 2015. After receiving treatment with Keytruda, he was declared 'cancer-free' by December of the same year.

Right: *Zimbabwean professional golfer Tony Johnstone was diagnosed with MS in 2004. He participated in trials of the new MS drug being developed in Cambridge, and won his first tournament on the European Senior Tour in 2008.*

BASF's pharmaceutical division. FDA approval for treatment of rheumatoid arthritis was secured in 2002, and adalimumab was given the brand name Humira (human monoclonal antibody in rheumatoid arthritis).

Humira was the first fully human monoclonal antibody drug to be approved by the US Food and Drug Administration (FDA).

Following additional clinical trials, Humira went on to gain approval as a treatment for psoriatic arthritis (2005), ankylosing spondylitis (2006), Crohn's disease (2007), psoriasis (2008), juvenile idiopathic arthritis (2008) and ulcerative colitis (2012). Since January 2013, Humira has been marketed by AbbVie, after parent company Abbott Laboratories split into Abbott and AbbVie.

Humira has become the bestselling drug in the world, with sales of $10.66 billion in 2013 and $12.54 billion in 2014.

Despite Humira 'leaving' Cambridge when its clinical development was taken over by BASF and then Abbott, the local impact of its early history can still be seen, as royalties from its sales have returned to Cambridge and fund not only new research in the MRC LMB, but also, through other channels, new research and further entrepreneurial activity in the field of antibody therapeutics. Two similar relationships between CAT and other companies also resulted in drugs reaching the global market – Benlysta (belimumab), a treatment for systemic lupus erythematosus, and Abthrax (raxibacumab), licensed in the US in 2012 for treating inhalation anthrax, both developed with Human Genome Sciences (HGS) and then GlaxoSmithKline (GSK) following its acquisition of HGS. In 2013, the US Government ordered 60,000 doses of Abthrax, a contract worth some $200 million to GSK.

LEMTRADA IS A STEP-CHANGE IN THE TREATMENT OF MULTIPLE SCLEROSIS

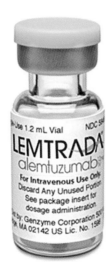

Lemtrada is another child of the LMB and the monoclonal antibody programme. A new drug for the treatment of relapsing-remitting multiple sclerosis (MS), a disease of the brain and spinal cord, Lemtrada was licensed in Europe, Canada, the UK and the US in the autumn of 2014. Unusually, it was licensed for first-line treatment despite a known risk

of complications – an indication of how significant it is as a new therapy.

Alastair Compston, Professor of Neurology in the Department of Clinical Neurosciences in the University of Cambridge, describes the arrival of Lemtrada on the market as a 'Cambridge story from start to finish', but that story started 40 years ago, has seen ten different companies hold varying levels of ownership, and has cost in the region of $1 billion.

What the Lemtrada story demonstrates is the tenacity of a few people who persisted in their work despite numerous knock-backs and dead ends – essential characteristics of the successful entrepreneur – because without the Cambridge team's refusal to give up, Lemtrada would never have reached the market.

It is hard to imagine how profound the impact successful treatment with Lemtrada for an MS patient can be. As professional golfer Tony Johnstone told the *Daily Mail* in 2008, 'One of the first effects of MS is to make you fade out of view as you physically and mentally decline. I'm in a unique position of knowing what it's like to come back.'

The following (approximate) timeline goes only part of the way to capturing the twists and turns as Campath-1H made its long and complicated journey to regulatory approval as a first-line treatment for MS.

1983
FIRST MONOCLONAL ANTIBODY, FIRST 'OWNER'.

Cambridge University and MRC assign rights for Campath-1 to the British Technology Group (BTG, formerly the National Research and Development Council), but crucially allow the team to continue work on the cell lines, even though BTG now 'owns' them. Campath-1 binds to IgM (Immunoglobin M) antibodies, renamed Campath-1M.

1985
THE NEXT OWNER, AND A NEW CAMPATH.

BTG licenses Campath-1M and Campath-1G (which binds to IgG antibodies) to Wellcome Biotech.

1988
THE HUMANIZING CHALLENGE.

Greg Winter and his team succeed in humanizing Campath-1G to create Campath-1H. BTG passes Campath-1H on to Wellcome Biotech, and extends their existing licences for Campath-1G and Campath-1M. Wellcome Biotech abandons work on Campath-1G in favour of Campath-1H.

1989
MS ENTERS THE EQUATION.

Alastair Compston joins the Cambridge University Department of Neuroscience. Both Compston and Herman Waldmann have separately identified MS, a disease with no effective treatment, as a potential target for monoclonal antibodies. Results obtained for vasculitis by Martin Lockwood indicate that Campath-1H might be effective in MS as well.

1990
ONE DOOR OPENS, ANOTHER DOOR CLOSES.

An MRC special grant plus contributions from Wellcome Biotech, the Wellcome Foundation, the Kay Kendall Trust and Cambridge University funds the establishment of the Therapeutic Antibody Centre (TAC) at Addenbrooke's Hospital in Cambridge, to produce antibodies of suitable quality for clinical research. Importantly, the group are still allowed to produce their own Campath-1G and 1H.

On the opening day of TAC, the closure of Wellcome Biotech is announced. It is to be reabsorbed into parent company Glaxo Wellcome, which then decides not to fund research into MS but instead chooses to fund clinical trials of Campath-1H in non-Hodgkin's lymphoma and rheumatoid arthritis.

1991
DIGGING IN.

Undaunted, Compston, Waldmann and the team obtain funding for initial trials from the MS Society of Great Britain and Northern Ireland, and treat their first patient under the named patient system. The patient improves so much they are able to go from extremely poor mobility before treatment to skiing a few months later.

1994
THE END OF THE ROAD?

Glaxo Wellcome abandons Campath-1H because there appears to be no commercial benefit in continuing. The Phase II trials for rheumatoid arthritis and non-Hodgkin's lymphoma are unsuccessful and reveal a number of complications from treating patients with Campath-1H, not least that it appears to be highly toxic to cancer patients.

The rights for Campath-1H revert to BTG.

TAC, the source of the antibodies, moves to Oxford, where Waldmann has already transferred.

Alasdair Coles joins Compston's team and they continue to seek funding for their own work on MS.

1997
ANOTHER YEAR, ANOTHER OWNER.

BTG licenses Campath-1H to US company LeukoSite. They plan to trial Campath-1H for B-cell CLL, as this condition has orphan drug status due to the potential market being too small for blockbuster – more than $1 billion – sales. Orphan status gives LeukoSite tax advantages for clinical trials and faster regulatory approval procedures. LeukoSite partners with ILEX Oncology to conduct the trials. Crucially, the assigned rights also allow LeukoSite to explore the use of Campath-1H for other diseases as well.

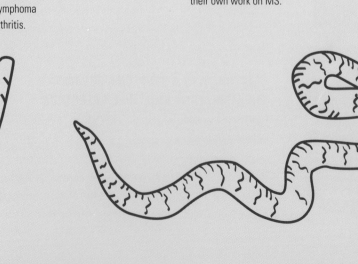

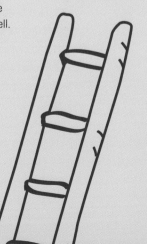

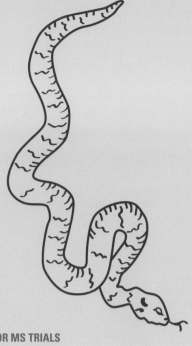

1999
HOPES FOR MS TRIALS ARE RAISED AND THEN DASHED.

Having initiated clinical trials using Campath-1H to treat patients with B-cell CLL in 1998, LeukoSite and ILEX Oncology now partner with Schering AG to fund clinical trials into MS, giving Schering an interest if the drug is commercialized. The project is risky because Schering has a veto on the trial programme.

Nevertheless, it looks like trials are going to go ahead, until LeukoSite is acquired by Millennium Pharmaceuticals, Inc. Efforts to persuade Millennium to move on to full clinical trials for MS appear to be unsuccessful.

2001
MS LOSES OUT TO B-CELL CLL.

FDA approves Campath-1H (now christened Alemtuzumab) for B-cell CLL as a second-line treatment. The EU approves Alemtuzumab (to be marketed as MabCampath) for third-line treatment.

2002
MS TRIALS RESCUED BY A CHANCE MEETING.

ILEX Oncology enters an agreement with Millennium to continue development of Alemtuzumab. A chance encounter between the CEO and President of ILEX, Jeff Buchalter, and one of Compston's MS patients, who is being treated with Campath-1H, persuades Buchalter to fund full clinical trials.

YET MORE OWNERSHIP COMPLICATIONS.

A Phase II trial for relapsing-remitting MS is prepared under the ILEX–Schering partnership, but ILEX is acquired by Genzyme before the trial starts. Genzyme inherits the relationship with Schering, but then Schering is acquired by Bayer and the relationship transfers to the new owners.

Genzyme are reluctant to proceed with clinical trials, but Compston and the Cambridge team make a strong argument for continuing, and Phase II trials go ahead. The results after five years are spectacular, and confound the statisticians.

Bayer sells their interest in the worldwide rights for Alemtuzumab to Genzyme in 2009.

2012
GREAT RESULTS – BUT THEY CAUSE PROBLEMS. OWNERSHIP CHANGES AGAIN.

Results of Phase III MS trials published in *The Lancet*, and the problem of how Genzyme will price Campath-1H for MS is raised. Because it is so effective, and treatment does not have to continue past the initial two sessions, they could charge a fortune. There are also concerns over whether Campath-1H (as Alemtuzumab) will still be available for B-cell CLL patients, for whom it is now approved as a first-line treatment.

Sanofi-Aventis (now Sanofi) acquires Genzyme for $20 billion, with $4 billion of that contingent on Alemtuzumab getting regulatory approval for MS. The deal means that Sanofi has essentially bought a ready-made but unlicensed product.

CHANGE OF USE.

Alemtuzumab as a treatment for B-cell CLL is withdrawn from the US and European markets prior to application for change of indication. Patients already prescribed Alemtuzumab for B-cell CLL provided with the drug free of charge through access programmes.

2013
LIGHT AT THE END OF THE TUNNEL – BUT HOPES DASHED YET AGAIN.

17 September: EU approves use of Alemtuzumab, now known as Lemtrada, as a first-line drug for MS. First-line status is very unusual for a drug with known potential side effects. Approval from the UK's National Institute for Health and Care Excellence (NICE) is similarly permissive.

The FDA refuses to license in the US, citing various concerns. This causes a backlash in other countries where licence is pending, resulting in applications either being paused, or given second-line licence (e.g. Canada). The FDA receives petitions from neurologists and the Multiple Sclerosis Society of America. European neurologists publish an open letter in *The Lancet*. The FDA asks for filing to be re-presented.

The first patient in the original clinical trials remains disease-free after nine years.

2014
FINAL HURDLE OVERCOME.

17 November: FDA approves Lemtrada.

1 December: first MS patient treated.

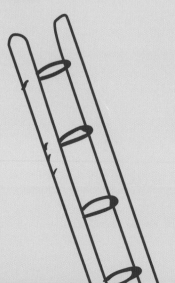

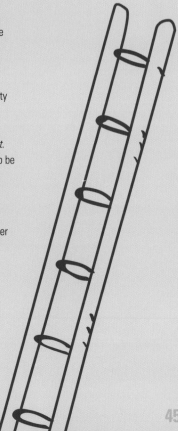

45

MEDIMMUNE CONTINUES TO GROW THE CAT LEGACY ON THE GLOBAL STAGE

The spirit, drive and determination of Cambridge Antibody Technology lives on through its heritage. Described as 'the jewel in the crown of UK biotech' by *The Independent* newspaper in 2008, CAT was acquired by AstraZeneca in 2006 and merged with another AstraZeneca acquisition, MedImmune, in 2007.

MedImmune Cambridge is a striking example of an international acquisition where the acquiring company has kept and grown operations in Cambridge. In fact, it has proved such a successful arrangement that AstraZeneca is setting up its new Global R&D Centre and corporate HQ in Cambridge.

There are now over 550 staff at MedImmune's new facilities on Granta Park. Along with its counterpart in Maryland in the US, MedImmune Cambridge comprises the biologics research and development operations for AstraZeneca. With a focus on the main therapy areas of oncology, cardiovascular and metabolic disease, and respiratory, inflammation and autoimmunity, the team in Cambridge has built leading expertise in antibody

discovery, protein engineering, disease understanding and biopharmaceutical development.

MedImmune's biologic drug candidates make up nearly 50% of AstraZeneca's total pipeline.

MedImmune's original human antibody phage display library contains over 10,000 million individual antibody fragments and was a fundamental breakthrough in generating antibody-based medicines. These libraries were sufficiently large that, for the first time, high quality drug leads could readily be isolated. The successful medicines Humira, Benlysta and Abthrax, as mentioned above, were all isolated using this technology. Humira's impact is well known, but Benlysta is also important as the first new treatment for lupus in over 50 years.

Now working as part of the global organization, MedImmune in Cambridge continues to generate, or make a significant contribution to the optimization of, the majority of the company's drug candidates. Almost 3,000 potential drug leads are expressed, purified and characterized every year as part of the organization's work on up to 60 different drug discovery and technology projects annually.

Tralokinumab, an anti-IL-13 antibody and one of the candidates that was discovered and optimized in Cambridge,

Far left: *Tristan Vaughan, Vice President R&D, Antibody Discovery and Protein Engineering, MedImmune.*

is now in Phase III clinical trials for severe asthma. Many lead molecules originally identified through work at MedImmune in the US, and by collaborations and partnerships around the globe, have been engineered in Cambridge to optimize their therapeutic potential. Two examples of these are durvalumab, an anti-PD-L1 antibody, now in Phase III clinical trials for a range of cancers, and mavrilimumab, an anti-GMCSF receptor antibody, which has completed Phase II clinical trials for rheumatoid arthritis.

MedImmune in Cambridge has established strong connections with its neighbours, and collaborates with a wide range of academics, researchers, charities, foundations and companies. The team also has a strong commitment to science education at all levels and believes inspiring the scientists of the future is key; community outreach activities include the University of Cambridge's annual Science Fair and more than 50 visits to local schools over a five year period.

The Cambridge-based MedImmune team has benefited from being part of the Cambridge community for over 25 years. And, in a world where partnerships and collaborations drive medical progress, becoming part of the Cambridge ecosystem was a contributing factor to the decision of AstraZeneca, MedImmune's parent company, to locate its new Global R&D Centre and Corporate Headquarters in Cambridge. This relocation to a new site next to Addenbrooke's Hospital, where colleagues from AstraZeneca and MedImmune will work side by side, is a clear signal of AstraZeneca's long-term commitment to the UK.

In 2014, a new collaboration was announced between MedImmune and CRUK in the establishment of the CRUK–MEDI Alliance Laboratory on Granta Park, where MedImmune has its Cambridge UK operations. The combined groups will focus on the diagnosis and treatment of cancer through novel biologics. The drug discovery process will involve a portfolio of cancer targets established by CRUK's network of principal investigators and MedImmune's world-class human antibody phage display libraries, with the goal of identifying primary cancer targets and honing in on the antibodies that will tackle them.

This unique partnership will bring together cutting-edge research with the most advanced antibody technologies industry can offer under one roof, to deliver significant output over a number of years.

Keith Blundy, CEO, Cancer Research Technology

"

In parallel with MedImmune's strategic focus on discovering and developing biologic medicines, the company places great importance on improving public understanding of science. The company maintains an active educational outreach programme, which encompasses visits to local schools and wider community-based initiatives, and also encourages the activities of university-level students studying life sciences subjects. We fully recognise the importance of inspiring the scientists of the future.

Jane Osbourn, Vice President Research and Development, MedImmune

ABCAM IS THE WORLD'S GO-TO PROVIDER OF LIFE SCIENCE RESEARCH TOOLS

Nearly half a million scientists around the world working in translational medicine and cellular biology use Abcam products in their research. 93% of Abcam's business comes from outside the UK.

Just as the development of monoclonal antibodies spawned research and clinical advances around the world, Cambridge (or rather, a Cambridge company) played a critical supporting role in those advances. Abcam was founded in 1998 by researcher Jonathan Milner and Tony Kouzarides, Professor of Cancer Biology at Cambridge University and now Deputy Director of the Gurdon Institute in Cambridge. The impetus to set up the company was born out of a very real problem for Milner's research into breast cancer genes.

I was constantly up against frustration in moving my research forward because of the lack of specific reagents and information about what was available… I got the idea of using a website to find them and I had been toying with the idea of setting up a business for years. I hadn't found an entrepreneurial atmosphere in the UK until I came to Cambridge.

Jonathan Milner, co-founder of Abcam, interviewed in 2001 by Lindy Beveridge

Of course today the idea of selling something over the internet is seen as normal but Amazon.com only launched in 1995, and although there were more internet users in the UK than, for instance, in Canada in 1998 (eight million versus seven and a half million), an online sales portal for such a complex product was not an obvious international business winner. Growth, not surprisingly, was slow, and at one point Milner was reduced to going to laboratories with an ice bucket and selling directly to his former colleagues.

But grow the company did. From a difficult patch in the early 2000s, Abcam went on to open its first overseas office in Cambridge, Massachusetts, in 2003. Further expansion to ten offices and facilities around the world and acquisitions followed, with a listing on AIM in 2005 – the same year that the company won the Queen's Award for Enterprise. By 2010, sales had reached over £70 million, with roughly 40% of those sales being in the US. Total product revenue for 2014–15 was almost double that at £135.4 million, with sales spread around the world.

A major part of Abcam's success is that it was the first company in this field not simply to describe its products, but also to add extensive data about their technical specifications, validation and usage. Researchers use antibodies to mark and identify specific, or target, proteins in a cell, which helps them understand how the cell functions normally and also when it is diseased. Good validation data helps them choose the right antibody for their work.

Introduction of knockout validation takes this important process to the next level, with antibodies tested against normal and 'knockout' cell lines. The knockout lines have had the gene that codes the target protein knocked out, and so the antibody should show no response if it is specific to that protein in the knockout line, while still showing a response in the normal cell line. A recent partnership with another Cambridge company, Horizon Discovery, will help Abcam to generate even more robust validation data for its existing products, and the two companies will join forces to create new knockout lines for new antibodies as they are developed.

Customers, too, play an important role in Abcam's success, not just by buying products and services, but because they become part of an interconnected scientific community that extends around the world.

Researchers who use Abcam products frequently submit 'Abreviews', where they list the experiment or test the Abcam product was used for, for instance Western blot, the other reagents and quantities used, experimental conditions, and any other relevant information. They also provide a star rating of how the product performed in the experiment. The more a product is used, the more information accumulates on the Abcam website, and the more benefits accrue to other researchers looking for the right product for their particular line

"

Our deep science base means we know what life science researchers need, we understand which biological pathways are important to them, and we know how to create the products and tools that will help them in their research. More than 20,000 published research papers have cited the use of Abcam's life science research tools.

Alan Hirzel, CEO, Abcam

Below: *Tony Kouzarides, co-founder of Abcam, with his medal for the 2013 Heinrich Wieland Prize.*

of research and experimental techniques. In this way, Abcam products become more valuable to customers the older they are and the more data is associated with them.

Since the acquisition of California company Epitomics in 2012, the company has offered proprietary RabMAb antibodies. This novel source is important because rabbits have a unique immune system, and antibodies derived from rabbits have higher sensitivity and stronger binding affinities than those derived from mouse cells. This characteristic means that it is possible to produce a wider range of monoclonal antibodies, which in turn increases the chances of finding a specific antibody that can perform a number of different functions. Abcam also has a RabMAb development laboratory in Hangzhou, and is the largest supplier of rabbit monoclonal antibodies in the world, with over 7,000 patented and validated RabMAb products in the catalogue.

Today, Abcam is the global market leader in supplying primary antibodies for research, and over half a million of the world's scientists researching proteins at the cellular level use Abcam research tools and services.

Allan Bradley, founder of Kymab.

THE ANTIBODY STORY CONTINUES TO INSPIRE ENTREPRENEURS

Researchers and companies around the world continue to seek to improve the efficacy and efficiency of therapeutic antibody treatments. Two particular goals are to create more fully human antibodies, and smaller molecules that contain only the active parts of the protein and can be delivered topically or orally, rather than intravenously as at present. A range of groups and companies in Cambridge are building on local, seminal expertise and experience to contribute to these goals. The presence of scientist entrepreneurs who have histories of successes behind them not only inspires the next generation of companies, but also encourages investment into Cambridge from funders and big pharma alike.

Greg Winter continues to be involved not only in the research of the MRC LMB but also in setting up new companies to exploit the latest technologies emerging from the LMB. **Domantis**, which he co-founded with LMB colleague Ian Tomlinson in 2000, worked on antibody fragments that were one-tenth the size of a normal antibody molecule. Therapeutic antibodies are large molecules and treatment has to involve transfusion, or injection at the very least; smaller molecules raise the possibility of topical or oral administration, making the process much easier and more convenient for the patient and their medical team. The importance of what Domantis was doing was indicated by the fact that, even before the company had any drug candidates in its pipeline, and at least one year away from any clinical trials, it was purchased by GSK. The £230 million GSK paid in cash for Domantis was considerably better than the £50–£100 million market capitalization that analysts forecast if the company had floated. The best return on venture capital investment for 3i in 2006, the *Financial Times* commented that the exit was 'an unusually fast turnaround for a healthcare investment'.

PanGenetics, although founded in Utrecht in the Netherlands, opened a development base in Cambridge to access technology there, and hired former CAT board member and CTO Kevin Johnson as its CEO. One of the first companies to adopt the 'no research, developmen only' model for antibodies, the plan was to identify and license early stage antibody drugs that showed great promise, and manage development up to proof of concept, at which point the bigger pharmaceutical companies would acquire the drug candidate and continue the clinical trial process.

In 2009, PanGenetics announced a unique deal with Abbott for a single antibody that was remarkable for the high upfront price of $170 million, subsequent milestone payments amounting to a further $190 million, and no royalties. The deal reportedly amounted to the biggest upfront payment for a Phase I product at the time. The antibody involved, PG110, binds to nerve growth factor and could play an important role in pain relief, a market estimated by analysts Decision Resources to reach around $21.6 billion in the US and major EU countries in 2022.

Kymab was founded in 2009 by Allan Bradley, a former director of the Sanger Institute, to exploit technology developed in his laboratory at the Institute.

The founding of Kymab marked another step in the quest to increase the efficiency of creating and isolating fully human monoclonal antibodies to target specific conditions and diseases. Kymab's transgenic human antibody platform, Kymouse, is a set of diverse mouse strains that helps the company to reduce the number of steps to finding potentially therapeutic monoclonal antibodies to a range of new diseases other than those with an inflammatory profile, such as rheumatoid arthritis.

Set up with initial funding from the Wellcome Trust Investment Division in its first example of venture capital investing with the intention of building a major pharmaceutical firm, Kymab has gone on to receive further funding from the Wellcome Trust, the Bill & Melinda Gates Foundation, Woodford Patient Capital Trust plc and Malin Corporation plc. Part of the funding from the Wellcome Trust is a grant to work on Ebola in a consortium with the University of Westminster, the Wellcome Trust Sanger Institute, and Porton Down, a facility of Public Health England. The Bill & Melinda

Gates Foundation contribution funds research into vaccine development for areas of high unmet medical need, with malaria and HIV being the first targets.

Kymab announced its first drug development partnership with Novo Nordisk in 2013.

Kymab also leverages its technology through Kymab Access, a global programme that provides access to Kymouse for leading academics and researchers working in the therapeutic antibody field, particularly those focused on orphan diseases and diseases common in the developing world. In March 2016, Kymab confirmed that David Chiswell had been appointed CEO. Previously, David was CEO at Cambridge Antibody Technology (CAT).

At the same time that Kymab was emerging from the Wellcome Trust Sanger Institute, the BBSRC Babraham Institute nearby was also giving birth to a company focused on antibody research, **Crescendo Biologics**; this time the target was antibody fragments. The potential benefits of antibody fragments, the smallest part of an antibody molecule that retained the ability to bind to a receptor site on an antigen and be biologically active, included the ability to penetrate tissues and tumours where traditional antibodies were too large to be effective.

Much of the work on antibody fragments relies on those derived from llama cells, which ultimately cannot be fully humanized, or phage display libraries, which lack sufficient efficacy. Crescendo Biologics was founded to develop a promising new technology platform from the Babraham Institute that indicated a possible way of generating fully human antibody fragments from transgenic mice.

The Crescendo Mouse produces only human antibody fragments, with no mouse antibodies to contaminate them. The Humabody molecules thus derived are smaller than traditional antibodies and expand the range of potential treatments because they can be administered by injection rather than via an intravenous drip, or applied to the skin.

One area Crescendo Biologics is focusing on is psoriasis. With around 125 million people suffering from this condition worldwide, and a market that is expected to reach $6.7 billion by 2018, current treatments do include monoclonal antibody therapy, but these have to be given intravenously, are expensive and are of limited application. A major advance would be to develop an appropriate antibody that can be applied topically rather than injected, and the fact that antibody fragments are small enough to make this possible indicates a great opportunity for Crescendo Biologics and their partners. Clinical proof of concept data is expected for Crescendo product CB001 by 2016, making it likely to be the first topical biologic to reach the market.

The company is also expanding its discovery programmes in oncology, with an initial focus on advanced prostate cancer. Prostate cancer is the top cause of cancer death among men in the UK, and the second highest in the US; an estimated 1.1 million men were diagnosed with the disease worldwide in 2012. Crescendo Biologics is examining opportunities for increasing the efficacy of therapies and also possibilities for treating the disease by targeting the immune system.

Bicycle Therapeutics, also founded in 2009, is yet another company co-founded by Greg Winter, this time with colleague Christian Heinis. Bicycle Therapeutics aims to move the antibody story into a new area — that of compounds that mimic antibodies in their selectivity and specificity, but which are much smaller and can be chemically synthesized. Known as bicyclic peptides, or bicycles, due to their shape, the option of chemical synthesis makes these compounds far easier and cheaper to produce than therapeutic monoclonal antibodies, and opens up a wider range of target options.

An additional benefit of bicyclic peptides is their potential role in improving compliance. One of the biggest problems in drug treatments is ensuring that patients take or receive the correct doses of the correct medicines at the correct times. Uncomfortable side effects or simply forgetting are two issues with compliance, and for drugs that require a visit to a nurse, doctor or hospital for administration, the barriers to compliance are even higher.

Christian Heinis, co-founder of Bicycle Therapeutics.

Small molecules such as bicyclic peptides are easier to administer than antibodies but can still be engineered to behave like them. Being small, they can sometimes penetrate tumour cells that normal therapeutic antibodies cannot. The size therefore could improve both compliance and treatment. Bicyclic peptides also have the advantage that they clear from the body within 24 hours, whereas it can take up to 21 days for therapeutic antibodies to leave the body, thus impacting on how often treatment can be given.

Abzena relies on a mixed model of providing research services to pharmaceutical companies along with using its proprietary discovery platform to identify antibody drug candidates that can be licensed out to partners. The company was formed when Cambridge company Antitope merged with a spin-out from Imperial College London, PolyTherics. The two companies consolidated at Babraham, Antitope bringing in particular its Composite Human Antibody technology and PolyTherics contributing enhanced conjugation and polymer technology, used among other things to produce antibody drug conjugates. The company floated on AIM as Abzena in June 2014, and acquired US companies PacificGMP and TCRS (The Chemistry Research Solution) in 2015.

The global customer base for Abzena includes major pharmaceutical companies, and ten antibody therapeutics developed with the Composite Human Antibody technology are in clinical trials with partners for a range of disease targets, including ulcerative colitis, chronic obstructive pulmonary disease (COPD), liver fibrosis and diabetic nephropathy.

XO1 AND ICHORCUMAB: SAVING LIVES WITH 'THE BLOOD OF THE GODS'

A new, synthetic fully human monoclonal antibody developed in Cambridge, ichorcumab – named after Ichor, the substance that flows in the blood of the Greek gods and gives them immortality – has the potential to profoundly impact death statistics and the economic burden of heart disease and stroke. If the new antibody lives up to expectations, it could be a game changer for millions of people.

Cardiovascular diseases are the number one cause of death globally, and the World Health Organization estimates that these diseases (including heart attack and stroke) accounted for 31% of all deaths worldwide in 2012. The Centers for Disease Control (CDC) states that one in every four deaths in the US, around 610,000 each year, is due to heart

disease. The cost of treating patients after a heart attack in the US has been estimated at over $11.5 billion, but this figure accounts for their inpatient treatment and hospital stays only and does not include rehabilitation, loss of productivity and the other costs associated with long-term chronic conditions. The CDC postulates that the total cost of strokes to the US economy, including non-treatment costs, is around $34 billion each year. Figures in other countries around the world show similar trends, and similar economic burdens.

The crucial mechanism behind deaths and disability due to heart disease and stroke is blood clotting, but medications to prevent clotting and so reduce the risk of heart attack or stroke – most commonly heparin and warfarin – increase the risk of uncontrolled bleeding, to the extent that minor surgery, such as having a tooth removed, could prove fatal.

Given the sheer numbers involved and the risks of current medications, any new treatment that could prevent blood clotting without promoting bleeding could have a profound impact worldwide.

A natural antibody that could do just this was discovered in 2008 when Trevor Baglin, consultant haematologist at Addenbrooke's Hospital in Cambridge, treated a patient who arrived in A&E with a head injury. Scans revealed a haematoma on the brain that might need surgical intervention, but a routine clotting screen revealed 'a degree of anticoagulation consistent with severe haemophilia', as Baglin reported. The patient seemed to have blood that could not clot. But, as Baglin observed, 'to our surprise the bleeding stopped quite normally.'

Baglin enlisted the help of a colleague, Jim Huntington, Professor of Molecular Haemostasis at the University's

Above: *XO1, left to right: David Grainger, Jim Huntington, Richard Mason and Trevor Baglin.*

Below: *Celltech Chiroscience.*

CHIROSCIENCE PRODUCES THE FIRST APPROVED BIOTECH PRODUCT FROM THE UK

Levobupivacaine, a long-acting local anaesthetic, was one of the first biopharmaceutical products from a UK biotech company to be approved in both Europe and the US. It was one of the first novel products developed by Cambridge company Chiroscience, founded by Chris Evans, Peter Keen and Andy Richards in 1992, and was licensed to what was then Zeneca Ltd in March 1998, with Zeneca buying shares in Chiroscience and agreeing to fund marketing and promotion worldwide except for Japan, with Chiroscience remaining responsible for gaining regulatory approval in the EU and US.

Chiroscience filed for approval for levobupivacaine in the US in April 1998. A further licence was granted to Maruishi in September 1998 for marketing in Japan. An initial approval from EU regulators was obtained in December 1998, but almost simultaneously Zeneca announced it was merging with Swedish company Astra. Both EU and US competition rules forced Zeneca to rescind its licence rights to the newly approved drug before the merger could be permitted to proceed. Chiroscience regained the rights and in 1999 gained US approval from the FDA. However, the uncertainty that the AstraZeneca deal created led to a merger between Chiroscience and another UK company, Celltech. A new licensing deal for levobupivacaine was essential, and Purdue Pharma took the US rights and Abbott Laboratories the licence for Europe and the rest of the world, excluding Japan.

Launched in the US and Europe as Chirocaine by the respective licensees in early 2000, levobupivacaine is still used around the world for a range of indications, and the founders and several former employees of Chiroscience have gone on to fuel the biotech boom in Cambridge.

Cambridge Institute of Medical Research, and together they discovered that the patient produced a unique antibody that had an anticoagulative effect when they tested it in the laboratory, but did not make the patient himself more at risk of excessive bleeding. In effect, the patient's own immune system had somehow solved the blood-thinning drug problem. If a synthetic antibody with a similar effect could be produced, it could have a significant impact on the treatment of patients where clotting was a major risk and the conventional treatment equally problematic.

In order to develop a therapeutic version of the antibody, venture capital firm Index Ventures took the unusual step of forming a virtual, single-asset drug development company, XO1 in 2013 with Richard Mason as CEO. Richard was formerly the CBO at Cambridge Antibody Technology. With a total investment of $11 million from Index Ventures, Cambridge Enterprise and other investors, and chaired by Index Venture partner David Grainger, a former Cambridge University researcher and entrepreneur, the entire focus of the company was to find a route to clinical trials for a synthetic antibody that performed in the same way as the natural one. The virtual model necessitated partnerships with service providers in the drug development space to create a preclinical model, with the hope of eventually finding a pharmaceutical company partner that would invest in clinical trials.

In March 2015, with preclinical work already showing great promise in animal models, XO1 was acquired by Janssen Pharmaceuticals, part of Johnson & Johnson.

Far right: Andy Richards, co-founder of Chiroscience.

53

ASTEX THERAPEUTICS DRAMATICALLY IMPROVES THE EFFICIENCY OF THE DRUG DISCOVERY PROCESS

Refining the drug discovery process was the goal of Astex Therapeutics.

Chris Abell and Tom Blundell in the University of Cambridge Chemistry Department had been working on enzyme inhibition in drug development, which looked promising for drug discovery. Working with Astex co-founder Harren Jhoti, they were able to demonstrate a methodology that would revolutionize drug discovery and succeed with an innovation that had long been postulated but not yet achieved.

To improve the rate and reliability of finding potential drug candidates, Jhoti and his team developed the novel Pyramid platform. The method uses high throughput X-ray crystallography and automated data collection to screen small molecules, or fragments, and analyse their binding properties against disease-causing proteins. Requiring fewer inputs and taking less time to identify promising molecules, the fragments

Above: *Tom Blundell.*

Left: *Chris Abell.*

Below: *Harren Jhoti, Astex co-founder.*

> **"**
> *Drug companies built libraries of a million or more compounds, and used robotic, high through-put screening to try and find a molecule that would interact with their drug target. This made little sense intellectually; we felt it was time for a new paradigm for drug discovery.*

Chris Abell, University of Cambridge Chemistry Department

can then be synthetically built on to create a molecule that has potency against the disease.

This method, now widely known as fragment-based drug discovery, clearly proved popular with big pharmaceutical companies, and companies such as AstraZeneca, Boehringer Ingelheim, Schering AG, Novartis, GSK and Janssen were soon queueing up to negotiate partnerships with Astex. Jhoti was named a World Economic Forum Technology Pioneer in 2005, and was the Royal Society of Chemistry's *Chemistry World* Entrepreneur of the Year in 2007.

Astex had found a better way to discover drugs, and had secured deals worth an estimated $1.8 billion before merging with SuperGen in 2011. The company was renamed Astex Pharmaceuticals, and eventually acquired by Otsuka Pharmaceutical in October 2013 at a valuation of $886 million, the seventh largest M&A deal in the life sciences sector that year. Otsuka were keen to maintain and build operations in Cambridge.

By the time of the acquisition, Astex had advanced eight of its own products into clinical development, including two in Phase II trials, and a number of others in the pipeline through its partnerships. The most advanced (LEE-011) from its partnership with Novartis has gone into Phase III and a number of others into Phase II, including AZD5363 in oncology and AZD3293 in Alzheimer's disease, both with AstraZeneca, and JNJ-42756493 in oncology with Janssen. Astex's most advanced compound, SGI-110, has also gone into Phase III.

As a consequence of Astex success, fragment-based approaches are commonplace throughout Pharma and Biotech, and the power of the technology is also recognized by academia and drug discovery institutes through the UK 3D Consortium, for example. While many companies have in-house capabilities, it is perhaps telling that GSK established a major fragment collaboration with Astex as their internal expertise was apparently not competitive. Importantly, fragments may open the door to blocking protein–protein interactions which would lead to totally new classes of therapeutic agents designed to meet the medical needs of the 21st century.

Former Head of Worldwide Discovery for Pfizer,
quoted in a Cambridge University Research Excellence
Framework impact case study, 2014

ARAKIS AND VECTURA PARTNER TO PRODUCE THE FIRST GLYCOPYRRONIUM TREATMENT FOR CHRONIC OBSTRUCTIVE PULMONARY DISEASE TO REACH THE MARKET

As big pharma companies seek to de-risk drug discovery by acquiring or licensing products from small biotech companies, those smaller companies also seek ways to de-risk their part of the bargain, not just by sharing the burden with big pharma, but also by partnering with other companies to help them punch above their weight. One example of this has been the way that inhaled glycopyrrolate, a maintenance treatment for chronic obstructive pulmonary disease (COPD), has come to market with sales expected to reach $750 million – based on innovation combining both drug discovery and delivery.

The successful arrival of this product as Seebri Breezhaler had its roots in a partnership between Cambridge company Arakis and Vectura, another company originally founded in Cambridge which had acquired drug delivery technology developed at Cambridge Consultants and from Bath University. Making such complex deals work challenges both the entrepreneurs and the big pharma companies they are planning to collaborate with.

Arakis was founded by Robin Bannister, Julian Gilbert and Andy Richards to work on reprofiling known drugs that the team recognized had potential for meeting unmet medical needs – referred to as performance enhanced medicines, or PEMs – which were often married with selected drug delivery technologies. The company had a number of products in its initial drug candidate pipeline, all being developed with a delivery partner. One of these was AD237, a potential treatment for COPD, being developed with Vectura, who brought the necessary inhalation technology, and together they demonstrated excellent Phase IIa clinical data.

A major boost was given to the Arakis–Vectura partnership when they jointly signed a licensing agreement with Novartis in April 2005 to commercialize AD237. At $375 million plus possible future royalties, at the time this was one of Europe's biggest biotech licensing agreements. In July 2005 it was announced that Arakis' original investors (the company had raised over £49 million in three private equity funding rounds) had accepted an offer from Sosei, a Japanese pharmaceutical company, to purchase the company for £106.5 million.

The AD237 licensing deal remained, with the compound now christened NVA237, and by October 2005 it was entering

Phase IIb trials under the auspices of Novartis. Subsequent Phase III trials proved successful and Novartis filed NVA237 and its proprietary delivery method with the regulators.

Seebri Breezhaler, based on the innovative pharmacology from Arakis and delivery technology from Vectura, was approved as a once-daily maintenance treatment for COPD in both Europe and Japan in 2012, the first approval for inhaled glycopyrronium anywhere in the world. This released substantial milestone payments and sales royalties for both Vectura and Sosei. Inhaled glycopyrronium became central to Novartis' respiratory strategy with a series of combination products being developed.

In 2015, Novartis announced that two products based on the Arakis/Vectura technology, the Seebri Neohaler and Utibron Neohaler, had been approved by the FDA. Sales outside the US for the first nine months of 2015 had topped $297 million, a growth of 174%, and entry into the US market, where an estimated 27 million people suffer from COPD, will add significantly to this. The FDA approval triggered further milestone payments to Vectura and Sosei of $22.5 million, with future royalties from commercialisation in the US.

Acacia Pharma, founded in 2007 by one of the original team from Arakis, Julian Gilbert, and Robert Gristwood, another Chiroscience alumnus, has also adopted the model of repurposing known drugs. Development costs for known drugs are lower because they have already passed safety and other tests for their previous use, therefore they may need less time to get to clinical proof of concept and have filing requirements that are less onerous – but the company has to ensure that what they develop from those known drugs is sufficiently novel to be patented and differentiated enough to be commercialized in its own right.

Acacia Pharma is focusing on supportive care, in particular potential treatments for post-operative nausea and vomiting (PONV), and chemotherapy-induced nausea and vomiting (CINV) in cancer. The company has four candidates in its pipeline: APD421 (Baremsis), in Phase III trials for PONV, and APD403 for CINV, APD515 for dry mouth (xerostomia) in advanced cancer patients, and APD209 for cancer cachexia (muscle wasting), all in Phase II trials. Results so far are very promising.

Whereas the Arakis model was to find partners to commercialize all four of its candidates, Acacia already has a US operation and plans to launch its own sales activities in the US following regulatory approval there, while it will seek partners to commercialize its products elsewhere in the world.

NAPP DEVELOPS THE WORLD'S FIRST CONTROLLED-RELEASE MORPHINE SULPHATE TABLETS

Cambridge has a long history of researchers and companies working in drug discovery, development and delivery, partly due to the arrival in 1983 of Napp Pharmaceuticals, a 60-year-old UK company that consolidated its three locations from around the country into a new and iconic building on the Cambridge Science Park.

Napp focuses on offering new medicines with important benefits for patients and supporting the NHS in delivering effective, sustainable healthcare. Among the company's notable successes has been a controlled-release technology, known as Continus, which has been used for a number of different treatments ranging from asthma to cardiovascular disease. Continus enabled Napp to develop the world's first controlled-release morphine tablet, making it possible to give morphine orally rather than only by injection.

Napp is privately owned and now part of the Mundipharma network of independent associated pharmaceutical companies,

Left: *Julian Gilbert (top) and Robert Gristwood (bottom), founders of Acacia Pharma.*

Above: *Napp Pharmaceuticals.*

on to play a key role in technology transfer out of Cambridge University, first with the Wolfson Cambridge Industrial Unit and then with Cambridge Enterprise. Thus the impact of Napp and the wider Mundipharma network includes not only products adopted globally, but also the growth of the Cambridge Phenomenon itself.

ARECOR WORKS ON A NOVEL TECHNOLOGY TO IMPROVE THE STABILITY OF BIOLOGICS

A much younger company looking into innovative ways to reformulate drugs for easier administration and improved efficacy is Arecor. A Unilever spin-out founded in 2007 and located on Cambridge's Science Park, Arecor focuses on peptides, proteins and biologics. One of the biggest problems with these drugs is their inherent instability in high temperatures or during prolonged storage, especially in solution form.

Arecor's novel Arestat technology produces reformulated liquid biopharmaceuticals such as monoclonal antibodies that can be more readily administered at home rather than requiring intravenous infusion in hospital. In addition, they can have less stringent requirements for temperature-controlled transportation and storage, potentially a major advance in supporting biologicals such as vaccines used in remote areas and inhospitable climates.

RARE AND ORPHAN DISEASES GET A NEW CHAMPION IN HEALX

Another twist in the 'new drugs from old drugs' story is emerging as young company Healx seeks to use advanced data analysis, machine learning and in-depth genomics to address the problems of rare and orphan diseases, where big pharmaceutical companies rarely direct their research.

Healx was set up with seed funding of £300,000 in April 2015, and went on to win the Life Science Business of the Year at the finals of the 2015 Cambridge University Entrepreneurs business plan competition. In March 2015, the company pitched at an Enterprise Tuesday event in Cambridge making it clear that they were not looking for investment, but looking for people to join them.

Healx matches trials data from existing drugs, or drugs that have been dropped out of the commercialization process when pharma companies decided the market was not big enough, with information on the genomics of the disease and patient groups. The core research for their technology was done in the

which has a presence in 51 countries and employs some 7,800 people worldwide. In 2013, the Cambridge site produced 21 million packs of medicines, which were supplied to wholesalers in the UK and over 40 countries across the globe.

Napp has provided a science education project across Cambridgeshire, the Science Ambassador Scheme, for over ten years. The scheme is delivered through 30 Napp Group volunteers (or Ambassadors) and offers Science Technology, Engineering and Medicine (STEM) educational events for schools throughout the county. The Ambassador Scheme has reached more than 10,000 students since it was launched in 2006.

The longstanding presence of Napp and Mundipharma on the Cambridge Science Park puts them at the heart of the Phenomenon's thriving life sciences community. It not only demonstrates their business models of partnerships and alliances in action, but also serves as a catalyst for new biotechnology and life sciences start-ups around Cambridge. A number of former Napp employees, including David Cavalla, Julian Gilbert and Robert Gristwood, have gone on to found companies. Another Napp alumnus, Richard Jennings, went

group of Andreas Bender in the Department of Chemistry at the University.

A key part of the business model for Healx is working directly with patient groups and charities set up to help those with rare diseases and promote research into their condition. The company's predictive technology has already been validated with experiments set up with a patient group in the US and the company has launched its first 12-month drug-repositioning programme.

Healx was also instrumental in setting up the Cambridge Rare Disease Network, to promote collaboration among researchers and pharmaceutical companies in this underserved area.

AFFINITY CHROMATOGRAPHY IS THE FOUNDATION STONE FOR A BILLION-DOLLAR COMPANY

Many of the world's major pharmaceuticals manufacturers rely on bioseparation techniques developed in Cambridge to extract proteins with potentially therapeutic benefits from natural and recombinant sources and purify them by removing other proteins, DNA, pathogens and other contaminants.

ProMetic Life Sciences Inc began as a joint venture between Cambridge company Affinity Chromatography Ltd and Canadian company Innovon Life Sciences. Affinity Chromatography Ltd was the first company spun out from the Cambridge University Institute of Biotechnology, under the direction of Chris Lowe, and was registered in 1987. It was co-funded by an angel investor, Kenneth Jones, an ex-Imperial Chemical Industries scientist, Vivian Stead and Chris Lowe. The company initially set out to exploit a raft of technologies based on triazine dyes and computer-aided design of small molecule mimics of Protein A for the binding of monoclonal antibodies. The Institute of Biotechnology and the University of Cambridge subsequently received the Queen's Award for Technological Achievement in 1996, in recognition of the novelty of the technology and its commercial success, the first such award for the University.

Innovon changed its name to ProMetic Life Sciences and listed on the Toronto Stock Exchange in 1998, and Affinity Chromatography became a subsidiary, with R&D in Cambridge and production facilities on the Isle of Man. ProMetic initially marketed its platform to pharmaceutical and drug discovery companies under a service and licensing model, but the company also used its technology to start building a pipeline of its own drug candidates.

"
Rare diseases affect 350 million people worldwide. 8,000 rare diseases have been diagnosed, but only 200 have a 'cure', less than 1%. But if we fail to treat patients with rare diseases, on average caring for them costs healthcare systems $1 million per year.

Tim Guilliams, Founder and CEO, Healx

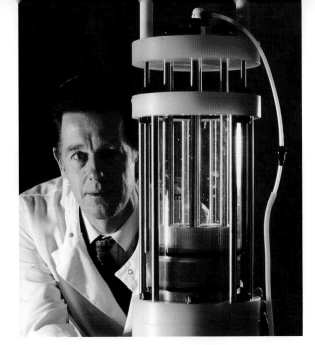

Chris Lowe.

ProMetic's proprietary technology platform, the Plasma Protein Purification System (PPPS), was developed in partnership with the American Red Cross to remove prions, infection-causing proteins associated with variant Creutzfeldt–Jakob disease (vCJD) in humans. The world's first prion removal system, ProMetic's P-Capt filter, received CE mark approval in the EU in 2006, and is used by national blood agencies to reduce the risk of transmitting vCJD through blood transfusion.

The PPPS technology is not only used to remove undesirable proteins from blood plasma, but also to extract other proteins with valuable and potentially therapeutic properties. Naturally derived, biological drug candidates face an easier and faster route to regulatory approval than synthetic drugs, and PPPS enables the extraction of multiple desirable proteins from a single sample. ProMetic's first potential drug candidate originating from this method is already in clinical trials for type 1 plasminogen deficiency.

Alongside the drug candidates derived from plasma, ProMetic also develops small-molecule drug candidates, which are designed to mimic antibodies, but much smaller and cheaper to produce than humanized antibodies themselves. ProMetic's candidates are targeted at underserved and rare and orphan diseases, and clinical trials are underway in fibrosis, chronic kidney disease and metabolic syndrome (which is associated with type 2 diabetes).

With a market capitalization of Canadian$2.06 billion (US$1.54 billion), as of 1 December 2015, several drug candidates already in clinical trials, and a new strategic alliance to manufacture and commercialize plasma-derived pharmaceuticals with Generium in Russia, ProMetic is anticipating the imminent arrival of its plasma-derived therapeutics on the market.

Far right: Louise Brown, the world's first 'test-tube baby', was born on 25 July 1978.

THE WORLD'S FIRST TEST-TUBE BABY IS CONCEIVED USING CAMBRIDGE TECHNOLOGY

Patrick Steptoe and Robert Edwards announced the birth of the world's first test-tube baby on 25 July 1978. Louise Brown had been conceived using pioneering surgical techniques developed by Steptoe, and a system that permitted a human egg to be fertilized outside the body created by Cambridge University physiologist Edwards, a method known as in vitro fertilization, or IVF.

Six months later, in January 1979, the birth of the first baby boy conceived using IVF was announced, again with the help of Steptoe and Edwards and their pioneering techniques. Australia was the next country to announce its first test-tube baby, in 1980, and the US followed in 1981. In 2013, more than 1.5% of all babies born in the US were conceived in this way.

Steptoe and Edwards opened one of the world's first IVF clinics at Bourn Hall, just outside Cambridge, in 1980, and continued to provide infertility treatments and conduct research into how to improve their techniques and increase the chances of success. Since then, additional interventions, such as using hormone treatments to stimulate egg production and freezing embryos, have been introduced, and many doctors and researchers around the world continue to develop associated procedures. Bourn Hall was also where the first successful conception and birth was achieved using a procedure to inject a sperm cell directly into an egg, and carries on with its work today.

Steptoe died in 1988, but Edwards was awarded the Nobel Prize in Physiology or Medicine in 2010 for the development of IVF.

Since Louise Brown's birth in 1978, around five million babies have been born worldwide using IVF.

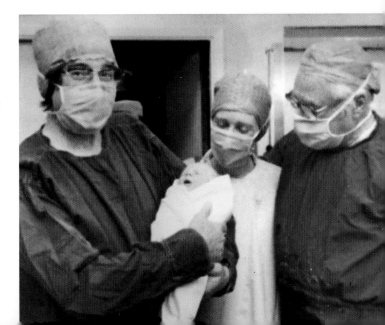

"

AstraZeneca's decision to make Cambridge the location of our global headquarters and the beating heart of our research and development reflects the importance we place on scientific excellence and the unique position of this amazing city as a hotbed of biopharmaceutical innovation. In Cambridge, we work side by side every day with world-leading scientific experts and collaborate with renowned academic research institutions, pre-eminent hospitals and cutting-edge biotech companies. We're delighted to be part of this tremendous ecosystem as we develop life-changing medicines for patients.

Pascal Soriot, CEO, AstraZeneca

Artist's impressions of the new AstraZeneca Global R&D Centre and Corporate Headquarters under construction on the Biomedical Campus in Cambridge.

61

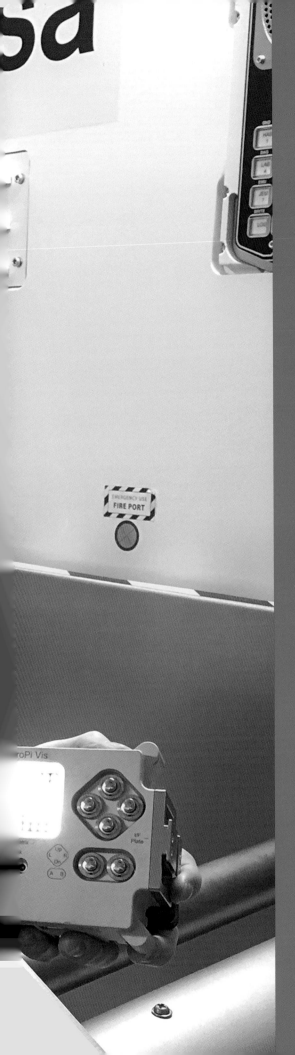

COMPUTING

An ARM chip in almost every smartphone in the world, 443 billion minutes of gaming time on RuneScape, seven million Raspberry Pi computers sold in less than four years – the list of computing successes coming out of Cambridge is long and varied.

Partly this is due to the establishment of computing as a discipline in Cambridge University, but equally it is because entrepreneurs in this sector have been exposed to computing through owning a BBC Micro from Acorn or a ZXSpectrum from Sinclair.

Today, although Acorn and Sinclair have long ceased to exist, their legacy is seen not only in the range of companies around Cambridge (and elsewhere) that point to the early home computers as inspiration, but also in the emergence of Raspberry Pi, and a whole new generation being introduced to coding at its most accessible and affordable.

British astronaut Tim Peake with a Raspberry Pi device.

THE CAMBRIDGE UNIVERSITY COMPUTER LABORATORY PUTS COMPUTING TO WORK FOR RESEARCH

When the Electronic Delay Storage Automatic Calculator, EDSAC, became fully operational in May 1949, it was the first time researchers had been given access to a stored-program computer to help them with their calculations.

EDSAC was built under the direction of Maurice Wilkes in what was then known as the Mathematical Laboratory of Cambridge University. The first program for EDSAC, to compute squares of numbers 0 to 99, was written by David Wheeler, the first PhD student to graduate from the Mathematical Laboratory. Wheeler and his colleagues developed subroutines that made EDSAC very user-friendly. Other significant contributions from the group included the Burrows–Wheeler Transform for data

Far left: *Sinclair ZX Spectrum.*

Below: *Maurice Wilkes (left) with the Electronic Delay Storage Automatic Calculator (EDSAC).*

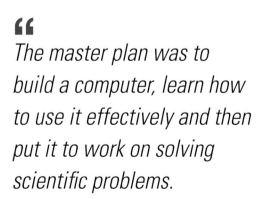

"

The master plan was to build a computer, learn how to use it effectively and then put it to work on solving scientific problems.

Haroon Ahmed, *Cambridge Computing: The First 75 Years*

encryption and the Tiny Encryption Algorithm (TEA), the latter still being used today.

The Cambridge college system, where people from different disciplines interacted on a regular basis, helped spread the word that there was a new machine available for anyone in the University to use, and EDSAC quickly became a victim of its own success.

The first conference on computing held outside the US was held in Cambridge in June 1949, and the first book on computer programming, *The Preparation of Programs for an Electronic Digital Computer: with special reference to the EDSAC and the use of a library of subroutines*, written by Wilkes, Wheeler and Stanley Gill, was published in 1951.

EDSAC and the Mathematical Laboratory played an important role in several Nobel Prizes, including those of Richard Stone (Economics, 1984), and John Kendrew (Chemistry, 1962), from the Cavendish Laboratory X-ray crystallography group, who used EDSAC for calculations in his work on the structure of myoglobin. Martin Ryle cited David Wheeler in his Nobel Prize lecture in 1974, for his work on developing the fast Fourier transform, a key algorithm for Ryle's research in radio astronomy.

Wilkes made a further major contribution to computer science and technology with EDSAC II, which introduced microprogramming, increasing operating speed and the number of instructions performed.

The Mathematical Laboratory also provided the first model for the University of interacting with business. Funding for EDSAC from J Lyons & Co evolved into a relationship with Wilkes and the Mathematical Laboratory to develop a computer for business use, under the LEO Computers (Lyons Electronic Office) brand.

The Mathematical Laboratory became the Cambridge University Computer Laboratory, and today, more than 200 companies have been started by its graduates. The first spin-out from the Computer Laboratory, Shape Data Ltd, was focused on computer-aided design (CAD), and developed Romulus, the first commercial 3D modelling software.

Data for the Computer Laboratory indicate that a disproportionately large number of companies which have been set up by computer science graduates become dramatically successful compared with the national average.

Haroon Ahmed, *Cambridge Computing: The First 75 Years*

> **"**
> *The development of aperture synthesis has therefore been very closely linked to the development of more and more powerful computers, and it is interesting to speculate how our work in Cambridge would have proceeded if, for example, computer development had been five years behind its actual course.*

Martin Ryle, Nobel Prize Lecture, 1974

65

The Computer Laboratory today has a 'Hall of Fame' listing companies that have been set up by graduates of the Laboratory in Cambridge and around the world. Among them are companies that have since disappeared, but had an impact at the time, such as Acorn (home computers, BBC Micro), FORE Systems (ATM network interface cards and adaptors, acquired by GEC for $4.5 billion in 1999), Shape Data (CAD, acquired by Evans & Sutherland Computer Corp. in 1981), and Virata (DSL and broadband communications, merged with Globespan in 2001).

The many major companies of today that owe their origins to the Computer Laboratory include ARM (a chip designer with a market capitalization of around $20 billion), CacheLogic (the technology behind the Velocix content delivery network, now owned by Alcatel-Lucent), DeepMind Technologies (an artificial intelligence company sold to Google in 2014 for a reported $400 million), Sophos (an antivirus technology company with 200,000 business customers and a June 2015 IPO on the London Stock Exchange (LSE) that gave it a market capitalization of over $1.5 billion), and SwiftKey (developers of a keyboard app for touchscreens voted one of the top apps of the year by both Google and Apple in 2014 and downloaded on over 250 million devices).

Of the companies awarded the Cambridge Computer Lab Ring's Company of the Year, half were started in Cambridge.

CAMBRIDGE GETS THE SEAL OF APPROVAL FROM MICROSOFT RESEARCH

The first research facility set up by Microsoft outside the US was located in Cambridge. One of the driving forces behind this initiative was Microsoft's desire to hire Roger Needham when he retired as head of the University's Computer Laboratory in 1995, and Needham did not wish to move to the US.

Needham was tasked with being a 'risk-taker' for Microsoft, and developed a broad range of disciplines and research areas among his teams, hiring ethnographers, economists, biologists and many others.

One result was an object recognition research project that led to the motion capture technology used in Xbox 360 Kinect, which allows players to interact with Xbox games via a webcam and movement instead of using a physical controller. The team behind the project, led by Andrew Blake, won the Royal Academy of Engineering MacRobert Award, the 'Oscar' of engineering.

ACORN AND SINCLAIR CREATE A GENERATION OF COMPUTER ENTREPRENEURS

In the late 1970s and 1980s, Cambridge was home to two of the most successful home computer companies in the world at the time, Acorn (makers of the BBC Micro) and Sinclair (makers of the Spectrum). Both had sales in the millions of units, and helped to create a generation of people whose first experiences with a computer were of writing code.

It is impossible to count the number of companies founded because an entrepreneur was inspired by a BBC Micro or a Sinclair Spectrum, but certainly in Cambridge examples include Adder Technology, a successful privately owned company,

Top left: *Roger Needham.*

Left: *Acorn BBC Micro.*

Above: *Hermann Hauser,*
co-founder of Acorn Computers.

Above right: *Clive Sinclair,*
founder of Sinclair Radionics.

Autonomy, which was sold to HP in 2011 for over $11 billion (a deal that later became subject to considerable controversy), games company Frontier Developments and encryption company nCipher. It is estimated that more than 100 successful companies owe their origins to Acorn or Sinclair.

While the founder of Sinclair Research, Clive Sinclair, went on to focus on various innovations in technology and personal transport, the founders of Acorn, Hermann Hauser and Chris Curry, continued to work in the Cambridge technology cluster. Curry founded several companies innovating in the areas of online payments and health technology, while Hauser expanded from investing in and helping new start-ups to a major role as a venture capital funder and champion of technology entrepreneurship. One of the first companies he founded after Acorn was ARM, and he has since broadened his interests to engage with life sciences companies, telecommunications, and organizations that promote entrepreneurship. Hauser is associated with some of the most successful companies in Cambridge and beyond, including ARM, Cambridge Broadband Networks, Solexa and Virata. He was awarded the KBE, an honorary knighthood (Hauser is Austrian), in 2015 for his services to engineering and industry.

KEYBOARD, VIDEO AND MOUSE ADD UP FOR ADDER

Adder Technology was initially funded from the proceeds of bestselling instruction manuals for the BBC Micro and Sinclair Spectrum, written by founder Adrian Dickens and fellow undergraduates at Cambridge University. Remaining privately owned over 30 years later, today Adder is a global name in KVM (keyboard, video and mouse) data switching technology, which originally allowed multiple computers to use a single printer, but now permits hundreds of computer users to connect with thousands of machines.

The largest KVM producer in Europe, and with offices and distributors all over the world, Adder products are used across a number of sectors, including finance, broadcasting, air traffic control, utilities and medicine. Customers include Illumination Entertainment, makers of the blockbuster movie *Despicable Me*, Lisbon Airport, HBOS, and the BBC, at the new MediaCity in Salford and Broadcasting House in London.

A key part of Adder's success has been its policy of manufacturing at its Cambridge headquarters, with a focus on maintaining the quality and reliability that keep its products at the top end of the market. Around 60% of Adder products are exported to Europe and the US.

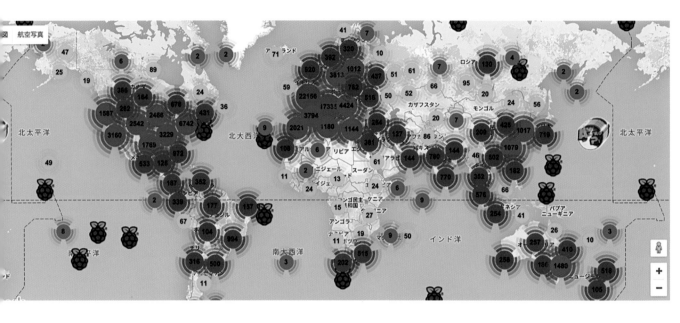

> **"**
> *We think that the lack of programmable hardware for children – the sort of hardware we used to have in the 1980s – is undermining the supply of 18-year-olds who know how to program, so that's a problem for universities, and then it's undermining the supply of 21-year-olds who know how to program, and that's causing problems for industry.*
>
> Eben Upton, founder of Raspberry Pi, quoted in *Linux User & Developer UK*,
> 29 February 2012

RASPBERRY PI GETS KIDS BACK TO CODING BASICS

The announcement of the BBC micro:bit in 2015 shows us that the Acorn and BBC Micro story is far from over, but while the micro:bit launch had to be delayed due to problems with the power supply, the newest manifestation of the Acorn/Sinclair legacy in Cambridge has already arrived in the shape of the global success that is the Raspberry Pi computer.

Intended to return coding to a central position in computer education in schools and increase the UK's competitiveness in the computing industry, more than seven million units have been sold around the world since the first Raspberry Pi was launched in 2012. This makes the Raspberry Pi the UK's fastest-selling personal computer, and it is rapidly catching up with the biggest-selling personal computer from the UK, the Amstrad PCW, which sold eight million units between 1985 and 1998.

Raspberry Pi came out of a growing recognition that coding skills among applicants to the Computer Science course at Cambridge University were declining. It looked like this was due to the changes in how people, especially children, interacted with computers, and the switch of ICT education from coding to the use of programs like Word and Excel. Similarly concerned individuals from the Computer Laboratory in Cambridge, Rob Mullins, Jack Lang and Alan Mycroft, were soon joined by David Braben, co-writer of seminal BBC Micro game *Elite*, and Peter Lomas, Managing Director of hardware design and manufacturing company Norcott Technologies, and the idea for Raspberry Pi was born.

Above: *Eben Upton, founder of Raspberry Pi.*

Above left: *The Rastrack Map, an idea originally thought up by 15-year-old Ryan Walmsley while he was waiting for his first Raspberry Pi to be delivered, allows owners around the world to add their computer to the map. Now supported by Google Maps and DigitalOcean, users can even drill down and see if there is a fellow Pi owner on their street.*

Over seven million Raspberry Pis have been sold since the first model was launched on 29 February 2012. Initial sales exceeded all estimates, and production had to be ramped up rapidly. When manufacturing was moved from China to Wales, production reached 40,000 per month.

It's actually cheaper for us to manufacture in the UK than in China, and a close involvement with the manufacturing helps us to better understand the processes involved and improve the design.

Eben Upton

The one-millionth Raspberry Pi was manufactured in the UK in October 2013, and barely a month later, the two-millionth Raspberry Pi had been shipped. May 2014 saw the three-millionth Raspberry Pi shipped, and sales of Raspberry Pi 2, launched in February 2015, reached one million in three months, by the end of April. Around 80% of sales are exports, with the company's largest market being in the US.

The success of Raspberry Pi has had a direct impact on component and distributor partners Premier Farnell Group and RS Components (both global companies with UK origins), who have benefited from expanding into a new market, adding skills and growing sales in the process.

Another impact of the launch of Raspberry Pi has been the number of new companies that have sprung up around it. Just as successful companies like Adder Technology and Frontier Developments were built on the success of the BBC

" The Raspberry Pi community… [has] changed the way people interact with computers.

Andy Harter, CEO, RealVNC, *Business Weekly*, February 2015

Micro and Sinclair Spectrum, Raspberry Pi also has an evolving ecosystem of value creation around it that extends beyond Cambridge. Three companies located around the UK, ModMyPi (Tunbridge Wells), The PiHut (Haverhill) and Pimoroni (Sheffield) have already gone from zero to £1 million turnover since the Raspberry Pi was launched. These three companies sell accessories for the Raspberry Pi, such as cases and add-ons. US company Adafruit Industries has also built sales of kits and add-ons since its involvement in the early stages of Raspberry Pi.

Booming sales and a thriving ecosystem mean that the original goal of the people behind Raspberry Pi, to promote the teaching of basic computer science in schools and

Right: *Assembling Raspberry Pis.*

developing countries, is becoming a growing success. The organization split in 2009 into a trading company that sells computers, and the Raspberry Pi Foundation, a registered UK charity that promotes education in programming through a variety of initiatives. In 2014, the trading company enabled the Foundation to launch its £1 million education fund, supporting projects around the world.

The Madanyu Education Programme is one of those supported by the Rasbperry Pi Foundation. The aim is to promote coding and computer skills in underserved areas, and the programme provides modified Raspberry Pi computers and training workshops tailored to local conditions in schools in remote communities in India and Kenya. Set up by two Cambridge University researchers, successful pilot projects in 2014 have led to more projects being set up, and expanding links with NGOs in both countries.

Much of the community activity around Raspberry Pi originates from users and volunteers sharing information and providing tutorials. As well as supporting this online community via its website and publishing the *MagPi* magazine, the Raspberry Pi Foundation also sponsors Picademy, a resource for teachers providing not only newsletters and regular updates, but also free training workshops for teachers to help them incorporate coding and the use of Raspberry Pi into lessons. Teachers have come to Cambridge for training from the US and India, and there has been interest from China, Singapore and Estonia for participation in future workshops.

In the first ten months of Picademy, around 200 teachers came to Cambridge for training. Picademy now has a relationship with Google Digital Garage to run courses for teachers from its new premises in Leeds, expanding the reach and accessibility of the Picademy programme in the UK.

Above: *Project Pi at the Khaya Centre, Lehae, Johannesburg, 2014.*

Above: *Steve Furber and Sophie Wilson, inventors of the ARM architecture.*

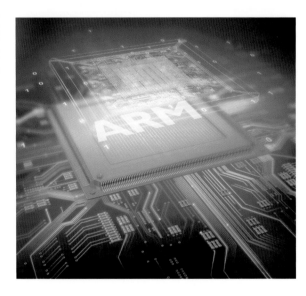

"

Today there are about two billion people who own a smartphone, and each of those smartphones contains at least one ARM-based chip.

ARM Strategic Report, 2014

ARM CHIPS WITH EVERYTHING

At 1pm on April 13th 1984, the first ARM microprocessors arrived back from the manufacturer – Plessey. They were put straight into the development system which was fired up with a tweak or two and, at 3pm, the screen displayed: 'Hello World, I am ARM.'
Steve Furber, *Electronics Weekly*, 14 May 2007

Over 60 billion ARM-designed chips have been shipped since that day in 1984 when the first ARM microprocessor said 'Hello' to the world – and the world responded by adopting ARM in ever-growing numbers. More than 95% of the smartphones on the planet contain at least one ARM-based component, analysts Canalys estimate that 80% of wearable devices sold in 2014 contained at least one ARM-based chip, and ARM chips are found in everything from everyday devices such as digital TVs and washing machines to the machines that host the cloud on the largest server farms. But, despite this ubiquity, as *The Observer* pointed out in a headline in November 2015, ARM is 'Britain's most successful tech company you've never heard of'.

Industry observers and investors, however, clearly have heard of ARM. In 2015, *Forbes* ranked ARM Holdings Plc as

the most innovative company in Europe, and the fifth most innovative company in the world. The company's market capitalization is north of $20 billion, and it is one of only two technology companies in the FTSE 100 – the other being business software company Sage.

Headquartered a few miles from the centre of Cambridge, ARM has come a long way since its first chip was shipped in 1991. It took ten years for ARM to reach the one-billion-chip milestone, but such was the explosion in mobile phones and then smartphones, one of ARM's key early markets, that it took just 13 more years to get to 60 billion. In 2014, the company reported that 12 billion ARM-based chips had shipped in that year alone, 16% more than in 2013, and almost twice as many as shipped in 2010.

> *"*
>
> *The impact of the Internet of Things is going to be profound. We already see ARM microprocessors going into sensors that help manage irrigation systems and use water more efficiently to increase crop yields, the infrastructure that is creating smart cities and improving energy efficiency, and wearables that save lives.*

Simon Segars, CEO, ARM

But the ARM story is about much more than smartphones: over half of ARM's designs go into a variety of other devices and applications. According to World Semiconductor Trade Statistics, around 33 billion of the 65 billion silicon chips manufactured in 2014 contained a processor, and with 12 billion such chips produced by ARM's partners, that gave ARM 37% of the total global microprocessor market.

One of the distinctive features of ARM chip design, and what made them so popular in the mobile market in the first place, is their low power consumption combined with high performance. While those features have been absolutely key to ARM's success in the world of portable and handheld electronic devices, they are also becoming increasingly critical in other applications, and designing processors for mobile phones is being superseded by other sectors.

One growth area is in servers. The seemingly inexorable rise of data transmission over the internet is putting more and more pressure on the data centres that process and route the data. The servers on which data centres rely are getting increasingly sophisticated and numerous as they evolve to deal with increasing loads, but simply adding more and more processors into the system to cope is not practicable, as cooling and power consumption become limiting factors. Low-power chips like those designed by ARM go a long way to mitigating these problems, and also provide the type of processing power that is used by companies like PayPal to track data and detect anomalies in real time.

The Internet of Things (IoT) is another major growth opportunity for ARM. Although Gartner has IoT at the top of the 'Peak of Inflated Expectations' in its 2015 annual 'Hype Cycle for Emerging Technologies', nevertheless the analysts predict that the IoT space will be worth $1.9 trillion in a few years' time. Others suggest even higher amounts: $7.1 trillion is cited by market researchers IDC, and $19 trillion by Cisco Systems. What is clear is that the size of the future market for IoT is unclear, but very large nonetheless, and ARM is among those companies positioning itself to take full advantage of the potential.

The computer power for the 'Things' in the IoT comes from microcontroller chips. These are tiny – two square millimetres, the size of a dimple on a golf ball – and their size, low power consumption and low cost mean that they are found in millions of everyday items, like the remote controller for your television, your car keys and even your washing machine. ARM's transition over the past four years to a 32-bit architecture has kept costs and energy consumption down, and computing power up for these chips, and ARM-based designs are found in an increasingly large range of embedded devices. But IoT is about far more than changing the channel on the TV or a fridge that orders more milk when supplies are low.

In 2015, Microsoft certified the ARM mbed Enabled development board as part of its IoT public cloud platform Microsoft Azure, and IBM added ARM mbed Enabled devices to its own platform, the IBM IoT Foundation. Salesforce.com is among other partners for ARM in the IoT space, all looking to

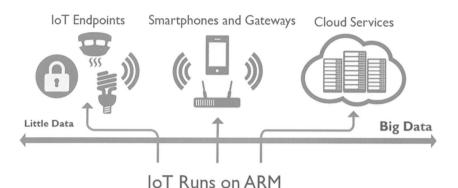

IoT Endpoints   Smartphones and Gateways   Cloud Services

Little Data   Big Data

IoT Runs on ARM

ensure the compatibility and connectivity of their products, from cameras to cars and from electricity meters to mobile health devices. As always, ARM's continuing ability to design chips that require very little power proves highly attractive to its customers.

The secret of ARM's financial success is its business model. Licences for its designs and royalties on every chip shipped mean that ARM designs have a 'long tail' – sales don't peak and then drop off a cliff when the next new design comes along, because the initial licence payment is followed by royalties when the design starts to ship in consumer and other products. Indeed, a significant proportion of revenues – more than half in 2014 – consist of royalties from designs licensed out five or more years ago.

Smartphones can change lives – we know that people who can connect to the world can get the information they need to make better decisions about the crops they're growing, get a better education, and build businesses and create wealth. But only two billion of the seven billion mobile phone subscribers globally own a smartphone. ARM chips are helping vendors develop smartphones that cost as little as $30 or $40, making the technology available to far more of the people who could most benefit from it.

Simon Segars, CEO, ARM

To meet rising demand, ARM is expanding. With nearly 4,000 employees in over 30 countries worldwide, the company is building new facilities in Cambridge to increase the headcount at its corporate HQ. The company is also increasingly involved in projects that unlock the power of its technology.
ARM is also dedicated to expanding the benefits of its technology to where it can create major societal impact,

Right: *Some of the countless products powered by ARM: the Samsung Gear S, the Amazon Kindle Paperwhite and the Microsoft Surface.*

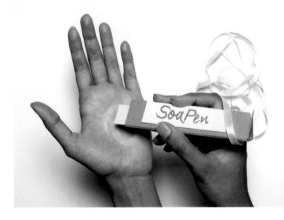

> Technology should be used to create opportunity for all; improving child health, education and prospects…should not be governed by economic status or geography.

Simon Segars, CEO, ARM

not only for human development, but also in the areas of conservation and biodiversity.

In May 2015, ARM and UNICEF announced a long-term partnership to identify ways the major needs of underserved populations can be met through technology and innovation, with a focus on access to healthcare, education and social support.

The relationship with UNICEF evolved from a maternal health project between ARM and UNICEF in Ghana, in collaboration with humanitarian technology company Literacy Bridge. The new, more expansive, partnership was launched with 'Wearables for Good', a call for ideas that addressed the health needs of mothers and children in parts of the world where these are most challenging, teaming up with global design firm frog.

The first Wearables for Good competition received 250 submissions from 46 countries covering six continents. Two winners were chosen from ten finalists, Khushi Baby and SoaPen, with each receiving $15,000 in funding and incubation and mentoring from UNICEF, ARM and frog.

In addition, ARM has teamed up with the Centre for Global Equality (CGE) in Cambridge and is establishing a Technology for Development Centre in collaboration with CGE, Trinity College and Redgate Software. The centre will host innovators from the developing world and help connect them with researchers and entrepreneurs in Cambridge so that they can work together in leveraging technology to address complex social and developmental challenges.

Above right: *The Literacy Bridge Talking Book project supplies illiterate and impoverished families with simple audio computers that are extremely intuitive to use and carry relevant and important information recorded in local dialects. The Talking Book is small, robust and requires very low power, essential for areas where there is no electricity – ARM technology makes it energy efficient and affordable.*

Above left: *One farmer in Ghana proved the value of the Talking Book to himself, using traditional methods for part of his crop, and following advice from the Talking Book for the rest. Overall results from a pilot project showed that farmers increased yields by 48% on the previous year by adopting new practices they learned about from the Talking Book.*

ARM also helped Cambridge-based global conservation organisation Fauna & Flora International to initiate a new conservation technology network to discover and develop technologies which could transform the conservation sector's ability to protect the natural world. This novel project has now developed into WILDLABS.NET project, a collaboration between seven major conservation organisations, with backing from Google and supported by The Royal Foundation of the Duke and Duchess of Cambridge and Prince Harry. WILDLABS.NET will create a multidisciplinary community, ranging from engineers and entrepreneurs to conservationists and development organizations, that will share information on major conservation and biodiversity issues and how best to address them. A series of innovation challenges will draw on the resources of the group to help find ways the latest technologies can help in efforts to protect threatened species and their habitats, and ARM will provide technical expertise and grant funding where appropriate.

Left: *Mike Hunter and Tim Spiers, founders of i2.*

GETTING ON SCREEN WITH DISPLAYLINK

Although it looks like a US chip company with operations in Palo Alto and a large proportion of its revenues coming from the US market, DisplayLink remains a Cambridge company at heart. But its outlook is always global, and counting the likes of Dell, Fujitsu, HP, Lenovo and Toshiba among customers for its USB network display technology means DisplayLink products are found in devices around the world. Allowing computers and other devices to link to multiple displays through a USB connection, DisplayLink's suite of semiconductor and software products provide NIVO (Network In, Video Out) technology in docking stations, monitors, projectors and zero client systems, among others.

Having raised over $60 million since it was founded as Newnham Research in 2003, DisplayLink has not only changed its name, but also pivoted to focus on the PC docking market since 2011, a move that has seen revenues grow three-fold and expansion into offices in Poland and Taiwan, as well as those in Palo Alto and Cambridge. The UK operations are now housed in state-of-the-art facilities on the Cambridge Science Park, and headcount has expanded to over 150 people across all four locations. With a new-found confidence, DisplayLink's product range has expanded to include support for mobile operating systems as well as wirelessly connected displays.

NCIPHER FINDS THE RIGHT KEY

The rise in online payments followed by the dawning realization of how vulnerable any data stored electronically might be were the drivers behind the growth of encryption company nCipher.

The company was set up by Alex and Nicko van Someren, two brothers who had talked their way into jobs at Acorn when they were still at school. nCipher developed hardware and software encryption technology to help keep payments secure for many major international banks and credit card companies, with household names such as Barclays, Bank of America, MasterCard and Visa among them. Billions of payments amounting to trillions of pounds every year relied on nCipher's technology.

nCipher was listed on the LSE in 2000, with a valuation of over £330 million. The same year, Microsoft announced that nCipher's hardware security modules would be incorporated into Windows 2000, a relationship that has continued into successive operating and server systems from Microsoft.

A number of high-profile data losses and thefts in the mid-2000s provided another important market for the company, as organizations sought to catch up with increasingly stringent regulations around the transfer, storage and encryption of data.

In 2008, nCipher was acquired by French company Thales for around £50 million, and cybersecurity development for Thales continues to operate in Cambridge.

THE WORLD OF INTELLIGENCE LOOKS TO i2

The first sale of i2's intelligence analysis software was to the Amsterdam Police Force. By the time the company finally became part of IBM in 2011, the software was used by the FBI, CIA, customs agencies, US Military Intelligence, the London Metropolitan Police Force, and major police forces throughout the UK, the Netherlands, Australia, New Zealand and Hong Kong.

Police forces and other agencies had used visualization techniques since the assassination of Bobby Kennedy, where tracking the movements of the assassin proved that he had been tracking Kennedy. However, by hand the process was laborious and required large amounts of space – the sequence of events in the 1990 Strangeways prison riot was visualized on paper to analyse what happened and when, but the large amounts of information could only be viewed by displaying it all on the walls of an empty gym.

The founders of i2, Mike Hunter and Tim Spiers, had heard about this technique from an ex-policeman and recognized that a simple software tool could make the process far more efficient. They demonstrated their first example on the Oracle stand at a police show, and a representative of the Amsterdam police signed up. The initial drawing tool became more complex after an evening in a pub with a detective, who described how it had taken six weeks to analyse the links

Right: *Ian Pratt, co-founder of Bromium.*

between four phone numbers in a case in Hong Kong. Over a weekend, the i2 team developed a database method that would complete the same task in four minutes.

Subsequent developments all aimed at improving the technology behind the tool without making the user interface too complicated, and included social network analysis – 30 years before the arrival of Facebook. Link analysis allowed users to produce networks based on the data, and eventually led to a time-based tool that was first used for murder enquiries.

In May 2000, the FBI used i2 software to track the 'ILOVEYOU' or 'Lovebug' computer virus to the Philippines within 24 hours, where they assisted the Philippines' National Bureau of Investigation in identifying the perpetrators. The virus forced computer systems around the world to be shut down, including the UK Houses of Parliament, the State Department in the US and the Dow Jones in Hong Kong, and caused billions of dollars' worth of damage.

i2 technology has been used to investigate major cases such as the Dr Harold Shipman murders in the UK, the Dunblane shootings in Scotland, and the so-called backpacker murders in Australia. Link analysis also helped US military intelligence to understand the relationships between tribal leaders in Afghanistan and identify those who did not pose a threat.

When i2 was first acquired by US company ChoicePoint in 2005, the technology was also applied to assessing risk for insurance companies using information published in US public records. The i2 operations were subsequently acquired by SilverLake, merged with Knowledge Computing Corporation (Tucson, Arizona), and then acquired by IBM in 2011. The technical team remain in Cambridge.

BROMIUM HAS A VIRTUAL APPROACH TO SECURITY

Three of the top five international insurance companies, one of the Big Four auditing companies, and two of the top three financial institutions use Bromium's vSentry as part of their defence against computer security breaches.

Bromium is a relative youngster on the Cambridge scene, founded in 2010 by some of the original team from XenSource – Ian Pratt, Gaurav Banga and Simon Crosby. Their experience with XenSource and Citrix led to them locating the headquarters for their new company in Cupertino, California, but the core team carrying out the R&D remain based in Cambridge. Listed in CNBC's 2013 'Disruptor 50' and recognized

"

vSentry is an intriguing product because of its unique ability to isolate and analyze the potential impact of very real attacks on your network. It's almost like performing preventative forensics, which is a very innovative capability, and incredibly valuable in today's carefully guarded corporate networks.

Sunil Seshadri, SVP & Chief Information Officer, NYSE Euronext, quoted in *InformationWeek*, March 2013

as a 'cool vendor' by Gartner that same year, Bromium has raised over $75 million from a sophisticated group of investors to fund development.

The Bromium technology uses micro-virtualization and isolation to enhance cybersecurity. Based on the Xen hypervisor but focusing on the end-user rather than the server, the idea is to stop incoming viruses at the task level and prevent them from getting into a computer's operating system. By running applications through a virtual machine, the true machine is kept safe from potential threats. Bromium counts the New York Stock Exchange among its early customers, a firm endorsement of their offering.

NEW COMPANY DARKTRACE IS ALREADY MAKING ITS INFLUENCE FELT

Being named Technology Pioneer at the World Economic Forum in 2015 puts Darktrace among the big hitters, with previous awardees including Google, Dropbox, Kickstarter and Twitter.

A new approach to cyber threats is that adopted by Darktrace, a company which already has an extraordinary track record despite its very short life. Founded only in 2013, barely two years later Darktrace has 18 offices around the world, and over 100 of the world's largest companies as its customers, including European energy firm Drax, telecoms giants BT and

T-Mobile, high-end cosmetics company Sisley, and major UK rail operator Virgin Trains. Darktrace also counts a number of banks and other financial institutions among its users, and Big-Four auditor and professional services company PwC.

The company's Enterprise Immune System is founded on Bayesian mathematics and advanced machine learning modelled on the human immune system. Machine learning algorithms enable the system to understand what is 'normal' traffic and detect any abnormal behaviour within a communications system. The Enterprise Immune System doesn't try to bolt the door to attacks, recognizing that many come from inside the enterprise, but focuses on finding and immobilizing threats.

The first investment for Invoke Capital, a new fund set up by Autonomy co-founder Mike Lynch, Darktrace has already raised $40.5 million in two funding rounds and is clearly going places quickly. As well as its remarkable roster of blue-chip customers, Darktrace has gathered a significant collection of industry awards, and was a Technology Pioneer at the World Economic Forum in 2015. Darktrace is also endorsed by the presence of the former head of MI5 and a leading expert from the NSA on the company's Advisory Board.

DESIGNING THE WORLD'S ESSENTIAL INFRASTRUCTURE: AVEVA

100% of the top 10 energy companies are AVEVA customers.

PFC Energy 50

90% of the top 10 global shipyards are AVEVA customers.

Clarkson's World Fleet Register

With a remarkable record of developing mission-critical engineering design and information management software, AVEVA started life in 1967 as CADCentre, a government-funded institution set up in Cambridge and tasked with boosting UK industry through the use of computer-aided design, CAD. Today, AVEVA is a truly global company, with 55 offices in 30 countries, a market capitalization of over $2 billion, and a standout roster of customers, some of whom have been using AVEVA software for over 40 years.

90% of our revenues come from outside the UK.

Richard Longdon, CEO, AVEVA

Left: *Nicole Eagan, CEO of Darktrace.*

Search Within 3D Model

Above: *AVEVA Engage software revolutionizes collaborative decision-making across capital projects and operating assets.*

One of the reasons Cambridge was chosen for the new government institute was because CAD research was already being undertaken in the University's fledgling Computing Department (then known as the Mathematical Department). A wise choice, as this readily available pool of expertise would be the foundation for CADCentre's, and then AVEVA's, long list of world firsts.

1976: World's first 3D plant design system (PDMS) – with object-based engineering database
1979: World's first intelligent P&ID (PEGS) launched at ACHEMA

With a couple of breakthroughs already under its belt, CAD Centre was privatized in 1983 and started to find its way as a commercial company.

1988: World's first plant walk-through visualization system
1992: World's first interactive full colour shaded plant design system

A management buyout in 1994 was the penultimate phase in transition from government-funded to commercial operation, and with its listing on the LSE in 1996, CADCentre was finally a public company.

1997: World's first internet-based collaborative design solution
2001: World's first plant design system for concurrent global project execution

CADCentre changed its name to AVEVA in 2002, to sever the last remaining link with its institutional origins, and also to signal to the world that it provided more than straightforward CAD. A series of acquisitions, starting with Swedish company Tribon Solutions in 2004, built AVEVA skills in complementary areas, such as marine design in the case of Tribon (Tribon's customers at the time of the acquisition included roughly three-quarters of the world's top 50 shipbuilders). AVEVA now has engineering, design and information offerings across oil and gas, power, chemicals, marine, and mining, among other capital industries. The company entered the LSE FTSE 250 in 2006.

2006: AVEVA Laser Model Interface provides world's first direct interaction with laser-scanned 3D plant models
2008: World's first open standards-based integration of P&ID and 3D design modelling

AVEVA is built on long-term relationships.
Richard Longdon, CEO, AVEVA

International links and having a long-term perspective on all relationships, whether with customers or employees, has been crucial to AVEVA's success. The core database that underpins AVEVA technology, Dabacon, was originally the result of a collaboration between AKZO Chemicals in the Netherlands, Électricité de France (EDF), Nottingham University and CADCentre in Cambridge.

Most AVEVA products are the result of pioneering new technology in partnership with one or more customers. For instance, the company's new decision support solution, AVEVA Engage, enables design and data access on giant touchscreen devices, and is the result of close collaboration with Shell, an AVEVA customer for over 25 years.

AVEVA software was also used by British Nuclear Fuels to design the Sellafield reprocessing plant – at the time the biggest engineering project in the world. This project made a major contribution to the globalization of AVEVA, as contractors

"

We started working with EDF when we were still CADCentre and still government-funded. EDF has been a significant partner ever since, particularly on nuclear projects, which are an order of magnitude more complex than anything else. They require exotic materials, and once you've switched them on, you can't go back in to make changes if it's not quite right. We have co-developed products with EDF and changed the way nuclear projects can be achieved.

Richard Longdon, CEO, AVEVA

who used the software on the Sellafield project took it into engineering applications and on to other projects.

2010: World's first automatic generation of finite-element models from 3D marine product models
2014: AVEVA E3D Insight, the world's first tablet app for project review and approval any time, anywhere

Given its global reach and multinational customers, AVEVA has to function and think globally, and has developed a comprehensive system of training and continuing professional development to integrate employees from around the world. This is particularly important to a company that functions the way AVEVA does, as there are often projects that interoperate between offices and don't necessarily involve the team at the Cambridge headquarters.

The management and work is distributed globally. We have 15 R&D locations around the world, but we don't outsource any more — all employees are AVEVA employees, wherever they are.

Richard Longdon, CEO, AVEVA

AVEVA also has long-term relationships in the education programmes the company supports in 26 countries around the world. AVEVA software is provided to institutions for a nominal amount or based on an exchange arrangement; for instance a Russian university received the software in return for the students helping to translate it into the Cyrillic alphabet. Many of the top people in shipping companies are alumni of a particular university in South Korea, and AVEVA's relationship with this university has proved of great mutual benefit.

Above: *AVEVA Marine vessel model. AVEVA Marine is the most powerful and comprehensive engineering and design solution available for the shipbuilding industry.*

Far left: *Richard Longdon, CEO of AVEVA.*

Right: *Elite: Dangerous was a 2014 'reboot' of the original.*

Below: *David Braben, Founder and CEO, Frontier Developments.*

ELITE CHANGES THE COMPUTER GAME PARADIGM

The computer game *Elite* changed the paradigm for such games when it was published in 1984. A genre-defining space game, *Elite* had no ending; a player could go on trading, travelling and perhaps fighting in space for ever – or for as long as their character lasted without getting wiped out by aliens.

So unusual it was turned down by traditional games publishers, who could not see the point of a game that did not fit the 'three-levels-and-reach-the-goal' model of the time, the co-developers, David Braben and Ian Bell, finally persuaded Acorn's publishing arm, Acornsoft, to take a punt on *Elite*. It went on to sell getting on for a million copies, proved the model for the game and led to Braben setting up game developer Frontier Developments.

In 1985, *Elite* became the first non-American game to become a bestseller in the US.

Elite was such a big seller partly because it was one of the first games to use wire-frame, hidden line removal, which marked a step change in the graphics experience for the player. Its unorthodox, open-ended format also meant the game got a lot of publicity in the gaming world, and it was rated very highly by commentators, adding to its success and subsequent influence on other game developers.

The influence of *Elite* has lasted long after the game itself became a curio for aficionados. It was rated the third most influential game ever by *The Times Online* as recently as 2007, more than 20 years after it was first published, 'best game of the 1980s' in 2008, and was one of only three games given a retrospective ten out of ten by *Edge* magazine.

Frontier Developments went on to produce games for the most important platforms in the world, including not only iOS and PC formats, but also Xbox Kinect. The *Kinectimals* children's game, released in 2010, won two BAFTAs, and is

also now on mobile platforms such as iOS and Android. Sales at over 1.5 million units as of October 2015 put *Kinectimals* in the top three of similar games according to video games tracker VGChartz.com (not that far off *The Sims*, at number one with 2.2 million sales).

The company has worked with games publishers such as Atari, Microsoft, Sony and Amazon as it has also moved into offerings in this space, for instance working with Amazon on transferring *Tales from Deep Space* to the Kindle Fire.

A 'reboot' of *Elite*, *Elite: Dangerous*, launched for Windows in 2014 and OS X and Xbox in 2015 (with a possible PlayStation 4 version after an exclusivity period with Xbox expires).

The new game is important not only because it is a return to a bestseller and already proving very popular, but also because it was partly financed by crowdfunding. Frontier wanted to publish the game themselves, rather than go through a third-party publisher, but couldn't justify the investment solely from the company's coffers. In addition, crowdfunding would serve as market research: given that *Elite* had so many fans from its earlier incarnations, a crowdfunding project would tell Frontier whether or not those fans had any appetite for a new edition.

Crowdfunding, if it proved popular, might also give Frontier a ready-made group of prelaunch testers for the early stages of the new game, and the funding targets were set accordingly – those who pledged above a certain amount would get additional rights to provide input into the game's development.

The crowdfunding launched on Kickstarter in 2012 and raised nearly £200,000 towards a target of £1.25 million on its first day. Frontier eventually raised £1.58 million over the 60-day campaign. More than 25,000 people contributed, and at the time it was the highest fundraising target for a project that had been achieved on Kickstarter. Later, in response to requests

RUNESCAPE

from those who had missed the crowdfunding window, Frontier added a 'Donate' button to their website and the total raised eventually reached £1.8 million. The company also listed on AIM in 2013, raising £4 million and giving the company a market capitalization of over £39 million (which has since risen to almost £80 million).

Around 2,000 of the Kickstarter backers paid £200, which gave them access to the beta version for testing, and more than 600 paid £300 and above, which put them on the 'design decision forum'. Frontier used this group to confirm the popularity of certain features, and it also led to them introducing other features and characters that the backers wanted – such as the return of the Thargoids, alien monsters from the original 1984 game.

Eventually, *Elite: Dangerous* raised £10 million in presales before its general release. Selling more than half a million copies by mid-2015, the game has been highly rated among games critics and analysts and potential revenues for *Elite: Dangerous* have been estimated by brokers Cannacord Genuity to range from a base figure of £24 million to a potential £240 million in 2017.

The fantasy universe of *Elite: Dangerous* recreates the Milky Way and has 400 billion astronomical features, such as star systems, moons and planets. The company claims it is the 'largest designed playspace in videogame history'. There are two ways to play, as an individual or in the massively multiplayer space. In the latter, each player's actions, their successes and failures, influence the rest of the game because the universe of the game is persistent, changes are 'saved' and it doesn't reset when a player starts again.

443 BILLION MINUTES OF GAME TIME PUT JAGEX GAME RUNESCAPE IN THE GUINNESS BOOK OF WORLD RECORDS

The other big games player in the Cambridge technology cluster is Jagex Games Studio, reportedly originally named for the slogan 'java gaming experts'.

Jagex game *RuneScape* is a MMORPG – Massively Multiplayer Online Role-Playing Game – that was certified by the *Guinness Book of World Records* in 2008 as the largest free MMORPG in the world. The total of 443 billion minutes' playing time was noted in July 2012.

RuneScape was released as a free online game in January 2001, and over one million accounts were registered within the first year. A subscription model was introduced in February 2002, giving members access to additional features, and had 5,000 subscribers in the first week, and 65,000 within a year. A pay-to-play version was published in 2003. In May 2007, the company recorded six million free and one million paying players; by July 2012, there were over 200 million registered accounts in 150 countries, supported by 139 servers around the world.

RuneScape isn't the only game in Jagex's stable. The company has developed and published more than 40 online games. It is the UK's largest games developer with around 480 staff, and was voted UK Games Developer of the Year in both 2009 and 2010. Jagex has also won numerous other awards in the gaming and enterprise sectors, including two Golden Joystick UK Developer of the Year awards, and has been listed in the Deloitte Technology Fast 50 and the *Red Herring* Global 100.

SMALLER AND NEWER PLAYERS IN THE GAMES WORLD PUNCH ABOVE THEIR WEIGHT

Guerrilla Cambridge, now part of Sony Computer Entertainment Worldwide Studios, develops games for PlayStation. The company started out as Millennium Interactive in Cambridge, and created the highly successful *Defcon 5*, *James Pond*, and *Creatures*. In the latter, players hatch and raise aliens known as 'Norns', look after them and teach them language. The Norns' 'brains' are modelled on neural networks and genetics, and can develop in unexpected ways if bred with different types of Norn. The game was a global hit, with over 100,000 copies selling in the US in just three months in 2007.

Guerrilla released *MediEvil* for PlayStation in 1998, and further editions in subsequent years. *MediEvil* was highly ranked by critics and commentators, and the first edition sold over one million units worldwide. A second edition, *MediEvil 2*, launched in 2000, won a BAFTA and sold over half a million units, with subsequent *MediEvil Resurrection*, launched in 2005, selling over three-quarters of a million units.

Ninja Theory developed *Kung Fu Chaos* for the Xbox in 2003 (when the company was called Just Add Monsters), and *Heavenly Sword* for PlayStation 3 in 2007. While the latter was not a huge seller, the developers worked with Oscar-nominated actor Andy Serkis on the motion filming and performance capture phases of development. Ninja Theory also helped develop the bestselling *Devil May Cry* for PlayStation.

Fen Research was founded by Andrew Gower, one of the co-founders (along with his brother Paul) of Jagex. The company focused initially on developing its own game engine and programming language, Fenforge, to make multiplayer games easier to develop and more varied. The company's first two games, *Solstrike* and a mysterious 'top secret' game, are currently in development. If the new game engine and language prove successful, Fen Research could start to realize radical ambitions for new games.

PlayFusion is a very new games company, co-founded by Mark Gerhard, former CEO of Jagex, David Gomberg, Rican Hodgson (also formerly of Jagex) and Justin Heimberg. The company is reported to be in 'stealth mode' at the St John's Innovation Centre, but is working on games technology that will combine digital games, toys and video content, so that the toys can be part of a child's interaction with the game.

Another relatively new games company is **Introversion Software**, which has offices in London but one of the co-founders, Chris Delay, remains based in Cambridge. Introversion launched *Prison Architect* in September 2012 in a paid alpha version. Sales reached an astonishing 1.25 million copies before the official launch in October 2015, grossing $19 million.

Another new game from Cambridge that could have significant impact but for different reasons is *Focus Pocus*, which is played wearing a headset to measure brain activity. Created by freelance developer PJ Belcher with Australian company Neurocog and US biosensor manufacturer NeuroSky, the primary purpose of the game is to help children with ADHD (attention deficit hyperactivity disorder) to moderate their behaviour by improving their concentration and attention.

MONEY MAKES THE WORLD GO ROUND, AND BRADY HELPS THE MONEY GO ROUND

Brady Plc provides trading and risk management software to the global commodity, recycling and energy markets, and is the largest provider by revenues in Europe for commodities trading.

The company has over 300 customers around the world, including some of the biggest names in finance, commodities and energy, such as HSBC, Standard Chartered, Deutsche Bank, Glencore, Rio Tinto, EDF and Norsk Hydro. Australia, the second largest producer of gold in the world, runs Brady software at the Australian Bullion Exchange (ABX).

Listed on AIM in 2004, the company started a string of strategic acquisitions in 2007 that expanded its offerings and helped it to broaden into new markets, such as scrap and recycling in the US.

Brady celebrated its 30th anniversary in 2015.

> **"** *The US scrap market is worth $100 billion in turnover, and 50% of this is already transacted using Brady software, with seven of the top ten recycling companies using Brady.*
>
> Gavin Lavelle, CEO, Brady Plc

MAKING MOBILE BILLS DO MORE WITH BANGO

More than 60% of all mobile network operators worldwide link to app stores via the Bango payment platform. Bango has a reach of more than 200 million billable mobile identities in over 140 markets in 60 countries.

Bango's technology is fast establishing itself as the industry standard, with six of the world's largest app stores, Amazon, BlackBerry, Firefox, Google, Microsoft and Samsung, all using the company's platform.

> "
> *15 years ago, 99% of the people I spoke to said we were idiots, companies like Nokia were the content keepers. Ten years ago 80% still thought we were fools, even after we joined the London Stock Exchange in 2005. Five years ago, 5% were saying we were probably right, but will we get there first? Now, the big players have absolutely bought into what we're doing.*

Ray Anderson, co-founder and CEO, Bango

The idea behind Bango, that people could buy things via the internet using their mobile phone and then have the cost included in their mobile phone bill, was highly contrarian when Ray Anderson and Anil Malhotra founded the company and began developing their payment software 15 years ago.

Bango was the first company to enable one-click mobile web billing in Europe, through Vodafone and Telefónica, then expanded into the US with AT&T, Sprint, and T-Mobile. Deutsche Telekom standardized on the Bango platform, as did Etisalat and du, mobile operators in the UAE.

But it is the rise of the smartphone and app stores that has provided the biggest opportunity for Bango. In 2014, 1.2 billion smartphones were shipped, and three mobile games, *Candy Crush Saga*, *Puzzle & Dragons*, and *Clash of Clans*, grossed more than $1 billion each. In 2015, Juniper Research predicted that carrier billing would grow to $13 billion by 2017.

Signing up BlackBerry World billing in 2011 was the start of a move into the big league of global players for Bango. Google Play signed up the same year, Windows Phone Store and Firefox Marketplace in 2012, Amazon Appstore and BlackBerry Messenger in 2013 and Samsung Galaxy Apps in 2014.

The Bango payment platform has been shown to increase conversion rates because it makes payment so much easier. Conversion rates where customers have the option of using

Below: Ray Anderson, CEO and co-founder of Bango, during an interview with Bloomberg News.

> **"**
> *The reality is that communication devices can replace banking systems and they are doing it. Bango takes friction out of the whole process of turning carrier billing on. They employ around 70 people, yet they service 100 carriers around the world.*
>
> Haydn Shaughnessy, quoted in *Forbes*, February 2015

a credit or debit card are typically less than 40%, and reach as low as 0.5% in markets where credit and debit cards are not widely used. Carrier billing for five app stores using the Bango Payment Platform in the first eight months of 2014 had conversion rates of up to 82%.

> *When Bango turns on carrier billing for Google, you see an increase in sales, anything from threefold to tenfold. Suddenly shopping is a whole lot easier. They get their transaction on their mobile phone bill.*
> **Haydn Shaughnessy, quoted in *Forbes*, February 2015**

Bango's newest product, the Bango Grid, launched in March 2015 and is a game changer for app stores. The problem Bango identified was that, with more than 700 mobile network operators globally all having different billing systems, content providers such as app stores would have to customize the interface with each network operator individually. This meant that it would be punishingly slow for the app store to achieve any kind of scale. The Bango Grid simplifies the process and activates carrier billing between app store and network operator with one click, allowing app stores to connect with many more network operators much more quickly. It also provides in-depth analytics, and can help network operators identify connection problems.

MONEY MOVER DOES WHAT IT SAYS ON THE TIN

Within a year since launching in 2014, Money Mover had already handled over €29 million in international transactions for SMEs (small and medium-sized enterprises).

Each year, SMEs account for over $5 trillion in international payments globally, with around $500 billion of that originating with UK SMEs. Such transactions can be disproportionately costly and complex for small companies. Hamish Anderson, who co-founded Money Mover with Andrew Comber, cites the example of a UK oncology company that receives research grants in US dollars, pays for drug discovery work in Indian rupees, and receives UK sterling and Euros from its European customers. The high costs of foreign exchange can equate to losing around 2% of the value of each international transaction, which puts a serious dent in a company's bottom line when so many such transactions are involved.

But SMEs are constrained by the lack of flexibility around terms and pricing for international payments currently available from the clearing banks, and peer-to-peer solutions, where a company in one country is matched up with another in the destination country to essentially 'swap' payments, lack certainty around timing and exchange rates. Money Mover was established to help SMEs get round these problems, and reduce the costs and risks of international payments.

RAISING FUNDS TO RAISE THE ROOF WITH SYNDICATEROOM

Since it was launched in September 2013, equity crowdfunding platform SyndicateRoom has notched up a number of world firsts, raised over £37 million for the companies selected to fundraise via the SyndicateRoom platform in just two years, and taken a lead position in the UK equity crowdfunding space.

The first movie to be financed with the help of equity crowdfunding used SyndicateRoom to deliver a chunk of the roughly £6 million budget. Hollywood blockbuster director Simon West (*Tomb Raider*, *Con Air*), hoped to raise £1.8 million through SyndicateRoom for his new film, *Salty*, but eventually raised over £2.29 million via the site.

Mill Group Residential used SyndicateRoom in the first example of a mixed IPO that offered shares to both institutional and 'retail' investors. Mill Group created a real estate investment trust (REIT) and promoted it to institutional investors via the traditional route of a roadshow and meetings with investor groups to explain the proposition, and also used SyndicateRoom to make shares available to the wider public.

Founded by Gonçalo de Vasconcelos and Tom Britton, and supported by a number of Cambridge Angels and other investors, SyndicateRoom is authorized in the UK by the FCA (Financial Conduct Authority). The company raised £10 million for its companies in its first year. Close competitors Crowdcube

and Seedrs raised £2.5 million and £1.5 million in their first years, respectively. But the models for the platforms are different – Crowdcube and Seedrs accept minimum investments of £10, whereas for SyndicateRoom the minimum is £1,000.

Apart from the size of minimum investment, the key differentiator for SyndicateRoom is that every investee company has a lead investor, either an experienced business angel or a venture capital or equity investment fund already involved with the company. Companies that come to SyndicateRoom are already revenue-generating, but looking to raise extra funds for growth. It is the 'endorsement' and the skills the existing investors bring to the table that makes SyndicateRoom's offerings more than just a step in the dark for investors. Their investments are de-risked by the participation of sophisticated investors, who have already performed due diligence of their own.

The UK Enterprise Investment Scheme currently accounts for around £3 billion in investments, venture capital investing for around £1 billion, and angel investing another £1 billion. So far, around £84 million has been raised through equity crowdfunding, so there is still plenty of room for SyndicateRoom to grow. And when some of the investments reach the exit stage, then it will be possible to get a clearer picture of the company's impact.

Above: *From left to right: SyndicateRoom CEO Gonçalo de Vasconcelos, Head of Capital Markets Tom Hinton and CTO Tom Britton.*

> **"**
> *Our reach is international. Only around 15% of the investments we have sponsored so far have been in Cambridge.*

Gonçalo de Vasconcelos, CEO, SyndicateRoom

Top right: *RealVNC helps Polar Bears International to track polar bears around the shores of Hudson Bay in Canada.*

Bottom right: *Telecom Cook Islands Ltd is the main provider for the 15 islands that make up the Cook Islands in the South Pacific, and RealVNC helps keep their engineers on dry land.*

THE BIGGEST CLOUDS DEPEND ON XEN

The Xen hypervisor, which saw its origins in a research project at Cambridge University, is now supporting the biggest clouds on the internet – such as Amazon Web Services, Rackspace Public Cloud and Verizon Cloud. The Xen hypervisor creates and runs virtual machines and a virtual operating platform that enables computing resources to be shared, and is supported by both Intel and ARM chips.

Originally developed by Ian Pratt and Keir Fraser as part of their research project in the late 1990s, Xen was released as open source in 2002, and had its first public release in 2003. Pratt and colleagues then founded Xensource in 2004 as a commercial entity to develop the system, although Xen hypervisor remained open source.

The Xen hypervisor was selected by Red Hat, Novell and Sun Microsystems for virtualization functions in 2005, and the company was acquired by Citrix in 2007 for $500 million. The first Xen cloud platform launched in 2011, and in 2013 the Xen Project became part of the Linux Foundation.

RealVNC GOES FROM FREEMIUM TO PREMIUM

We could not launch without VNC.

NASA

RealVNC is the de facto standard for remote control, with over two billion copies downloaded or built into devices worldwide. The software is part of the internet, being the origin of the remote framebuffer protocol, RFC 6143. Used by industry, government and the education sector, RealVNC software is also found embedded in many vertical markets, such as consumer electronics and in vehicles.

Intel, IBM, Philips, Comcast, the Royal Shakespeare Company, Dublin City Council – RealVNC has a diverse roster of customers using its technology for remote access and computer support. Google has built RealVNC technology into its Chrome browser and operating system, allowing users to access other applications on their other devices, not just Google applications from the cloud.

Virtual Network Computing, VNC, had actually started as a project in the AT&T Laboratory in Cambridge in the mid-1990s, and the team had released their handiwork as a free download in 1998. With hundreds of thousands of downloads in just a few months indicating they could be on to a winner, when

AT&T announced the closure of the Cambridge Laboratory, a group of the staff had no hesitation in setting up a new company, and, in 2002, RealVNC was born.

Although free downloads proved the popularity of their technology, they did not pay the wages, and so the company was the first to develop crowdfunding for a technology business – before it was even termed 'crowdfunding'. 'If you love our software, why not buy the t-shirt?' Merchandising (t-shirts, baseball caps, mousemats and more) raised several hundred thousand dollars, but then users said they had enough t-shirts, and could they just donate some money? So RealVNC put a 'Donate'

"

We are thrilled to tap into RealVNC's proven technology and expertise to complement our existing initiative.

Google

"

RealVNC was an early pioneer of the 'freemium' model.

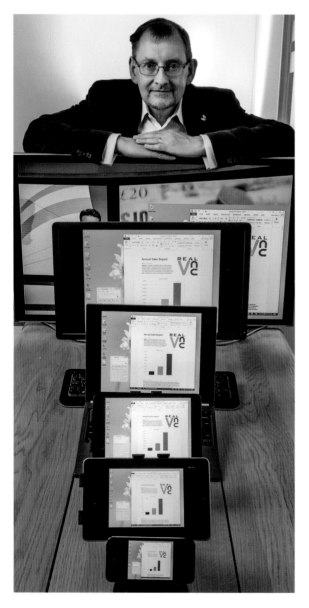

button on their website, and raised hundreds of thousands of dollars more. Growth has been organic ever since, with no need to raise venture capital or seek investment via a stock market listing.

The crowdfunding campaign also provided RealVNC with an opportunity for some free market research, and the people who had bought the merchandise obliged by telling them what they used the software for, and, more importantly, what they wanted to use it for, which informed the development roadmap.

Since they already knew they had a market, RealVNC used the money raised via their rather unorthodox methods to develop a better version of the software that they could charge for. It was estimated that it would take a couple of years, and the money, plus some from UK Government grant systems and EU project money, was used to hire some additional engineers.

Since then, the company has experienced compound annual growth of 50% every year, and royalties from OEM licences have overtaken revenues from direct sales. Licensees include many of the world's major technology companies, such as IBM, Philips, Siemens, Texas Instruments, Cisco, Dell, Citrix, Microsoft and Symantec. Philips, for instance, build RealVNC into their MRI and X-ray machines, so that their technicians can troubleshoot, test, and calibrate the machines remotely.

RealVNC has received three Queen's Awards for Enterprise, and in 2013 won the Royal Academy of Engineering MacRobert Award, the UK's top engineering prize, joining the likes of internationally renowned previous winners such as Jaguar Land Rover and British Aerospace.

1SPATIAL PUTS THE UK ON THE DIGITAL MAP

Going from mapping the tracks of ionized particles in bubble chambers to creating the first digital database for the UK's Ordnance Survey was an unexpected turn for the parent company of 1Spatial, Laser-Scan, but it marked the start of a long association between Cambridge companies and the world of digital mapping.

Laser-Scan was originally founded out of the Cavendish Laboratory in 1969, to develop a method based on lasers for tracking ionized particles in bubble chambers. The Sweepnik followed the lines of the bubbles' tracks on photographs. A military client asked if their technology could follow the lines on maps, and, having worked out how their laser device could do this, the company moved into digitizing maps.

At the same time, it emerged that their laser technology could also be used for secure printing – for items such as banknotes,

Far left: *Andy Harter, co-founder of RealVNC.*

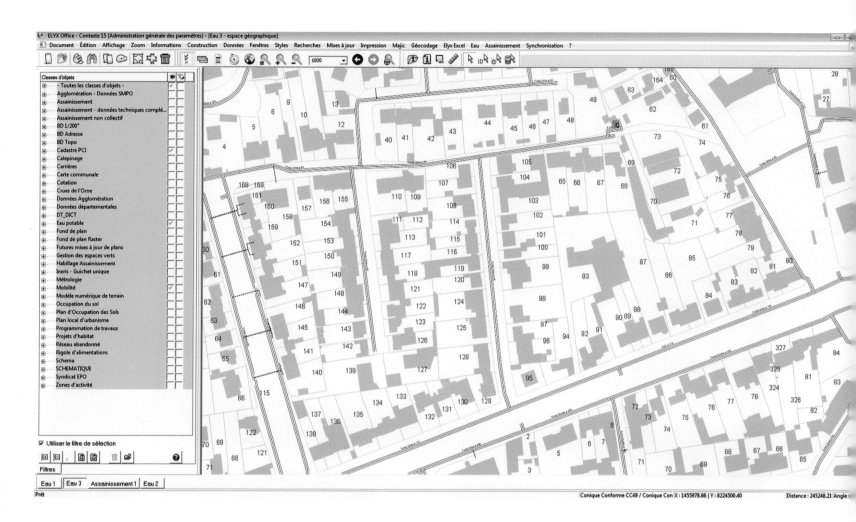

Above: *1Spatial's Elyx Office provides a wide range of functionality via an office interface.*

passports and driving licences, and one of the world's major secure printing companies, De La Rue, became a customer. It was estimated that Laser-Scan equipment was used to design around a third of all the banknotes used in the world in the 1970s. De La Rue continues to print the majority of the world's banknotes.

Winning the contract with Ordnance Survey Great Britain in 1979 to create a national mapping database was a major coup and started Laser-Scan down the road to becoming an international success in digital mapping.

In 2005, the company split into Laser-Scan Engineering Ltd (hardware) and 1Spatial (software). Laser-Scan Engineering continued to develop the laser technology that had evolved in the 1970s into a significant player in the security printing and engraving sector. Laser-Scan security printing is today used by global secure printing providers Giori for many of the world's banknotes, passports and driving licences.

1Spatial continued the success in digital mapping, and the Ordnance Survey remains a customer. Many more customers demonstrate the breadth of uses for digital mapping technology, and the roster includes Verizon, VINCI Autoroutes, Vodafone, the London Metropolitan Police, EDF, the Swedish Maritime Association, the Queensland Government, the National Geographic Institute, and the National Geospatial-Intelligence Agency in the US.

SMALLWORLD IS BIG IN THE WORLD

Smallworld is another international success story that emerged from the days of the CADCentre in Cambridge University. Dick Newell and colleagues spun Smallworld out of CADCentre in 1989, in order to develop and commercialize their GIS software. The company was acquired by GE Energy in 2000, part of General Electric. At the time, Smallworld had over 750 utility customers and 120 telecommunications, broadband and internet customers worldwide, and what is now known as GE Smallword remains a global market leader for GIS in utilities and communications.

FINDING 100 MILLION LOCATIONS IN 4.5 SECONDS: GEOSPOCK

A demonstration from young company GeoSpock at the end of the TechStars accelerator programme in 2015 showed their technology searching for and finding 100 million constantly moving locations around the globe in 4.5 seconds, a speed 15 times faster than that of the current market leader in tracking very large numbers of assets or locations.

GeoSpock describes what they do as 'extreme-scale, real-time geo-spatial and multi-dimensional big data applications'. A cloud-based system, the technology has multiple potential applications among a huge variety of big data challenges, including modelling the weather and human genome sequencing.

Big data can be an asset, but it can also be a big headache without the technology to analyse and use it. The data often comes from multiple types of sources, and is difficult to integrate and then understand – turning data into information is particularly tricky. The GeoSpock Engine is a database that works with archived and live data, based in part on founder Steve Marsh's PhD research into developing an extreme-scale supercomputer for simulating brain function.

GeoShock founder Steve Marsh at Web Summit 2015.

The GeoSpock location database service deals with massive data sets exponentially faster than the traditional NoSQL service.

ViewRanger, an off-road satellite navigation device developed by Augmentra.

Founded in February 2013 and backed by some of Cambridge's most experienced and successful entrepreneurs, GeoSpock has early adopters for its technology from the insurance, mapping, security and logistics sectors. The company is also partnering with the Ordnance Survey and Future Cities Catapult in location data innovation projects.

As the Internet of Things arrives and more and more devices have GPS location sensors built in, being able to tackle massive geospatial datasets will only get more important.

VIEWRANGER SAVING LIVES WITH OFF-ROAD GPS

ViewRanger, an off-road satellite navigation service developed by Augmentra, is used by over 200 search and rescue teams in Europe and the US.

As a mobile phone app, ViewRanger is also marketed to the travel, leisure and adventure sectors. It features a global directory of routes, utilising data from the UK's Ordnance Survey and the US Geological Survey, among others. In 2014, 750,000 people per month accessed ViewRanger's trail guides

and shared routes with friends and fellow hikers. Used in 20 countries and with 500 partners publishing via the app, ViewRanger has created a global community.

Founded in 2006 by a group of keen hillwalkers, Augmentra was the first company to create panoramic mapping, the first app to bring Ordnance Survey outdoor recreational mapping to mobile phones, and the first mapping and navigation app to gain Symbian Signed certification. Augmentra also developed the first mobile travel guide for the UK's Automobile Association, and the first mobile travel guide for Ordnance Survey Ireland.

ViewRanger has won numerous awards, including a Google Play Top Developer Badge in 2015 (fewer than 500 app developers worldwide have received this accolade), the Mobile App World 'Best Independent App' 2010, and the Ordnance Survey's Most Innovative Product in the Navigation Sector. It is the number one bestselling app on the Apple iPhone in 20 countries, and number one in the sector in the Apple iTunes store. The app also has multiple number one rankings in the Google Play and Nokia OVI app stores.

TELECOMMUNICATIONS

I f you use a smartphone, you almost certainly hold one or more ARM chips in your hand every time you use it, but there's also a high likelihood that you'll be taking advantage of Bluetooth technology from CSR or VideoCore media processing from Alphamosaic (both Cambridge Consultants spin-outs) in the same device. Your wireless keyboard and mouse could represent a little part of Cambridge on your desk, and the signal you get when out shopping may well be coming to you from a 3G small cell developed by a Cambridge company.

An 'RFeye Array', generically referred to as a 'direction finder', made by CRFS. They are used in radio spectrum monitoring and surveillance for detecting and locating unauthorized, suspicious or interfering transmitters.

If you attended the 2012 London Olympics, the 2014 Sochi Winter Olympics or any of a number of other major international sporting events, the radios used by the security and emergency personnel keeping you safe came from Sepura. If you have any financial investments that operate wholly or in part through the stock markets, such as a pension, the electronic trading systems that help grow your money – or give you the excitement of playing the markets yourself – rely on Solarflare to protect the networks and keep your trades safe and compliant.

Cambridge companies were behind the first commercial internet service provider (ISP) in the UK, leaps in Asynchronous Transfer Mode (ATM) and Asymmetric Digital Subscriber Line (ADSL) connectivity, and, more recently, other improvements to broadband connections and functionality.

If you drive one of the top brands of car, the manufacturing processes that produced it may well have been optimized and monitored by the Ubisense Smart Factory system, as might the manufacturing of the Airbus you flew in on your last trip. And when the Internet of Things (IoT) starts to improve all our lives, it may well be Cambridge technology from ARM that makes things happen.

From the early days of radio to the first live outside broadcast of the famous Boat Race shown on television, and from the world's first webcam broadcasting over the internet to the latest microwave backhaul technology improving network coverage inside buildings and shopping centres, Cambridge technology underpins how we communicate and receive data, information and entertainment around the world.

Cambridge also saw its first billion-dollar company in telecoms company Ionica which, although it did not survive a string of eventually insurmountable challenges, had a lasting impact on the development of the Cambridge Phenomenon. Ionica not only demonstrated that it was indeed possible for Cambridge to create a billion-dollar company, but it has had an enduring legacy in the companies and technologies that grew up around and after it.

The companies discussed below are only part of the Cambridge telecommunications story. The other part of the story is the role of the technology consultancies, and their not insignificant part in the wired and wireless revolutions is covered on pages 117–18.

Above: Sepura provided radios for the security and emergency personnel at the 2012 London Olympics.

TELECOMS PIONEERS SET THE SCENE
FOR THE SEPURA GROUP

The Sepura Group was founded in 2002, but its origins can be traced back to Pye Radio Ltd, founded in Cambridge in 1896.

Pye was producing more than 40,000 radio sets per year by the mid-1930s, and its television receivers became the basis for the radio sets used by the British military in World War II. In 1955, the first broadcast from ITV, the first commercial television station in the UK, relied on Pye cameras and studio equipment. By 1960, around 15% of the UK's radio and electronic exports came from the various Pye companies.

Pye was eventually acquired by the Dutch company Philips, and was gradually broken up as globalization changed television and electronics manufacturing models. But its legacy lives on in Cambridge in form of the Sepura Group. The company was founded when private equity firm Kelso Place rescued the TETRA radio business from the ailing Team Simoco, the last incarnation of Pye. Sepura floated on the London Stock Exchange in 2007, valued at £200 million.

Sepura came into a nascent market. The TETRA standard had been established just a few years earlier in 1995 by the European Telecommunications Standards Institute for government and emergency services. The technology, and robustness, of the company's radios proved a success and Sepura went from strength to strength, becoming market leader in 30 countries.

More than 1,000 organisations in over 100 countries use Sepura TETRA radios in one or more critical functions, such as emergency services, policing, border control or utilities.

The number of Sepura TETRA radios in operation around the world more than tripled between 2008 and 2014, from around 400,000 radios to over 1.2 million, with the company shipping its millionth radio during its tenth anniversary year. In 2014, Sepura confirmed its global status with sales in 83 countries, 22 of which generated over €1 million of revenues.

Sepura TETRA radios are used by every police force in England, Scotland and Wales, as well as every ambulance and every paramedic. Global sporting events, such as the 2008 Beijing Olympics, the 2010 World Cup in South Africa and the 2012 London Olympics, have based their security and emergency provisions on Sepura communications

Below: *Norwegian policemen equipped with Sepura radios.*

"
The next time you see a policeman on the street or a paramedic in an ambulance, the radio they carry on their lapel to send emergency messages will most likely be made by Sepura.

Financial Times, April 2015

technology. The 2016 Rio Olympics will also be using Sepura communication systems.

Other customers range from Disneyland Paris to Audi, New Jersey Transit and Pan American Energy.

At CERN (the European Organization for Nuclear Research), Sepura's technology has helped to overcome a unique, and particularly demanding, set of challenges. The site covers 60km^2, comprising 600 buildings on the surface and 50km of underground tunnels, including the circular Large Hadron Collider, which is approximately 27km long and sits 50–175m below ground. The surrounding rock, and presence of powerful magnets, has a significant impact on radio reception.

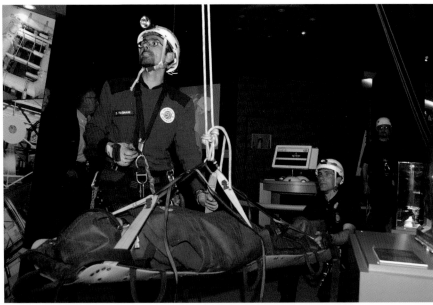

Right: *Sepura products are used by CERN's specialized fire brigade.*

Below: *New Jersey Transit are just one of Sepura's many prominent customers.*

Above: *The Panama Canal relies on Sepura communications technology.*

Sepura products are used by CERN's own specialized fire brigade and the organization's maintenance and security personnel, both above and below ground. One of the key functionalities at CERN is accurate location data, which Sepura technology provides – even deep underground, where GPS signals cannot reach.

Heathrow Airport, the Panama Canal, platinum mines in Australia and the oil and gas rigs of the North Sea also rely on Sepura communications technology, as did the 2015 G7 summit of world leaders in Bavaria, Germany, where almost 18,000 Sepura radios were in use every day. Even Lord's, the 'home of cricket' in London, uses Sepura for its communications.

A remarkable feature of Sepura's growth is perhaps not its obvious success, but the fact that, until very recently, it was denied the potential of the extremely lucrative markets of the US and Canada. This was due to TETRA radio being prohibited by North American regulators the Federal Communications

Commission (FCC) and Industry Canada because of concerns about interference with other radio bands and interoperability.

In 2011, the FCC and Industry Canada permitted a temporary waiver of the relevant regulations, allowing TETRA pilot programmes in particular bands. In 2012 this arrangement was made permanent – although TETRA is still prohibited from the public safety spectrum, thus Sepura's focus is on other critical communications sectors, such as public transport. In 2014, Sepura reported its first infrastructure win in North America – the Toronto Transit Commission, the third largest public transportation system in North America, which moves over 460 million passengers per year on buses, subways and trams.

Today, Sepura's market capitalization sits at around half a billion dollars, despite the North American markets only just opening up to TETRA technology. The company estimates that this new opportunity raises its addressable market from around $0.5 billion dollars to $2.5 billion.

CAMBRIDGE AND THE DIAL-UP DAYS – UNIPALM-PIPEX IS THE FIRST COMMERCIAL ISP IN THE UK

Unipalm was the first commercial internet service provider in the UK, launching in 1992, and the flotation was intended to fund the expansion of Pipex – the Public IP Exchange – which had been set up by Unipalm in 1990. The company became Unipalm-Pipex in 1995, and in November of that year was sold to UUNet for £150 million, becoming UUNet/Pipex.

Unipalm was originally set up by Peter Dawe to sell American networking software to businesses which used Ethernet technology to connect computers and save the time and hassle of sharing documents via floppy disks. The software could connect up to ten computers in a single office, but went no further.

The software Unipalm was selling was soon superseded by proprietary networks that linked different offices together via telephone lines, but the links were very slow, and companies were reluctant to sign up to a system that was only useful if the companies they wanted to connect to were also participants.

Efforts to persuade major telecoms providers in the UK, BT and Mercury, to set up a public network that would help

"

The first internet-related company to be listed on a stock exchange anywhere in the world was Cambridge's Unipalm Group, which was floated on the London Stock Exchange in 1994.

Unipalm joins 'superleague'

CAMBRIDGE computer firm Unipalm is one of the fastest-growing companies in the United Kingdom, according to a recent study.

The company was included in a "superleague" survey by the 3i Cranfield European Enterprise Centre which examined 3,500 medium-sized firms which achieved a minimum turnover growth of 25 per cent over a two-year period.

The study comes at the end of a successful year for the Unipalm Group, the country's leading PC to enterprise networking software specialist.

Earlier this year it announced a record turn over of £8.4 million, an increase of 59 per cent over last year and launched two new companies. Computer

College and Unipalm Consulting, to specialise in IT training and consultancy.

The group has also seen a 50 per cent growth this year in the number of employees at its headquarters on the Cambridge Science Park.

Joint managing director Peter Dawe said: "This superleague of fast-growing UK companies has proved that even medium-sized companies like ourselves, who are in a niche market, can be successful.

"1993 has been an eventful and exciting year for Unipalm and one in which we have seen the company continue to expand beyond its traditional boundaries and diversify into new areas."

According to the 3i research, the group of fast-growing companies doubled its aggregate turnover to £18.4 billion.

Eventful and exciting year . . . Peter Dawe, joint managing director.

sell the new technology met with no success, and so Unipalm led a group of organizations that decided they would have to do it themselves. The group leased lines from BT to provide the physical infrastructure, and using a Unipalm-Pipex hub networked a few thousand buildings.

The biggest part of the emerging network was in the US, which had originated in the Advanced Research Projects Agency Network, ARPANET, funded by the US Government and the first to use the TCP/IP protocol suite, the foundation of the internet. By the 1990s, the ARPANET connected a number of corporate and educational establishments in the US, organizations that British companies wanted to connect to, and so, in 1992, Unipalm-Pipex leased a 64k line from London to Washington to access the American network. At the same time, Unipalm-Pipex also connected to the UK government's network that connected research and educational establishments, JANET. (By this time, a few universities in the UK had set up their own lines to the US, also for the purposes of connecting academic researchers.) With a connection to Washington, UK companies and customers could send emails to US organizations – novel at the time.

In 1995, Unipalm-Pipex was the biggest commercial ISP in the world for customers, revenue and geographical reach.

An early customer for Pipex was Demon Internet, which captured a large proportion of the dial-up internet access market in the UK in the 1990s. The network grew at 10% a month, and by the time Unipalm-Pipex was sold to UUNet, it was the biggest ISP in the world for customers, revenue and geographical reach, having partnered with associate companies in South Africa, France, Germany, the Benelux countries and Italy, with countries in the Gulf region about to join. In addition, non-associate companies used Unipalm-Pipex to network to the rest of Europe.

A crucial contribution of Unipalm-Pipex was to drive the concept of neutral interconnections. Prior to the advent of the internet, network providers negotiated one-on-one with every other provider to exchange traffic. This could work if a country had only one network provider, but when the numbers of providers was much higher, the process became highly fragmented and inefficient. Pipex promoted a model for networks that replicated a telephone exchange, and LINX was born.

The London Internet Exchange, or LINX, began with a Cisco Catalyst 1200 switch donated by Pipex that linked five ISPs in the UK and enabled them to interconnect without having to go via the costly, and slow, US connection. The establishment of LINX as a not-for-profit company to provide neutral interconnections between its members has proved an enduring model.

LINX was the first internet exchange in the world to deploy a 100-megabit switch in 1996, and the first exchange to operate 10Gb Ethernet.

When LINX was set up, there were about 2,700 websites worldwide; in September 2014, Tim Berners-Lee tweeted evidence from Internet Live Stats that the number of websites had surpassed a billion. The original LINX operation used one cabinet in a largely empty data centre building, Telehouse in London's Docklands, and is today spread across several centres in the UK and one in the US. LINX is now one of the largest internet exchanges in the world, with over 650 members from more than 65 countries.

The no-settlement model was another area where Pipex lobbied for, and eventually succeeded in, persuading ISPs that it was against their interests to charge each other for interconnections, since it involved the costly step of counting data packets, and would distort prices for smaller players in the field.

The Pipex name lived on in several different ownership structures and incarnations, eventually ending up as a residential business that was absorbed into the Carphone Warehouse's TalkTalk service in the UK.

Peter Dawe, founder of Unipalm-Pipex and the driving force behind many of the early commercial models for ISPs, went on to help set up the Internet Watch Foundation (originally known as the Safety Net Foundation) when the legal issue of whether or not ISPs were publishers arose in the UK in the mid-1990s. If ISPs were seen as publishers, this implied that they were responsible for the information and images transmitted over their networks, and thus liable for prosecution under obscenity laws where pornographic images were involved. Internet Watch, a collaboration between police, government and industry, serves to help ensure reported illegal content is taken down. With numerous other ventures to his name, Dawe is most recently the founder of Cambridge TV.

Far right: *Peter Dawe, founder of Unipalm-Pipex.*

KEEPING UP WITH RAPID CHANGE: ATML, TO VIRATA, TO GLOBESPANVIRATA

Another Cambridge company that is no longer operational but played an important role in the development of telecommunications started out as Advanced Telecommunications Modules Ltd (ATML), and ended up as GlobespanVirata.

ATML secured the first investment from a Silicon Valley VC into a UK company.

ATML was the first spin-out from what was then the Olivetti Research Laboratory in Cambridge (itself a legacy of Acorn Computers). The company was set up in 1993, after a consortium of around 1,000 companies endorsed Asynchronous Transfer Mode (ATM) as the standard for networking. ATML focused on 25Mb ATM networking equipment at a time when Ethernet was only delivering 10Mb. Investors into a first round which raised approximately $11.25 million included Silicon Valley's Oak Investment Partners and New Enterprise Associates.

When Ethernet started delivering speeds of 100Mb, ATML was suddenly in a difficult position: despite its other multimedia attributes, who would be interested in buying slower technology?

With Charles Cotton as the newly appointed CEO, the company split and regrouped, pivoting the business model from ATM networking to the new standard for dial-up connections, Asymmetric Digital Subscriber Line, or ADSL, which promised a leap in telephone connection speeds from 56kbps to 500kbps or more. The company changed its focus to modems using ADSL semiconductors and software, and changed its name to Virata.

The technological driver for this change was that the link layer for an ADSL modem used ATM, and only Alcatel and the newly named Virata had the required technology and motivation to pursue ADSL at the time. Virata sold software licences to more than 250 companies looking to enter the ADSL modem market, and since the software only ran on Virata's semiconductors, developed a strong revenue stream.

Virata defied conventional wisdom for UK companies and listed on NASDAQ, a bold and pioneering move.

Virata took the unusual step for a UK company at the time of listing on NASDAQ in 1999, with its valuation soaring to more than $5 billion in early 2000. This move later encouraged other Cambridge companies, such as ARM and Abcam, to list in the US instead of or as well as the UK, gaining not only access to a larger and more sophisticated investor network, but also greater exposure to the potentially lucrative American market.

Another unusual step was to pull back from an 'arms race' with American competitor Globespan. The two companies were essentially complementary, with Globespan the market leader in the physical layer semiconductors and Virata offering the software and chips necessary for modems, but they were each trying to eat the other's lunch by buying up companies to fill the gaps between them: Globespan was trying to outplay Virata at its own game, and Virata was doing the same in reverse. The logical, but perhaps counter-intuitive move, was a merger between the two companies, which took place in 2001. The new organization, GlobespanVirata, was market leader in the DSL (Digital Subscriber Line) space in 2002, with combined revenues of more than $500 million.

As well as demonstrating the value of making the right pivot at the right time, and 'normalizing' listing on NASDAQ for other Cambridge companies, the Virata experience continues to have an impact on Cambridge and on the world. Although Cambridge operations for the descendant of GlobespanVirata, Conexant, were shut down in 2005, the people involved have gone on to invest in or start more companies in Cambridge and beyond.

The experience also created strong links between Cambridge and Silicon Valley, in particular with several VC investors, and also between individuals, providing a conduit for investing in and promoting Cambridge that remains active to this day. One of the companies that has benefited from the relationship is Solarflare, another example of a Cambridge company that has merged with a counterpart in California and leveraged the best of both worlds.

"

Solarflare is the de facto standard in the financial sector, with 98% market share worldwide. The vast majority of electronic trades made on a daily basis around the world rely on Solarflare's technology.

SOLARFLARE HAS THE FINANCIAL MARKETS SEWN UP

Yet another example of what happens in Cambridge when one door closes – the redundant and dispossessed go on to do something bigger and better.

Steve Pope and Derek Roberts lost their jobs when AT&T Laboratories closed, and promptly set up a new company in Roberts' garage with associates from the Cambridge University Computer Laboratory, David Clarke and David Riddoch.

The project Pope and Roberts had been working on at AT&T was to create the 'fastest LAN [Local Area Network] on the planet', and now they decided to repeat the exercise, but this time producing a LAN that worked across the internet. The company, Level 5 Networks, with Charles Cotton as chairman, was set up as a fabless semiconductor and software developer with the intention of developing Ethernet network interface cards that worked via copper and fibre connections and would dramatically increase transmission speeds. A similar company in California, Solarflare, was working on the same technology, but transmitted over unshielded twisted pair wire connections.

Getting to know about each other, the two companies merged in 2006. In a novel arrangement, no shares or cash changed hands, and both companies' investors, led by Oak Investment Partners, provided new funding for what was now called Solarflare.

The technology evolved from simply accelerating data transmission to participating in what happened to that data afterwards, and the Solarflare network 'super-adapter' was born.

Solarflare created the first distributed, active security solution that is implemented within network servers.

Nowhere is this capability more important than the financial sector. Not only do fast transmission speeds spell the difference between a successful, timely trade and a slow, potentially loss-making trade, but the data being transmitted has to be secure, monitored and stored to meet increasingly stringent regulatory requirements. On top of that, complex and vast sets of market data analytics play an ever-more important role in the success of financial institutions.

Growth in the financial sector for Solarflare literally skyrocketed, from fewer than 200 customers in 2012 to over 1,400 in 2015, and today the technology supports the platforms in every major exchange and hedge fund in the sector.

We got to the point where customers were telling OEMs [Original Equipment Manufacturers] to incorporate Solarflare technology in their servers. It's very unusual for a small company like Solarflare to be calling the shots when dealing with global conglomerates.

Russell Stern, CEO, Solarflare

With customers in 82 countries, Solarflare has proven their proposition in the financial sector, but its technology is applicable in all areas where transmission and security are critical, which could be boiled down to any commercial use of the internet.

The market for innovative security products is growing very rapidly, with examples like Target, The Home Depot and TalkTalk demonstrating that security breaches are getting bigger and more damaging. The old model for security is like having guards patrolling the perimeter, and is very software-oriented. But many threats come from within –

"

…just two guys sitting in a shed with a SMART award…

Steve Pope, co-founder of Level 5 Networks

"

*We wouldn't be an integral part
of the New York Stock Exchange
if we weren't getting it right.*

Russell Stern, CEO, Solarflare

from a compromised laptop or a disgruntled employee – and
software always has vulnerabilities. Hardware has been
underexploited for security, but the network adaptor is the
gateway into the server, which makes it one of the most critical
components in the servers and telecommunications functions
for a new, hardware-oriented security model.

Data centres and clouds in particular also need high
transfer rates and low latency, and face another problem as the
laws of physics start to bite.

Now that more and more interactions go through
servers made up of many microprocessors, the physics of
semiconductors becomes a limiting factor because it is
inevitable that Moore's law will reach its end point and the

only way to increase speeds would seem to be to increase
the number of microprocessors. But this in turn will ramp
up the temperature in servers and the costs of cooling will
be prohibitive, thus function will be impaired. Solarflare's
technology provides an alternative way of networking data
through the system, steering it to the right place.

Now adding other markets, Solarflare has already gained
customers in sectors that deal with large quantities of data,
such as the UK, Canadian and US governments, security, big
pharma, utilities and companies that transmit video and other
rich media.

Above: *Solarflare employees
outside the NASDAQ stock market
in New York.*

Far left: *Russell Stern,
CEO of Solarflare.*

Above: *Stan Boland, founder of Element14.*

Bottom right: *Steve Barlow (left) and Robert Swann, Alphamosaic.*

ELEMENT 14, YET ANOTHER LEGACY FROM ACORN

The impact of Element 14 might be seen as a flash in the pan, since the company as an entity existed for less than two years, but we all rely on Element 14 technology every time we connect to the internet via broadband.

Arising from a management buyout for the princely sum of £1.5 million, Element 14 emerged out of the remnants of Acorn Computer Group when the company was broken up in 1999. The company had seven co-founders, including Stan Boland, and was acquired by Broadcom for $642 million just 15 months later. What was so special about the tiny Element 14 that attracted such an enormous offer from one of the world's top semiconductor companies?

It has to be remembered that among the team at Acorn were the developers of the original Acorn RISC Machine chip, which led to the setting up of ARM, a Cambridge company with a market capitalization of over $20 billion today. While ARM chips power electronic devices like mobile phones, wearables and connected devices in the IoT, Element 14 focused on DSL chipsets, software and chip design for the multimedia and digital TV markets.

With its purchase of Element 14, Broadcom gained the expertise of Sophie Wilson, designer with Steve Furber of the original Acorn RISC Machine chip and subsequently chief architect of what became the Broadcom FirePath processor. In 2012, Wilson was named a Fellow of the Computer History Museum in Mountain View, California, one of a select group of people who are recognized as having changed the world with their innovations in computing. She was also named a Broadcom Distinguished Engineer, and is a Fellow of the Royal Academy of Engineering and a Fellow of the Royal Society.

The technology developed by Wilson and the team at Element 14 was the basis for Broadcom's FirePath processor,

and underpins the world's broadband DSL infrastructure, enabling digital data to be transmitted over telephone networks.

According to a 2012 report from analysts Point Topic, globally, broadband access is still dominated by DSL via copper wires, although the percentage serviced by cable and fibre connections is slowly rising. In 2013, it was claimed that Element 14 technology still powered 90% of broadband to the home worldwide.

ALPHAMOSAIC BECOMES ANOTHER CAMBRIDGE FEATHER IN BROADCOM'S CAP

Spun out of a different organization, Cambridge Consultants, Alphamosaic was another company whose potential was spotted early by Broadcom. Founded by Steve Barlow and Robert Swann in 2000, the company specialized in multimedia processors for mobile devices. Alphamosaic had only 57 employees when it was acquired by Broadcom in 2004 for $123 million. The employees of Alphamosaic became Broadcom's Mobile Multimedia Group on the Cambridge Science Park.

Their novel 2D digital signal processor architecture, termed VideoCore and launched in 2002, was another Cambridge innovation that was noted for its low power processing capability. The new architecture was designed for images and video, and first appeared in Apple's video iPod. It also featured in the Nintendo Gameboy video and music accessory, and numerous mobile phones, including from Samsung.

AMINO TECHNOLOGIES IS BECOMING MUCH MORE THAN A WORLD-LEADING SET-TOP BOX SUPPLIER

It may seem normal today to be able to access impossibly huge numbers of channels on a TV, pause or rewind a live television programme, or connect various monitoring devices around the home to a single screen, but this 'new normal' is the result of rapidly changing technologies. The way content is sent to our television screens has expanded from an old-style antenna on the roof to include satellite, cable and the internet, among others, and how we access that content has evolved accordingly, driving the development of the set-top box into something much more complex than a TV tuner.

Amino Technologies Plc has won numerous awards for its Internet Protocol TV (IPTV) set-top boxes, including the prestigious Red Dot award for design in 2003 for the AmiNET100 and the Good Design Award for the A130 in 2008. Founded in 1997, the company was ranked by analysts ABI Research as the world's leading IPTV set-top box supplier for three consecutive years from 2006 to 2008.

But more recent awards indicate how the company has evolved and expanded its offerings as IPTV, video streaming and the concept of the connected home have taken off. In 2014, the Amino Home Reach system, provided via a USB dongle that integrates home monitoring devices with the Amino set-top IPTV box, won both the Best Digital Home Service Innovation at the TV Connect Awards and the Best IPTV Technology or Service at the prestigious international CSI awards.

To date, over seven million Amino devices have been sold to more than 1,000 customers in 100 countries. Customers include network operators, broadcasters and hospitality providers and enterprises. AIM-listed since 2004, revenues in 2014 were over £36 million, and Amino's list of partners includes global names such as Adobe, Broadcom, Dolby, Ericsson and Intel.

Two strategic acquisitions in 2015 mean that Amino is keeping up with and ahead of the way video and other content is being delivered. The acquisition of US competitor Entone Inc increased Amino's range of hybrid devices, which combine both broadband and standard TV reception, and connected home capability. Integrating Entone also expanded Amino's global footprint, bringing new customers and new opportunities. The share placing initiated to provide some of the funds for the $73 million acquisition of Entone was oversubscribed, suggesting that Amino's shareholders agreed that the acquisition was an important move.

The acquisition of Finnish company Booxmedia added extra capacity in 'over-the-top' (OTT) services, enabling customers to deliver a TV experience direct to mobile devices, smart TVs, gaming consoles – as well as set-top boxes – and meet the growing consumer appetite for video consumption on any device, anywhere, anytime. Booxmedia provides live streaming, video recording, video-on-demand and catch-up services all via the cloud, and was recently chosen by Delta in the Netherlands and RTL Belgium to provide services encompassing live-streaming of TV programmes and also libraries of content for catch-up viewing. With analysts predicting that mobile devices will account for up to 20% of our viewing time by 2025, Booxmedia's capacity to provide TV via such devices will be an important part of Amino's 'TV everywhere' mix in the future.

As the set-top box evolves into a hub that not only provides anytime, anywhere, any device content but also connected home functionality, the next major step on the horizon is 4K Ultra High Definition (UHD) TV. Although 4K is not predicted to hit the mass market until 2017 at the earliest, Amino is already developing products that meet the recently defined High Efficiency Video Coding (HEVC) standards so that its customers will be ready when 4K arrives.

Above: *The Network Operations Centre at Velocix.*

VELOCIX HELPS ALCATEL-LUCENT BECOME KING OF CONTENT DELIVERY

'We run a 24/7 operation centre, managing networks on a global basis for the likes of Time Warner Cable and Liberty Global – the biggest cable operator in the world, across 12 countries in Europe – and a whole host of others…we're the number one company in the world in the technology we provide.'

Paul Larbey, CEO, Velocix, and President of Video Business, Alcatel-Lucent, *Cambridge Business* May 2015

Cisco has estimated that over 80% of internet traffic will be video content by 2019. They have also forecast that 72% of all video content will be delivered over content delivery networks, or CDNs, by then. In other words, CDNs will be delivering over half of all internet traffic by 2019, and a large proportion of that traffic will use Alacatel-Lucent's Velocix technology.

Velocix, which started life as CacheLogic, a spin-out company from Saviso Consulting, has been an innovator in the CDN space since it was founded in 2002. Recognising that the biggest problems with delivering the large files that video required would be speed of downloading and security, the Velocix technology got round this problem by developing a way of 'cacheing' or storing encrypted video content at distributed points in networks, so that it could be downloaded quickly from a cache rather than from a central location.

We expect our content to be delivered not only quickly, but also to different devices in different locations – gone are the days of the family sitting together to watch the same programme at the same time. In the 1970s, around 20 million, or over a third of the UK's population at the time, would simultaneously watch TV programmes such the *Morecambe and Wise Christmas Show*. Today, audience figures are made up not only of those who watched a show when it was first broadcast, but also of viewers who watched afterwards, on their computer, on a tablet or even on a smartphone. In 2014, video already accounted for around 75% of network traffic for mobile service providers.

Velocix operations in Cambridge have grown from 35 people to more than 120 since the company was acquired by Alcatel-Lucent in 2009. In 2014, Alcatel-Lucent was ranked the top vendor of 'on-net' CDN products by analysts SNL Kagan MRG. On-net CDN products are those installed within the networks of pay TV companies and other operators, as opposed to 'off-net' services, which are provided by third-party suppliers. If Cisco's predictions about the rise in video traffic are even approximately accurate, Alcatel-Lucent and Velocix are extremely well-placed in the CDN space.

"

It would take an individual over five million years to watch the amount of video that will cross global IP networks each month in 2019.

Cisco Visual Networking Index: Forecast and Methodology 2014–2019

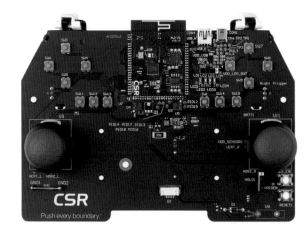

CSR MAKES BLUETOOTH A REALITY

The world's first Bluetooth system on a single chip, BlueCore 1 from Cambridge Silicon Radio, shipped in 2000. The 100 millionth shipped in 2005, the one billionth in 2008, and the two billionth in 2010. The three billionth chip was shipped in 2012.

Cambridge Silicon Radio, or CSR as it is better known, revolutionized communications. CSR was the first to market with a Bluetooth device on a single chip, which paved the way for the earpieces that allowed hands-free mobile use in cars, and spread into many of the different devices we use today, from wireless keyboards and computer mice to fitness wearables, wireless video game controllers and the connection between smartphones and in-car entertainment and monitoring systems.

CSR created, under the technical direction of James Collier, the world's first Bluetooth device on a single piece of silicon at 2.4GHz (a licence-exempt frequency band) incorporating the XAP processor core, which was licensed from Cambridge Consultants, digital logic and analogue radio frequency electronics – all on one very small piece of silicon.

Founding Managing Director Phil O'Donovan,
Business Weekly, May 2015

What was remarkable about CSR's single-chip Bluetooth device was that everyone told them it couldn't be done. Bluetooth

operates at a very high frequency, 2.4GHz, and no other semiconductor manufacturers were addressing that segment because they believed it was too difficult.

CSR was founded as a spin-out from Cambridge Consultants, by three founding directors, Phil O'Donovan, James Collier and Glen Collinson, who had been working on a number of projects in the ISM band, where users do not require a licence. The group had developed design tools at Cambridge Consultants to develop 2.4GHz chips, with the designs based on CMOS chips – important because CMOS was the standard, comprising 99% of all chips made, and because it was cheap and wouldn't add any unusual costs to the final product.

Phil O'Donovan, one of the founders, argued that to have any chance of success with the technology, the only option was to create a spin-out: they needed to be a separate entity to raise the money they would need. A sale and purchase agreement that comprised a mixture of patents, licences, technology, key people, some equity for Cambridge Consultants and goodwill (important for potential investors) was drawn up, and CSR was born.

CSR raised its first £12 million from Cambridge funder Amadeus Capital Partners, Gilde and 3i. Of that initial funding,

Above: *The founders of Cambridge Silicon Radio (CSR).*

Above left: *CSR wireless gaming controller board.*

Right: *The Nike FuelBand uses CSR's Bluetooth Smart.*

Left: *Joep van Beurden, CEO of CSR.*

"
Our BlueCore4-ROM chip is the biggest selling Bluetooth chip in history.

CSR Annual Report, 2007

they spent $1.6 million on equipment to test the chips they were designing, because they had no experience of actually making chips and needed to be able to test them in Cambridge at the time. Later, when the company began its long-running manufacturing and testing partnerships with Taiwan Semiconductor Manufacturing Company (TSMC) and Advanced Semiconductor Engineering (ASE), the testing was transferred.

Having a head start over other chip manufacturers – not least because they thought it couldn't be done – meant that CSR got there first with its single-chip Bluetooth device, and quickly achieved market dominance. This rapid growth was helped in part by the introduction of legislation mandating hands-free operations for mobile phones in cars, with CSR's technology being the instant solution. Dongles, too, were a major early market for CSR, and the company subsequently designed a card with Bluetooth that could be built directly into PCs.

The company remained as world leaders in Bluetooth technology in mono headsets for mobile phones with around 80% of the market, and in 2007 it had over 1,000 employees in ten countries and revenues of $849 million. In that year, CSR shipped over 50% of the world's Bluetooth chips, and its technology was designed into approximately 60% of all Bluetooth products.

In 2007, under the leadership of new CEO Joep van Beurden, CSR acquired another small Cambridge company that had big customers, Cambridge Positioning Systems (CPS). CPS counted

Ericsson, Samsung, HP and Texas Instruments among its clients. Founded in 1993 to develop low-cost location services for vendors and manufacturers of mobile phones, CPS was behind giving mobile phones GPS capability and allowing users to find their location. The acquisition for CSR meant it could now incorporate geolocation into its world-beating Bluetooth chips.

In 2009, CSR recorded more Bluetooth design-wins than all of its competitors combined.

In 2012, revenues were over $1 billion, CSR had more than 2,000 employees in 26 offices around the world, and the company had shipped its three billionth chip since 1999. To keep up with ever-changing markets, CSR was already shifting away from concentrating on handsets to multifunction platforms, where the technology was more complex and margins were higher. As part of this reorganization, CSR sold its handset connectivity and handset location business to Samsung for a headline figure of $310 million, with Samsung also buying shares in CSR, giving it a 5.98% stake. The sale created the Samsung Cambridge Solution Centre.

CSR was then able to focus one of its new business groups, Core, on growth sectors, including automotive, consumer, indoor location and voice and music, and also to develop the new Bluetooth 4.0 standard. Known as Bluetooth Smart, the new device is ultra-low energy, and used for short-range wireless connections such as for a mouse and keyboard.

Bluetooth Smart is also integral to devices such as Nike+ shoes and the Nike FuelBand, and in 2013, Google announced that the next generation Android operating system would be Bluetooth Smart ready, it being already supported by Apple's iOS 7.0.

By now, the customer list for CSR read like a who's who of the world's top electronic device manufacturers, and included (among many others) Dell, LG, Motorola, NEC, Nokia, Panasonic, RIM, Samsung, Sharp, Sony, TomTom, Toshiba in mobile communications and computing; Audi, BMW, Ford and Toyota in automotive; Beats, Bose, Sony and Philips in hi-fi; and the Sony PlayStation among gaming devices.

In 2015, CSR was acquired by Qualcomm, also a fabless semiconductor company, which at the time was capitalised at $130 billion on the NASDAQ stock exchange and already had a mobile and telecoms research base on the Cambridge Science Park. The deal valued CSR at $2.5 billion.

UBISENSE MAKES SENSE FOR AIRBUS, ASTON MARTIN, BMW…AND MANY MORE HOUSEHOLD NAMES

Vehicles and utilities are two of the largest markets in the world, and any downtime for them is extremely costly. A small Cambridge company, Ubisense, with 240 employees and offices in the US, Canada, Japan, South Korea, Philippines, Singapore, France and Germany, is providing the answers.

Major automotive companies have complex, distributed and time-critical production lines that have to be managed and understood at granular levels, especially as increasing customization means that multiple permutations must be available for each model, making the production process even more complicated.

Utilities and communication networks have assets distributed over many thousands of square miles that they have to keep track of and repair when necessary, as quickly as possible.

Founded in 2002, Ubisense for a while was a company with a great technology but no clear direction as to where its market lay. The answer came when Ubisense completed a Smart Factory project with BMW in 2008 and the value of the technology – sensors, monitors and analytical software that could also interact with a customer's own monitoring equipment – became clear.

Among its more than 500 customers in 50 countries, Ubisense counts most of the top ten global automobile manufacturers, heavy vehicle manufacturers such as Komatsu, CLAAS and John Deere, more than 40 telecoms network operators, and utility companies in a number of countries, including the US. Airbus uses Ubisense technology at ten of its manufacturing sites.

Ubisense is another Cambridge company that, despite its relatively small size, has productive relationships with some of the largest companies in the world. It is a Google Enterprise Partner, and partners with Atlas Copco in a tool location system – a useful relationship with the company that can claim one in three cars in the world is assembled using its tools.

The company is also involved in the Manufacturing Technology Centre in Coventry, alongside others like Siemens and Rolls-Royce, and is supplying tracking and monitoring systems for the Factory 2050 initiative, a project of the University of Sheffield Advanced Manufacturing Research Centre.

Above: *VectaStar ODU-S Access Point.*

CAMBRIDGE BROADBAND NETWORKS GO THE LAST MILE

For people living far from metropolitan centres, the 'last mile' of any communications network is the most critical, but it is also the hardest for operators to reach, as the core network breaks into subnetworks at the edges and each subnetwork must be served without data or signal loss. However, it is a legal obligation for the providers to ensure that data sent via their networks reaches the subnetworks and the final recipient. Backhaul, the connection that links subnetworks to the core network, is the crucial function here.

Cambridge Broadband Networks Limited (CBNL) developed VectaStar, a microwave system for backhaul, which has proved particularly successful in developing countries especially in Africa.

The launch of the iPhone in 2007 and the rise of the smartphone have driven up demand for data transmission dramatically, particularly as accessing media-rich sites such as Facebook and news channels via mobile devices becomes the norm. This puts far greater loads on networks, and on their furthest reaches in particular.

That CBNL are successfully addressing this problem is reflected in their position as market leader in point-to-multipoint microwave, with VectaStar microwave backhaul networks operating in 42 countries for more than 70 service providers. CBNL counts seven of the world's top ten mobile operators among its customers, even though it has only recently begun to address the North American market.

Right: *AlertMe energy monitoring system.*

THE ENTHUSIASM FOR WIRELESS, AND ITS POSSIBILITIES, REMAINS UNDIMMED

Cambridge has no shortage of start-ups in the wireless space, as more and more opportunities – and new technologies – present themselves.

Founded in 2010, **Cambridge Communication Systems** offers the world's first self-organising small cell microwave backhaul system for mobile networks. The number of awards it has already won for its technology suggests that the system is promising. Not only that, but the team behind it inspire confidence, with co-founders Steve Greaves and John Porter being previously in the founding teams of CBNL and Adaptive Broadband, and telecoms heavyweights on the board including Robert Sansom and David Cleevely.

The first commercial deployment of Cambridge Communications Systems' product, Metnet, was by China Mobile, the world's largest mobile operator, and this was one of the first live deployments of outdoor cells in the world.

AlertMe focused on the smart meter sector as a way to combine wireless communications and software to make home energy use more efficient. Early strategic partnerships with home improvement giant Lowe's in the US, and British Gas, which, at ten million registered homes, is the largest domestic energy provider in the UK, proved significant.

Turnover reached £18 million and the system was being used by 150,000 British Gas customers by the time British Gas decided to extend its partnership arrangement into an acquisition. AlertMe was sold to British Gas for £44 million in 2015, by which time co-founder and serial Cambridge entrepreneur Pilgrim Beart was already well on the way with his next company, 1248.

Another company in the smart metering space is **Cyan Technology**. Their focus is power saving and low costs, and their products are aimed at emerging economies. The company's mesh-based wireless technology and software package can be retrofitted on to legacy systems, without necessitating major re-engineering or replacement, and is designed to make upgrading to smart cities easy and affordable. The technology was recently recognized by the industry, winning the European Utility Week 2015 award for Smart Metering, ICT & Data Management. Cyan is starting to extend its reach in emerging and growing markets, with a subsidiary in India serving customers such as Tata Power Mumbai and CESC in Mysore, relationships with Egyptian contractor El Sewedy and Adenco in South Africa among others, and partnerships in Brazil and China.

NEUL GOES FROM WHITESPACE TO CELLULAR NARROWBAND IoT

Neul was an early pioneer in a new opportunity for telecommunications: white space, the unused frequencies in the radio spectrum. As television and radio transition to digital signals, more such channels are becoming available for exploitation.

Potential uses of white space are many, and include rural broadband, data networks in cities or on large campuses, and machine-to-machine communications, the Internet of Things or IoT. Part of the attraction of the technology is that it is far too expensive to use mobile broadband networks to support such communication networks.

Co-founded by two of the founders of CSR, James Collier and Glenn Collinson, the intention for Neul was to explore ways of exploiting white space. Following a number of trials, Neul decided to focus on low-power area networks. Such networks are intended as the basis for the IoT, because they are ideal for devices that are not required to transmit data continuously, for instance sensors that transmit one reading per day.

"

The new standard will unlock a huge market. Huawei has the capability and outreach to bring Neul technology to that market. Neul has grown 50% in the last 12 months; to continue our growth we moved to new premises on the Science Park. This is hugely exciting, for the company and for Cambridge.

Henk Koopmans, CEO, Neul

Neul became a wholly owned subsidiary of Huawei in September 2014, reportedly for $25 million. The company had around 30 staff at the time and Huawei announced that it was intending to develop a global research centre in Cambridge for IoT, with Neul as the foundation stone.

This enabled Neul to engage with 3GPP and lay the foundation for a new standard called Narrow Band IoT (NB-IoT), to be published in 2016. NB-IoT networks can be rolled out very quickly because they are created through upgrades of existing cellular base stations.

Above: IoT & Street lighting solution (300,000 nodes and counting) developed by TTP and Mayflower, deployed into Hampshire, saving 4,000 tonnes of CO_2 per annum.

CW CONNECTS THE WIRELESS WORLD

One of the most influential organisations in mobile is a non profit organisation. We are not talking about Sony Mobile but Cambridge Wireless.

www.theregister.co.uk

Robert Driver, CEO of CW.

What is now known as CW started in 2000 as Cambridge 3G, set up as a forum for 3G companies to test their applications, with the aim of making Cambridge the leading test bed for 3G in Europe. Along with Cambridge names such as ARM and CSR, the first meeting in September 2000 attracted international names BT and Vodafone. The original 3G demonstrator was developed at technology consultancy Scientific Generics (now known as Sagentia).

In 2005, the group was rechristened Cambridge Wireless, to reflect the fact that it had broadened its remit from 3G to include other wireless technologies being developed in Cambridge, acknowledge the complex interfaces between different technologies – electronics, software, chip architecture – that are needed to create a wireless network, and recognize that wireless technology was no longer just about telecommunications, but was increasingly important in numerous vertical industry sectors.

CW is a not-for-profit organization that is owned by its members, with a governing board that is elected by the membership. Members are drawn from all parts of the wireless enabled world, from securely connected devices, networks, smart phones, software and applications, through to data analytics, content delivery, telecommunications and satellites.

www.cambridgewireless.co.uk

Acknowledging the explosion of wireless from not simply being a telecommunications niche, but growing rapidly in other markets, the first Special Interest Group meetings were held that year to bring together members from different areas. Soraya Jones, CEO from 2007 to 2015, grew corporate membership from 70 to 400 over seven years, and expanded activities to include 19 Special Interest Groups. Partnerships with CommNexus in San Diego and the development of an annual international conference increased the reach of members and opened up opportunities worldwide.

In 2013, rebranding the name of the company to CW acknowledged the fact that 60% of the group's 400-plus corporate members are based outside Cambridge, with 17 countries represented. In 2014, 39 meetings across 19 different Special Interest Groups were held, along with a European start-up competition and a major international conference, bringing together different industry sectors that have their own wireless technology requirements with small start-ups, global corporations, R&D organisations, regulatory bodies and operators.

"

Mutual collaboration between business leaders, entrepreneurs and academics to track emerging technologies and understand their commercial consequences lies at the heart of the Cambridge Phenomenon. But in the world of wireless technology, these principles and culture have carried far beyond Cambridge.

Robert Driver, CEO, CW

Time lapse photograph of communications satellites.

TECHNOLOGY CONSULTANCIES

A distinguishing feature of the Cambridge Phenomenon is the presence of a thriving mini-ecosystem of technology consultancies. Indeed, many claim that it was the founding of the first, Cambridge Consultants, in 1960 that sowed the seeds for the technology cluster of today, and there is certainly a rich legacy of growth, product successes, spin-outs and investments that can be traced all the way back to the founder of Cambridge Consultants, Tim Eiloart.

Cambridge technology consultancies work across many different sections, including electronics, telecommunications, drug discovery, and health care.

Today, Cambridge has its own 'Big Four' in the shape of the largest and oldest of the technology consultancies, Cambridge Consultants, PA Consulting, Sagentia (originally Scientific Generics) and TTP, in order of founding. The four are all 'related', with the late Gordon Edge leaving Cambridge Consultants to set up PA Technology for PA Consulting, and subsequently founding Scientific Generics, and the founders of TTP coming out of PA Technology.

Alongside the Big Four, there are a number of other, smaller consultancies, often set up by former employees of the bigger organizations who have decided to go it alone, and frequently specializing in a particular technology area. For instance, Team Consulting focuses on medical devices, Sentec (recently sold to a subsidiary of US company and long-term client Sensus) on smart metering, and Plextek on electronics. Cambridge Design Partnership recently spun out Gmax Technology, which applies GPS and sensing technology to the equine world, providing the system via which Coral Champions Club members track the fitness of racehorses in the UK, and the first handheld ECG for vets, which is in use at Dubai Equestrian Club's International Endurance City racing venue. Depending on exactly how they are defined, Cambridge is home to around 20 technology consultancies.

Peter Marsh of the *Financial Times* and long-time observer of the Cambridge Phenomenon estimated combined sales for the Big Four in 2008–09 at £140 million, with more than 70% of this amount being generated outside the UK. More recent estimates put the figure at over £250 million across the entire Cambridge technology consultancy sector.

As for the financial impact of the consultancies in the wider world, it has to be remembered that they develop products and technologies for their clients, and confidentiality means that, in most cases, it is hard to estimate the impact the consultancies have on the bottom line for their clients. However, it must be assumed to be substantial, given the calibre of clients that are named and the nature of the technologies the consultancies work on.

But the impact of the consultancies is not just about their attracting international companies to Cambridge to seek answers to complex technological problems, but also in the levels of employment they generate in the region, in themselves and in spin-outs, descendants and contractors. In 2008, the Centre for Business Research estimated that around 7,000 people were employed in technology consultancies and their spin-outs around Cambridge. Analysts SQW indicated the powerful attraction the consultancies have for recruits, finding that fewer than half (41%) of consultancy employees in 2000 lived within easy commuting distance when they took the job.

The consultancies also encourage or provide sources of investment and incubation. Over the years, all of the Big Four have had venturing arms, and all have nurtured teams and ideas that have gone on to form spin-outs or become key parts of other companies.

A business model worth hundreds of millions of pounds to the Cambridge economy, spin-outs whose combined capitalization exceeds $7 billion, technologies that have changed lives: the technology consultancies are a major driver in the success of the Cambridge Phenomenon.

Above: *Cambridge Consultants' rapid prototyping facilities help principal engineer Fred Hamlin turn ideas into commercial products.*

Far left: *Tim Eiloart, founder of Cambridge Consultants.*

CAMBRIDGE CONSULTANTS

Working with blue-chip clients, developing groundbreaking technologies, spinning out billion-dollar (and more) companies – Cambridge Consultants has spearheaded a technology consultancy model that has had, and continues to have, multiple impacts locally and internationally.

Founded in 1960, the original business model for Cambridge Consultants combined providing fee-for-service technology, the creation and exploitation of intellectual property through licensing and spin-offs, and product development, and would go on to be copied multiple times around Cambridge.

From its origins as a business founded to 'put the brains of Cambridge at the disposal of British industry', Cambridge Consultants has evolved into an asset-backed, full-service innovative product development company. It has more than 530 staff, who represent a wide range of disciplines and operate out of state-of-the-art facilities whatever sector they work in, from life sciences to optics, and from wireless processors to antenna development, with rapid prototyping capabilities alongside to demonstrate proof of concept and product viability.

Cambridge Consultants has a reach that extends to the US and Asia, which it uses not only to open up new markets, but also to gain insights into the latest technology developments and future needs around the world. The company enriches its services by developing its own intellectual property in a variety of fields.

Cambridge Consultants works across the consumer, defence and security, digital health, digital services, industrial and energy, medical technology, oil and gas, and wireless communication sectors, and supports these with core skills that range from mechanical engineering to software, and from physical sciences to human factors – using the understanding of how people interact with technologies and systems to guide better design.

Although much of the company's work for clients remains confidential, a few examples demonstrate the divergent areas in which Cambridge Consultants has created ripples around the world. Alongside client projects, the company also has space for its own blue-sky thinking in areas where it sees unmet or potential needs, or simply interesting technological challenges. The history of past projects of this nature demonstrates that such activity frequently leads to unexpected benefits down the line.

SATELLITE COMMUNICATIONS – A LONG-TERM COMMITMENT TO THE IRIDIUM NETWORK

Cambridge Consultants has a long-standing relationship with Iridium Communications and has been its virtual design team in more than 50 projects for its satellite communications network, including the latest generation handsets, ground station infrastructure, modems and systems, and the world's first configurable push-to-talk network.

Iridium is unique because it is the only commercial satellite operation that covers the entire world, including the oceans and the North and South Poles. Thus it extends vital radio coverage to the 90% of the world's surface that does not have good cellular coverage. This makes it a crucial service for many industries and sectors, including aviation, maritime, oil and exploration, and research bases such as the Amundsen–Scott South Pole Station. Iridium has 66 satellites in orbit in its network, plus a few extra in case one fails.

The variety of technical challenges is immense. The satellites travel at around five miles per second – faster than a bullet – so the technical specifications for handsets, for instance, have to be very much higher than those for

Right: *Cambridge Consultants works with Iridium Communications to develop its satellite communications network.*

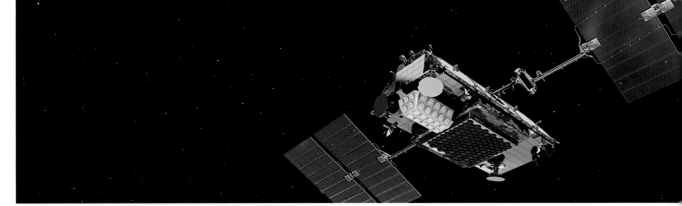

static networks. Handsets also have to be extremely rugged, adaptable for other possible uses, and suitable for volume manufacturing. They have to be extremely reliable, as they serve as a lifeline for users in remote and inhospitable locations. Cambridge Consultants has been involved in everything from software and technology design to choice of manufacturing partner, design of production and testing systems, and preparedness for high-volume manufacture.

Iridium systems were recently adapted to create a maritime product, OpenPort, which uses the network to provide a broadband satellite voice and data communications system for seagoing vessels.

XAP PROCESSORS LICENSED FROM CAMBRIDGE CONSULTANTS ARE FOUND IN AROUND 2 BILLION PRODUCTS

In the early 1990s, 20 years before the Internet of Things, Cambridge Consultants began designing mixed signal application-specific integrated circuits (ASICs), which had applications in sensors and wireless systems. One strand of this work was to enable products that needed a little intelligence and extremely long battery lives – ten years or more. Processors at the time were 32-bit and power hungry, but projects such as electronic energy meters (for instance British Gas' Quantum Smart Card-operated meters), pagers, and water meters needed a low-power alternative.

James Collier, who was later part of the team that spun CSR out of Cambridge Consultants, Steve Barlow (who subsequently founded Alphamosaic) and Alistair Morfey (now a Technology Director at Cambridge Consultants), came up with the architecture for a small and extremely power-efficient 16-bit microprocessor called XAP. The original XAP and later iterations up to the most recent, XAP6, have been licensed to many companies, including 3M, Cyan, Danfoss and Ericsson. XAP was also one of the two fundamental pieces of IP that Cambridge Consultants licensed to CSR when it spun out, and accelerated the development of CSR's products and its establishment as world leader in single-chip wireless technology.

CAMBRIDGE CONSULTANTS PLAYS A CRITICAL ROLE IN AIR TRAFFIC CONTROL WITH PARK AIR SYSTEMS

NATS Services, which provides air traffic control to 14 UK airports including Gatwick, Heathrow and Stansted and

handles over two million flights per year, uses radios from Park Air Systems, a subsidiary of Northrop Grumman and a long-term development partner of Cambridge Consultants. Available data suggests that around 70% of all traffic flying in the US and EU uses radios designed in Cambridge. The proportion in Asia is likely to be similar. The NATO Kandahar air base in Afghanistan was another Park Air customer.

The Park Air T6 is described by Bloomberg as 'the world's most widely deployed ATC radio'.

The 1990s saw a change in Air Traffic Control (ATC) radio standards, as airport communications were switched from analogue to digital. The biggest problem for achieving the switchover was the period of change, during which some aircraft to airport communications would still have to use the old analogue system until the planes were refitted with new radios. The new system, therefore, had to work with analogue

Above: Tim Fowler in the Satimo Stargate 64 anechoic radio test facility – one of only a handful in the UK – used to maximize the performance of wireless products.

"

I don't think many people thought we could actually do it.

Neil Upton, Technical Director, Northrop Grumman Park Air Systems

and digital signals at the same time, and, with the help of Cambridge Consultants, Park Air won the contract to provide radio coverage for the US and Europe.

More recently, the next-generation T6 has been co-developed by Cambridge Consultants, with a brief of not only improving the underlying technology, but also making it half the size and more efficient in power consumption.

HELPING ASTHMATICS TO TAKE THEIR MEDICINE

The inhaler for asthmatics seems ubiquitous, but a closer look reveals that there are many different types of inhaler, used for different formulations of medication and by different populations, with differing dosage and usability needs. Analysts Future Market Insights estimate that the combined global market for all three types of inhaler – dry powder inhalers, metered dose inhalers and nebulisers – will reach $43 billion by the end of 2025, driven largely by the increase in not only asthma, but other respiratory disorders such as chronic obstructive pulmonary disease (COPD) and fibrosis.

Cambridge Consultants developed a novel dry powder inhaler for emerging Italian company Chiesi Farmaceutici SpA. The NEXThaler delivers extra-fine particles of the active ingredients, which leads to better delivery and means the dosage can be reduced. It also tracks compliance by the patient, as the dose counter only counts correct doses delivered.

Launched in the EU in 2013, as the Foster NEXThaler it is now marketed in 47 countries and Chiesi reported an increase in sales for Foster, NEXThaler and related brands of 21% in 2014 over 2013. The NEXThaler was the first dry powder inhaler launched in the UK that delivered extra-fine drug particles, and it was indicated for regular treatment of adult asthma patients.

Chiesi is currently conducting further clinical trials intended to broaden its market by demonstrating that use of the NEXThaler can be extended to treating those with severe asthma and COPD.

GETTING TO THE BOTTOM OF THE LUNGS

The Starhaler, which Cambridge Consultants helped developed for India's largest pharmaceutical company, Sun Pharmaceuticals, was designed to overcome a number of problems associated with delivering drugs via inhalation for patients with COPD.

The drugs for COPD need to be delivered deep into the lungs to be effective, but normal inhalers tend to force the dose to the back of the throat, and the amount of active drug that reaches the lungs can be insufficient. Another issue is lactose: since the drug is made as an extremely fine powder, it is typically bound to lactose molecules to help delivery. A build up of lactose residues in the throat can lead to problems for patients with an intolerance.

The Starhaler was designed to be breath-activated, only releasing the dose when the patient breathes in and thus helping to deliver the drug into the lungs. It also used a novel de-agglomeration technology to separate the active drug from the lactose particles, helping to avoid problems for lactose-intolerant patients. Tests demonstrated that the Starhaler was so efficient that only half the usual amount of the drug was needed to achieve the correct therapeutic dose.

Having launched the Starhaler in India, Sun Pharmaceuticals has applied for approval to conduct clinical trials in Germany prior to launching in Europe, and has filed for Investigational New Drug (IND) status in the US with a view to launching there in the future.

Far right: The Starhaler, developed in partnership with Sun Pharma Advanced Research Company Ltd, delivers drugs via inhalation for patients with COPD.

119

CAMBRIDGE CONSULTANTS WORKS WITH START-UPS IN CANCER DIAGNOSIS

Cambridge Consultants has helped Clearbridge BioMedics, a spin-out from the National University of Singapore, to develop a novel diagnostic instrument for detecting the presence of cancer cells in the blood.

Circulating tumour cells indicate that a cancer is spreading, or metastasizing, and it is this that is often the eventual cause of death for a cancer patient. Launched commercially in 2014, the ClearCell FX system co-developed with Cambridge Consultants uses biomechanical properties rather than biochemical markers to isolate circulating tumour cells – and can detect them at concentrations as low as one in a billion. The device is already used by the Singapore General Hospital to monitor cancer patients, and has started to notch up sales worldwide.

Another start-up in Singapore with a cancer focus is Endofotonics, which has worked with Cambridge Consultants to develop a novel endoscopic device that is the world's first real-time, in vivo molecular diagnostic system. Based on Raman spectroscopy, a fibre optic probe linked to a customized software algorithm can 'fingerprint' tissues during an endoscopic examination and provide surgeons with instant feedback on the presence or absence of cancerous tissue. Initial trials with more than 800 patients have proved the laboratory prototype, and work now continues on commercialization and addressing the necessary regulatory requirements.

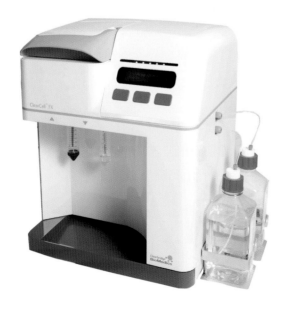

GETTING TO THE HEART OF THINGS WITH A NOVEL PACEMAKER

A collaboration between Cambridge Consultants and US company EBR Systems has developed the world's first wireless cardiac resynchronization therapy (CRT) system that is implanted in the left ventricle.

Implantable pacemakers have been around for several decades, but current models have a number of issues. They depend on electric leads to transmit pulses to the heart, but there is a real risk of the leads deteriorating in the body, leading to failure of the device. Practical considerations mean that pacemakers are implanted in the right ventricle, but studies have demonstrated that synchronizing the left and right ventricles can be more effective, particularly where heart failure is concerned. However, inserting conventional leads into the left ventricle is difficult and highly risky to the patient, and the only other wireless pacemakers on the market to date are implanted on the right ventricle.

Furthermore, conventional pacemakers provide no benefit for around 30% of patients, and fail in a further 5–10%, meaning, for instance, that more than $1 billion of the $3.5 billion spent annually on CRT devices in the US brings no benefits to patients. The American Heart Association estimates that there were 5.1 million people in the US suffering from heart failure in 2013.

The new system, named WiSE for 'wireless stimulation endocardially', consists of a tiny electrode implanted in the left ventricle. With every heartbeat, it receives a synchronized ultrasound signal from a small transmitter placed between two ribs. The sound waves are converted to electrical energy, which provides the cardiac pacing. The technology eliminates the need for a left ventricular lead and is designed to let the doctor place the simulation point at an optimal, patient-specific location inside the left ventricle – which could potentially be more effective.

WiSE has recently achieved European CE mark approval, meaning it complies with EU legislation and can now be

Above: *Endofotonics develops ground-breaking endoscopic instruments to improve pre-cancer diagnosis.*

Bottom left: *A cancer diagnostic device developed by Clearbridge BioMedics in partnership with Cambridge Consultants.*

Right: *Cambridge Consultants ensured that Acorn Computers got a bank loan it desperately needed by demonstrating that a technical problem with the new BBC Micro could be solved. The result was hundreds of thousands of happy customers – and a long legacy of companies founded by BBC Micro users.*

Far right, above: *Hoppier beer font. Blue-sky thinking has led Cambridge Consultants to design a way to customize the flavour of beer using the principles of the coffee machine – with a few technological tweaks.*

Far right, below: *Free app Instant Wild gives anyone with a smartphone anywhere in the world access to near real-time tracking of endangered species in a number of countries. In a project with the Zoological Society of London, Cambridge Consultants developed a motion-triggered camera system that can withstand extremes of temperature and upload images via Iridium satellite link.*

assessed and used in Europe. Easier to implant because of its small size and lack of electric leads, and powered by Cambridge Consultants' own XAP processor technology, the system has already been trialled in the US and, of those patients who are six months or more past the implantation date, 81% have improved symptoms.

SPIN-OUTS MAGNIFY IMPACT

Spin-outs have been a way for Cambridge Consultants to maximize the impact of some of its own innovative teams when a market opportunity has been identified and a professional services approach is not the most interesting commercial solution. For instance, James Collier's team had become the repository of the most advanced capability for implementing single-chip wireless solutions on CMOS when the Bluetooth standard was announced. Their initial differentiation came from implementing a single-chip CMOS solution (hence lower power, lower cost) when the rest of the world was doing two-chip solutions. The company they launched, CSR, is discussed in more depth in the Telecommunications section (see pages106–107).

Six of the seven companies that were spun out of Cambridge Consultants between 1996 and 2002 have gone on to be highly successful. Four Cambridge Consultants spin-out companies – CSR, Domino, Vectura and Xaar – have achieved market capitalizations of more than $1 billion. Domino, spun out in 1978, kick-started the inkjet printing sector (see pages 142–144), and was later followed by Elmjet, Xaar and Inca Digital in the same sector (with Domino itself spinning out Xennia in 1996). Alphamosaic and Cyan were also Cambridge Consultants spin-outs.

Other spin-out-like events have occurred when teams from Cambridge Consultants have been 'acquired' out of the parent company: for instance the Vivid drug delivery group and technology became part of the pharmaceutical start-up Vectura.

HCO UOVISION-LolCam2   10.23.2014 15:20:21   ●30 024°C 075°F ▢

This was to enhance value through combining formulation and device technology to optimize therapy, and Vectura has now grown into a full FTSE-listed company. Similarly, the ZigBee development team and IP became part of the US start-up Ember, which was later acquired by Silicon Labs.

Adding up the various acquisitions, flotations and revenues of the Cambridge Consultants spin-outs reaches into the billions of dollars, and the technologies they have launched (Bluetooth, inkjet printing, VideoCore multimedia processors and more) are found in billions of devices and applications around the world.

PA CONSULTING GROUP

PA Consulting Group (PA) traces its origins back to World War II and efforts to improve productivity in munitions factories, and kept a firm basis of manufacturing and technology expertise whilst growing to become a significant management consultancy by the early 1970s. At around this time, Gordon Edge and Roy Hawkins, who were both working at Cambridge Consultants, started looking for new opportunities and ways to improve the technology consultancy model.

Negotiations with PA led to the establishment of the PA Technology Centre, or PAT Centre as it came to be known locally, in 1970. PAT Centre was to be the technology 'arm' of PA Consulting, and created multiple opportunities for synergies between the disciplines of hard-core technology development and management consulting.

PAT Centre started to rack up 'firsts' for the group. The coin-operated, vandal-resistant payphone that the company designed for Plessey in the 1970s helped Plessey win a large British Telecom contract (beating the much larger GEC). The PA-designed payphone went on to be the most successful product in Plessey's history, and is still in use around the world.

PA was the first of the Cambridge technology consultancies to win a Queen's Award for Technological Innovation. The award was given for the development of an electronic digital micrometer for Moore & Wright in 1978, which went on to sell around the world in the hundreds of thousands.

Now known as PA's Cambridge Technology Centre, the company employs around 500 people in Cambridge, the majority being scientists, engineers and technologists working in state-of-the-art laboratories and workshops. *The Independent* newspaper reported revenues for the technology group of around £40 million in 2010, and, like the other consultancies, the majority of revenues come from overseas customers. PA Consulting Group as a whole employs some 2,500 people worldwide. Over the years, PA has supported and backed a number of its employees in creating new spin-out businesses, generating approximately £300 million for the firm in total. New in 2016, and very positive for PA's continued global impact, is a partnership with, and significant investment from, the global alternative asset management firm Carlyle, which has taken a 51% share in the company that the *Financial Times* reports values PA at $1 billion. The partnership extends PA's global client network and ability to acquire, grow and build out around the world.

THE WORLD'S FIRST FULLY AUTOMATED INJECTION CYCLE IN A SINGLE-USE, DISPOSABLE SYRINGE

Many people have to inject themselves with medication, sometimes on a daily basis, but this can be difficult for those who have a fear of needles or who worry about getting their injection wrong. The problem of compliance with medication is well known, and fear of needles makes this an even more challenging problem.

Working with Janssen Research & Development, part of Johnson & Johnson, PA was tasked with coming up with a method of injecting medication that was reliable and also worked without the patient having to see or touch a needle.

The answer was the SmartJect autoinjector, which was the world's first pre-filled, single-use, disposable autoinjector with a fully automated injection cycle. The patient, or carer, simply removes the cap, presses the SmartJect against the skin where the injection is to be administered, presses a button and the SmartJect does the rest – it even retracts the needle so the patient doesn't have to withdraw it after the dose has been administered.

The prototypes for the SmartJect were created with a 3D CAD-enabled printer – PA had the first US Viper 3D printer

Far left: *Gordon Edge, who set up PA Technology for PA Consulting.*

Above: *The CleanSpace Tag is a portable air quality monitor.*

Far right: *PA Consulting worked with Oday Abbosh, inventor of Ora kitchen towels, from the design idea to prototype.*

Each 'clean' journey earns CleanMiles, which can be exchanged for rewards. Community members are also provided with information about the air they are breathing that can inform their travel plans and also show the effect the community as a whole is having on air quality.

PA assembled a multidisciplinary team with the commercial understanding and range of technology expertise needed to develop CleanSpace with Drayson in under nine months. The PA team used a flexible business model to work with Drayson as the project progressed, gradually handing over areas of development as Drayson recruited more skills and expertise of its own. PA supported Drayson by co-developing the portable air quality sensor, the smartphone application and the cloud-based internet services to support the user community. The solution has now been launched in London and will be introduced to other cities worldwide.

PA HELPS AN INVENTOR, A RETAILER AND THE ENVIRONMENT – BY REINVENTING THE KITCHEN TOWEL

It might not seem like the loftiest of technology, but Euromonitor International reported that the global retail value of kitchen towels sold in 2015 was over $11 billion – and yet the sector has seen very little innovation in years. So to get a completely new and extremely innovative product from idea to supermarket shelf in this sector in less than 12 months, as PA did with the Ora kitchen towel, is remarkable on many levels.

The distinctive feature of the Ora kitchen towel is that it is round rather than square. Clever folding means that the round towels are stackable in cones and can be used with one hand. One roll of Ora is equivalent to two rolls of normal kitchen towels, and requires 20% less packaging – which has knock-on savings for transportation and the environment. More towels

in Britain in its Cambridge Technology Centre. This speeded up the process, reducing the time to build prototypes down from weeks and months to days. PA's design and development process took into account the needs of commercial production, and contributed to the development of automated manufacturing equipment.

Pre-filled syringes are one of the fastest growing markets in healthcare, with the BCM Group estimating that 3.59 billion units were sold in 2015, up from 2.45 billion units in 2011, and the SmartJect can be used for a number of conditions where drugs cannot be taken as tablets.

CLEANSPACE™ AIR QUALITY NETWORK – FROM CONCEPT TO REALITY IN UNDER NINE MONTHS

The World Health Organization estimates that seven million deaths worldwide each year are attributed to air pollution, with nearly 30,000 deaths in Britain alone. Drayson Technologies conceived the idea of CleanSpace, technology that would connect and empower people to take action against air pollution. CleanSpace is a combination of smart phone application, portable air pollution sensor and cloud-based software services, and supports a community of like-minded individuals who want to improve air quality in urban environments by choosing non-polluting modes of transport.

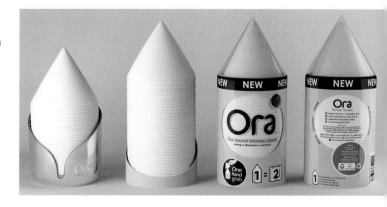

per roll also take up less shelf space in the supermarket, a key factor in efforts by supermarkets to maximize revenues per unit area of shelf.

PA was approached by the inventor of Ora, Oday Abbosh, and worked with him from the design idea through to prototype, initial production and then mass production. Finding a way to take the delicate paper towel discs and fold and process them into stacks required a completely new manufacturing process as there was no pre-existing way to do it, and no machines that could be adapted or built on. The PA team worked hard together with Abbosh's founding design partner, Acumen, to find a series of creative solutions to bring Ora to life.

Even when the principles of the process were understood, it wasn't obvious that it could be scaled up to mass production. PA first built a single pilot machine to demonstrate the concept, and then translated that into a manufacturing operation. This was all the more challenging given the tight deadline to produce sufficiently large quantities of Ora to keep up with an increasing store ramp-up schedule that had been agreed with Tesco, and the manufacturing processes had to be developed almost in parallel with the pilot machine build.

In October 2014 Ora was Winner of the prestigious Grocer New Product Awards (Household Category), and was recognised by City A.M. and Mishcon De Reya in January 2015 as a 'Leap 100 company', one of the UK's 100 most exciting fast-growing firms. Ora is currently shortlisted for a DBA Design Effectiveness Award.

HELPING TO REDUCE ENERGY USE IN 10 MILLION HOMES

Landis+Gyr, an international manufacturer of gas and electricity meters, needed a new ecometer. Studies have shown that ecometers and smart meters lead to a reduction in household energy use and can help towards reaching targets for reductions in emissions. The UK Government mandated that all homes in the UK should have smart meters by 2020 and Landis+Gyr's customer was the UK's biggest energy supplier, Centrica.

PA developed the product – widely seen on TV – to be as attractive to use as a mini iPad but at a fraction of the cost, so it could be given away free of charge. The device shows the homeowner how much energy they are using, what the bill will be, and enthusiasts (usually the teenagers) can set targets for reduced consumption. Developing this meant PA pulling together skills in behavioural science, electronics, radio, mechanics, and industrial, user-interface and software design. To save development time and coordinate across sites and with manufacturing contractors, the project used sophisticated computer-aided design, with rapid prototyping (above and beyond 3D printing) to illustrate key decisions.

Above: *PA Consulting worked with Land Rover BAR to identify technologies that would give Ben Ainslie's boat an edge over the competition.*

Below left: *For philanthropic eyewear company Adlens®, PA Consulting combined mechanical engineering skills with product design and commercial manufacturing expertise to help create AdlensFocuss™, a variable power optics range of glasses, launched in the US consumer market in 2015.*

SETTING SAIL FOR THE AMERICA'S CUP WITH LAND ROVER BAR

Ben Ainslie, who has won more Olympic medals than any other competitive sailor, has taken on the challenge of winning the America's Cup, sailing's most coveted trophy, for the UK, and in January 2014 launched Land Rover BAR (Ben Ainslie Racing).

Today's America's Cup boats are high-spec catamarans that travel at upwards of 50mph, and the old days of being able to study the boat's performance by following in a chase boat are long gone. As PA telecoms specialist Phil White told *The Times*, 'It's really difficult to do anything out [on a chase boat]. It's cold, wet, bouncing around — it's hard enough to stand up, let alone calculate anything.'

But studying every aspect of the boat in action is what is needed in the long development and training process leading up to the races that decide the Cup. It is the Formula 1 of sailing: small tweaks can mean the difference between winning and losing at this level.

Enter the virtual chase boat. And enter PA Consulting, who chair the Technical Innovation Group (TIG) for Land Rover BAR. Although Land Rover BAR have much of the design and

engineering expertise for the project, bringing in PA Consulting was seen as a way to add expertise, skills and technologies from other areas outside the marine industry. PA's job was to work with Land Rover BAR to identify technologies in other sectors that could give the team the edge; a cross-disciplinary, horizon-scanning role to make sure nothing was missed in the development of a winning boat.

To get the virtual chase boat from the drawing board and onto the desks of the sailing technologists, a number of elements that were well within PA's skill set were needed, including setting up the boat itself with multiple sensors to collect information, including video, on how the boat is performing, and data links sufficiently robust to survive conditions on the boat and relay information back to shore via a suitable radio frequency and antennas that could find line-of-sight from boat to shore, whatever the sea conditions.

PA's first system was installed on the team's first trial boat, Testing Boat 1 or T1, launched in October 2014. Successful trials with T1 have led to the system being installed on T2, launched in autumn 2015. All we can know is that it transmits all the data collected from the sensors and cameras on the boat and transmits it to the team's 'Mission Control' at the teams base at Camber Quay in Portsmouth. There, analysts and engineers are able to study the data in real-time and at length to identify opportunities to enhance the performance of the boat.

SAGENTIA

Sagentia is another of the Cambridge technology consultancies with a distinguished pedigree and a long line of innovations and inventions that are in use around the world.

Founded in 1986 as Scientific Generics by Gordon Edge and a group of colleagues who came out of PA Consulting, the original business model was to provide technology consultancy but also to actively incubate technologies and form spin-out companies when the technology was mature. The first spin-out, Diomed, emerged before the end of the 1980s. Several more followed, including Absolute Sensors, TurfTrax, Sphere Medical, CMR Fuel Cells, and Atraverda in the early 2000s.

The company rebranded as Sagentia to mark its 20th anniversary in 2006 and move away from the growing association of the word 'generics' with generic drugs. Sagentia also took the strategic decision to redirect resources to the consultancy side of the business and make that the primary focus. As a consequence, the venturing arm, Generics Asset Management, was spun out as Chord Capital the same year to separate it from the parent company.

Martyn Ratcliffe acquired a majority shareholding in 2010 and became chairman of the company. Sagentia's consulting fees in 2011 were reported up 22% on the preceding year, with around 77% representing overseas customers and 72% of this being from the medical sector, the company's greatest strength at the time.

The medical sector, particularly medical devices and the new area of mobile health applications, continues to be a strength, with recent projects including Cevira, a non-surgical treatment for precancerous lesions of the cervix developed with Photocure and currently in Phase III trials, and VeriHaler, a connected health system that uses sensors in inhalers which connect to an iPhone app via Bluetooth to help patients and healthcare providers

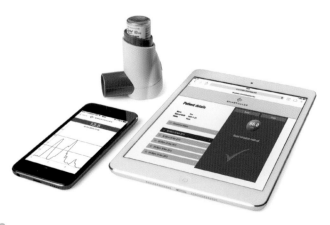

monitor compliance and effectiveness of treatments for chronic obstructive pulmonary disease (COPD) and asthma.

Strategic acquisitions have started to balance out the offerings from Sagentia. The first was OTM, an oil and gas consultancy, which was acquired in 2013. 2015 saw two more acquisitions, Oakland Innovation (consumer and healthcare) and Leatherhead Food Research (food and drinks sector). With these acquisitions, the company now has core offerings across the medical devices, consumer, industrial, and oil and gas markets.

The newly christened parent company, Science Group, has more than 350 employees and facilities in the US, UK and Dubai. The Cambridge operation serves as Science Group headquarters and its research and development centre. Revenues in 2014 were just shy of £30 million, with the company's market capitalization around £56 million.

AUTHENTICATING AND DISPENSING THE RIGHT DRUG FOR ASTRAZENECA

AstraZeneca's Diprifusor is a target-controlled infusion system used around the world to deliver precise dosages of the anaesthetic Diprivan (propofol). It was the first such system to gain regulatory approval, and won AstraZeneca a Queen's Award for Technological Innovation. In 2004, it was reported that more than 13 million doses of anaesthetic had been delivered using the Diprifusor.

The original IP came out of the University of Glasgow, but AstraZeneca came to Sagentia for help with developing an automated system that verified the authenticity of the Diprivan being used and delivered the correct concentration of the anaesthetic to the patient.

Sagentia's own, patented programmable magnetic resonance (PMR) technology was adapted for the Diprifusor. A

Above: *Using technology adapted for the Diprifusor by Sagentia, a PMR label is encoded with information and attached to a pre-filled syringe.*

Far left, below: *The VeriHaler, a connected health system that uses sensors in inhalers that connect to apps.*

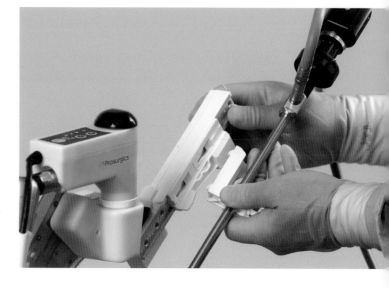

small, acousto-magnetic PMR label is encoded with identifying information and attached to a pre-filled syringe. When the syringe is inserted into the Diprifusor's infusion pump, the label is read automatically to ensure that it contains genuine Diprivan, and operating software only allows the drug to be administered if this information is correct. The syringe cannot be reused with unvalidated medication because the label is wiped once the dose has been delivered.

The project for Sagentia went all the way from adapting their own IP to high-volume manufacturing, and resulted in a licensing arrangement with AstraZeneca for the PMR technology.

GIVING SURGEONS A FREEHAND

Laparoscopy, or keyhole surgery, has many benefits for patients, but brings difficulties of its own to those carrying out the procedure. One of these has been holding the camera telescope steady during potentially long operations, normally the job of a surgical assistant who has to be instructed where to move the telescope. Alternative robotic systems are bulky and expensive, but steady camera work can lead to faster procedures and better outcomes. One study demonstrated that up to 7% of keyhole operating time can be taken up with removing the telescope to clean it, a problem typically caused by unnecessary movement.

Prosurgics, now OR Productivity, a healthcare robotics company, had a first-generation product, the EndoAssist, already on the market, but recognized the need for a second-generation product that was smaller, easier to use and more affordable. They developed a first prototype for this new product, but came to Sagentia for subsequent iterations to better meet the complex specifications they required.

The result was the FreeHand, a unit that fixes to the operating table and is controlled by the surgeon's head movements: the surgeon wears a wireless controller either fixed to their surgical cap or on a headband that sets the direction of movement of the telescope, and the surgeon uses a foot pedal to activate the movement.

The US Society of Laparoendoscopic Surgeons named FreeHand its 2008 Innovation of the Year.

Far right: Sagentia worked with Prosurgics (now OR Productivity) to develop instruments to improve stability for laparoscopy.

Below: *FreeHand is controlled by a surgeon's head movements.*

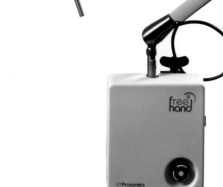

Approved for a range of minimally invasive surgical procedures, the FreeHand was the first affordable robotic assistance product on the market. It is so compact that it is portable – one consultant laparoscopic surgeon told the ITN Healthcare News Channel that he took it with him when he travelled to mentor and train other surgeons.

M-PESA FROM SAGENTIA MAKES PAYMENTS SAFE AND EASY

Within three years of launching in Kenya in 2007, payments sent via Sagentia's M-Pesa mobile phone system amounted to more than 12% of Kenyan GDP. The impact on rural households in Kenya has been life-changing, increasing incomes by up to 30% because transferring money has become safe, easy and cheap.

With many Kenyans travelling from rural areas to work in the cities, sending money home to their families had long been a difficult and even dangerous business. With no cheap means of transferring money, workers often had to resort to trusting their cash to someone who would take it personally to their home village. Risks of theft and the commission paid to the messenger were just two of the problems this method entailed.

Originally a UK Government Department for International Development (DFID) project to help make micro-finance loan payments easier, and funded with £1 million from DfID and similar from Vodafone, the objective was to find a way to help people in developing countries, particularly Africa, get better access to loans and become less dependent on cash transactions. Testing and pilots quickly demonstrated that users wanted to do more than simply take out loans with the

127

new technology, and the project evolved into how best to transfer money, whatever its purpose.

Within a year of launch in Kenya, 20% of Vodafone's Safaricom subscribers had registered. By year three, half of all adults in Kenya, some 10 million people, were registered, and there were more than 5 million transactions per day. By the end of 2011, there were 17 million registered subscribers in Kenya, more than two-thirds of the adult population, and 25% of GDP was being moved using M-Pesa.

The product was subsequently launched in Tanzania and South Africa, and gained five million subscribers in Tanzania by May 2013. M-Pesa has been slower to take off in South Africa and elsewhere, a situation ascribed to different and more complex regulatory regimes around money transfer.

One unintended consequence of the launch of M-Pesa in Afghanistan in 2008 was the discovery of large numbers of non-existent policemen. The system was initially used to pay the salaries of the Afghanistan police force, and revealed not only that around 10% of the workforce did not exist, they were 'ghost' officers, but also that very few policemen actually knew what their salary was. Many thought they'd been given a pay rise, because they hadn't been aware of how much of their salary was siphoned off before they received it.

M-Pesa continues to be rolled out in other countries, launching in India in 2011, Mozambique, Lesotho and Egypt in 2013, Romania (2014), and Albania (2015).

AWARD-WINNING REVAMP OF A 50-YEAR-OLD TOY

Scalextric racing cars were first launched at the Harrogate Toy Fair in 1957. Model cars with electric motors that picked up current from a groove in a specially configured track, they were a huge success, but as the 21st century approached, the toy started to look dated and racing two cars in parallel around a track had lost its appeal.

Sagentia helped the owners, Hornby Hobbies, to develop Scalextric Sport Digital and Scalextric Sport World systems, which introduced far more complex technology into the toys – using digital technology and internet connectivity – and allowed racers to change lanes and race four or even six cars against each other at the same time. There was even a mode that allowed players to race against the system itself, with a 'ghost' car programmed and run automatically. Importantly, older models of Scalextric cars can be modified to run on the Digital system.

Scalextric Sport Digital was the unanimous winner of the 'Best New Toy Design' at MAX-IT, the Marketing Awards for Excellence in Toys, in 2005, and Hornby's market capitalization improved by £2 million following the product's launch.

Above: Sagentia helped develop Scalextric Sport Digital, which introduced 21st-century technology into a 20th-century toy.

ADDING THE FROTH FOR THE MARS DRINKS FLAVIA

Getting the froth on coffee just so is important, but technologically tricky when the coffee comes from a drinks dispensing machine. Mars Drinks had launched the FLAVIA vending machine but wanted to improve the milk froth it produced, to make the cappuccino the machines dispensed more like the 'real thing' that the customer would receive in a coffee shop. In order to do this, the machine needed to be capable of generating a 'dry' head of foam on top of the coffee.

The 'traditional' method, as used by baristas, is to run steam through liquid milk to heat and froth it up, but the end result from a vending machine is a wet foam that doesn't hold its shape and soon merges with the coffee, rather than sitting on top. Sagentia developed an entirely new milk system for the FLAVIA machines which produced the right type of foam using powdered milk and, importantly, no additives to make it froth or hold its shape. The system was incorporated into the machine, which has been selling successfully around the world ever since.

Right: *Sagentia worked with Mars Drinks to improve the froth in their cappuccinos.*

Far right, below: *Aqualisa is the UK's leading brand of shower, and in 2001 launched the first digital shower, which remains a bestseller today. Sagentia developed a new valve for the shower, designed innovative control electronics, and supported the subsequent transition to manufacturing and compliance with electrical and mechanical product safety requirements. The Aqualisa digital shower won 'Best Consumer Product' at the 2004 UK Design Business Association's Design Effectiveness Awards.*

GETTING CLOSER TO NON-INVASIVE PRENATAL DIAGNOSIS OF DOWN'S SYNDROME

A recent development is one that has the potential to revolutionize prenatal screening for the genetic conditions Down's syndrome, Edwards' syndrome and Patau syndrome, chromosomal abnormalities that can cause devastating disabilities from birth.

Sagentia helped Premaitha Health, a Manchester Science Park-based molecular diagnostics company, to develop the IONA test. IONA is the world's first non-invasive prenatal test (NIPT) to match the stringent requirements for the European CE mark and was launched commercially in February 2015.

Although the chromosomal abnormalities behind the three syndromes are well known, current testing for pregnant women involves a combined test which signals those at risk, who then undergo invasive prenatal tests such as amniocentesis and chorionic villus sampling (removing cells from the placenta). But the combined test produces a large number of false positives, leading to a large number of unnecessary amniocentesis procedures, which in themselves carry the risk of inducing a miscarriage or causing infection.

From a maternal blood sample it is now possible to isolate and sequence fetal DNA and identify whether there are any abnormalities with the chromosomes known to be important, for instance chromosome 21 for Down's syndrome.

In November 2015, an independent multi-site, blinded study of the IONA test in the UK reported 100% accuracy in identifying the three syndromes, and 0% false positives. Since launch, a number of partnerships and arrangements have already been put in place in Europe and further afield.

With over three million such tests carried out in Europe every year by around 600 laboratories, and the worry, time and expense of the large number of unnecessary invasive procedures, the IONA test has the potential to make a step change in prenatal screening for genetic abnormalities. More than 200 of the laboratories that specialize in such screening have already expressed an interest in IONA.

The technology is already available in the US and China, and laboratories in Europe have until now had to send samples to these countries for analysis.

Accuracy is critical, and Sagentia helped to develop a custom clinical bioinformatics analysis application that performs the test analysis, computes the test results and generates reports. The software had to be developed to meet all regulatory requirements, including the standards required for CE validation and FDA submission, among others.

In July 2015, Premaitha started offering its IONA diagnostics as a service to deal with the demand for its tests, and has since opened a Care Quality Commission-approved clinical laboratory on the Manchester Science Park to increase capacity.

TTP GROUP

Originally founded as The Technology Partnership, which is still the largest subsidiary, TTP now operates as a group of companies, including TTP Labtech, Tonejet, TTP Meteor and Melbourn Science Park. The youngest of the Big Four at a mere 28 years old, over the course of its existence TTP has had a profound impact in a number of areas. It has also spun out companies which have created their own impacts, and incubated and retained other technologies as platform technologies and subsidiary companies within the group.

With an international reach, and roughly 70% of its business from overseas, TTP has been particularly strong in Japan since the early days. The pioneering members of the new company chose to go and investigate the Japanese market because they thought it would be a good fit for their digital printing and communication technology skills. The approach was to ask, 'What can we do that is of value? Who is going to use it? Where are they?' — and then get on a plane to go and find them. Early projects in Japan for the copier businesses of Fuji and Ricoh were just the start, and since then TTP has delivered projects in telecommunications and drug delivery, among others, for Japanese companies.

The latest arrival in the TTP Group is TTPMeteor. Set up in 2015, the new company encompasses TTP's inkjet team, and thus is built on more than two decades of experience in the

sector. TTPMeteor offers off-the-shelf printheads and drivers, and also bespoke systems. Customers already include some of the world's biggest names in inkjet printing, including Ricoh, Toshiba and Xaar.

TTP LABTECH PLAYS AN IMPORTANT SUPPORTING ROLE IN DRUG DISCOVERY

TTP Labtech invents and develops the instruments and equipment that make step changes in some of the underlying processes behind identifying drug targets and new ways to tackle them.

With turnover at around £20 million, TTP Labtech customers include pharmaceutical companies and academic research institutes in over 20 countries. The company also has a joint venture in Shanghai, and most of TTP business in China comes through Labtech operations.

TTP Labtech launched comPOUND, the world's first modular storage system for biological samples in 2001. Holding 100,000 samples and designed to build with additional modules up to capacity for one million samples, comPOUND also features an automated 'cherry-picking' system that enables required samples to be withdrawn without disturbing conditions for the rest of the samples.

World-leading protein research tools company Abcam uses comPOUND to store its antibody and protein reagents, with installations in both the UK and the US. Danielle Miller, Head of Operations at Abcam, points out that comPOUND not only reduces picking time for each vial from around 30 seconds to 5 seconds, allowing the company to maintain its fast delivery

Above: *TTP's skill base and experience covers innovation in lens design and wavefront optics through to addressable laser arrays and manufacturing innovation.*

Far left: *Peter Taylor, Managing Director, TTP Group.*

Left: *TTP has been involved in the development of over 25 inhalation devices, including the K-Haler®, the first ever inhalation device to offer breath actuation.*

promise to customers, but also enables Abcam to store the samples at −20 instead of −80 degrees Celsius, since the inert environment inside the comPOUND storage chamber removes the need for lower temperatures but still ensures sample integrity. With each vial of product selling for around $350 and Abcam delivering around 6,000 vials each week worldwide, proper storage and efficient picking are essential to the products' reliability and Abcam's reputation.

TTP Labtech's lab2lab helps companies like Novartis speed up drug discovery. Novartis uses the pneumatic lab2lab system to link several laboratories at its Horsham Global Discovery Chemistry site to a central analytical laboratory. The company reports that the system increases the productivity of its staff of around 100 chemists, because it enables them to carry out more procedures per day, and also improves the efficiency of machine usage in the analytical centre.

Protein crystallography screening is another important area that TTP Labtech serves. The company's mosquito LCP liquid handling technology was used to help obtain the first high-resolution X-ray crystal structure of one of the most important types of protein receptors in drug development and discovery. The first identified structure of a class B G-protein-coupled receptor (GCPR) was announced by drug discovery company Heptares and published in *Nature* in 2014. GCPRs are linked to a great number of diseases, and six of the ten bestselling drugs in the US in 2010 were developed to target GCPRs. But the proteins are very hard to develop drugs against, as they lose their shape once outside the cell

and their activity is lost. Identifying the structure opens up opportunities for applying different, structure-based drug discovery techniques and should increase the possibilities for novel drugs targeting these proteins.

THE WORLD'S BESTSELLING DISPOSABLE INHALER

The Hovione TwinCaps inhaler was developed by The Technology Partnership initially for the Japanese market in response to the global threat of a flu pandemic in 2006.

Warnings of the potential for a major pandemic prompted governments to respond by ordering stockpiles of treatments, and one of these was Inavir, developed by Daiichi Sankyo, the second largest pharmaceutical company in Japan. It had to be delivered as a dry powder using a pre-filled, single-dose disposable inhaler, which in turn had to be easy to manufacture and easy to use. Hovione, tasked with developing the delivery system, came to TTP.

An elegantly simple solution was found. The inhaler contains two doses in two separate compartments, one for each nostril. The patient pushes one side of the inhaler in to release the dose. This action simultaneously creates a highly turbulent environment in the compartment, ensuring that the drug is dispersed as very fine particles. Once the first dose is administered, the drug compartment is pushed from the other side, and the process repeats.

The TwinCaps subsequently became the world's bestselling disposable inhaler. Also launched in the US and Europe, sales of Inavir reached over $130 million in 2013.

TTPCOM DISRUPTED THE MOBILE PHONE MARKET AND OPENED THE DOOR FOR BLACKBERRY, SAMSUNG AND OTHERS

In 2004, mobile technology from TTP spin-out TTPCom was found in around 40 million devices around the world.

The company had been demerged from TTP and listed on the London Stock Exchange in 2000 in the heady days of the internet stock bubble, with a valuation of over £540 million. In 2001, RIM, the makers of the BlackBerry smartphone, announced that they would be incorporating TTPCom's GPRS and wireless email technology into their devices. The BlackBerry became so ubiquitous among business users keen to access their email at all times that it was nicknamed the 'CrackBerry'.

Other companies, including Samsung and Sharp, followed RIM and used TTPCom's technology to join the big players in the smartphone market. In the mid-2000s, TTPCom's revenues came almost entirely from exports.

One of the reasons for TTPCom's success was that the company had targeted the new GSM standard, and developed chip technology and software development tools that meant the standard wasn't only accessible to the top-tier mobile phone companies with large R&D budgets. This enabled second-tier companies to participate and the opportunity to seize the initiative proved decisive for several of them.

TTPCom had grown to 600 employees by the time it was acquired by Motorola for over £100 million in 2006, but the new owners made the decision to wind operations down a couple of years later.

In its heyday, TTPCom was the leading independent supplier of mobile phone technology and a key player in expanding the mobile telecoms market. Its eventual closure was not necessarily a bad thing for Cambridge. Following the closure, the founder of TTPCom, Tony Milbourn, told *Electronics Weekly*, 'it's good for Cambridge, there'll be ten start-ups as a result of TTPCom closing.' Milbourn himself was behind two of the companies that emerged after TTPCom, Camitri Technologies and Cognovo, which he co-founded with Gordon Aspin, Richard Fry, Mark Collins and Pascal Herczog, all former colleagues from TTPCom. Cognovo was acquired by Swiss company u-blox in 2012 and continues its development operations at Melbourn.

IP.ACCESS BRINGS THE MOBILE PHONE SIGNAL IN FROM THE COLD

If you remember the days of having to go outside to get a signal on your mobile phone, you'll probably be grateful to ip.access, another part of the TTP–TTPCom jigsaw which launched one of the first small cell systems to extend networks inside buildings in 2007. ip.access had been part of TTPCom when it spun out of TTP, but was not included in the Motorola acquisition of TTPCom and struck out on its own.

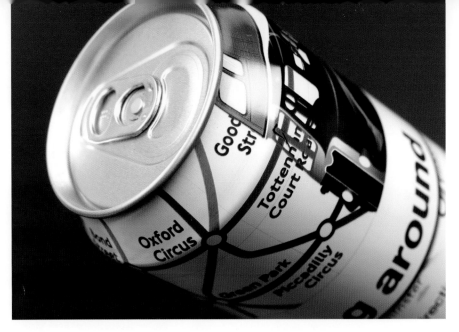

Above: *A beverage can printed using Tonejet technology.*

Today, when you visit a shopping centre and find that you are being sent vouchers and offers to your mobile phone from nearby shops, that may well be because your location is being tracked over one of ip.access' indoor small cell networks. Combined with data about your age, gender and shopping habits, the information enables retailers to tailor offers they think you'll like. Not all of us think this is a good thing, but it makes commercial sense to retailers and network providers.

The Oyster 3G small cell system from ip.access was one of the first commercially available when it was launched in 2007. By 2011, ip.access was the market leader with the most femtocells deployed worldwide, not least because it was used by Cisco for AT&T systems, and popular with global network providers such as Vodafone.

The many other customers for the company's 2G and 3G picocells and femtocells include over 50 mobile network operators from around the world, such as Batelco in Bahrain, T-Mobile in numerous locations and French company Bouygues.

In 2013, ip.access became the first 3G small cell provider to ship one million units.

Investment from Cisco and technology development agreements with Qualcomm once again demonstrated how small companies from Cambridge have the technological know-how to attract the largest global players. In August 2015, ip.access won a major investment from Zouk Capital and entered into a partnership with global organization Amdocs.

ip.access is part of the European Commission-funded Horizon 2020 consortium seeking to develop the infrastructure for 5G in an €8 million pilot project.

TONEJET ON THE CUSP OF THE NEXT PRINTING REVOLUTION

Using electrostatic rather than hydrostatic forces to print on difficult materials may well open new markets for printing of packaging as Tonejet begins to commercialize the world's first industrial digital printing system for beverage cans.

The arrival of inkjet printing signalled a step change in a process that had been used for hundreds of years, but the model of applying ink to a surface continues to present challenges. Laser printing involves contact between the printer and the surface to be printed, which puts constraints on the range of applications, whereas inkjet printing does not involve contact – but again, there are constraints, such as the fact that the surface to be printed on has to be able to absorb the ink.

A major driver of printing innovation is marketing – being able to generate fast and responsive printing on packaging helps to move consumer goods by making them topical and attractive. But while this represents a huge potential market, doing short print runs and changing designs and promotions quickly is not possible with conventional printing methods, partly because short print runs are not economical for packaging print companies, but also because not all types of packaging can be printed successfully. Inkjet printing on metal beverage cans, for instance, is not feasible because the metal cannot absorb the types of ink that are suitable for the process.

With a long interest in printing technologies of various kinds, TTP recognized a novel opportunity with an 'electrostatic spraying' system that was being developed for improving the performance of liquid ink laser printers.

This led to the idea for a system that was very different from other inkjet systems, using electrostatic rather than hydrostatic forces to generate and deliver droplets of ink on demand. Being contactless, the system can print with very thin, but dense, layers of ink, and also cope with difficult materials, such as printing heat resistant inks onto glass and ceramics. The project was incubated within TTP as a joint venture for some years before becoming demerged as a subsidiary, Tonejet, in 2004.

While the new method has a range of potential applications, the initial focus is on packaging, and Tonejet has had a development relationship with Europe's largest beverage can manufacturer, Ball Packaging Europe, since 2008. Around 370 billion cans are used each year worldwide just for beer and beverages. In the UK alone, Coca-Cola produces 2.6 billion cans each year across all its brands. But the technology will also help smaller beverage producers, such as the 'craft' drink makers, where the move to selling their drinks in cans will be helped by shorter production runs that are still economically viable.

133

42 TECHNOLOGY

From malaria testing to payload mechanisms for a reusable satellite launcher, 42 Technology tackles a wide range of industrial and technological challenges with a team of full-time consultants and a pool of associates with specific expertise on tap. International sales account for more than half of 42 Technology's revenues, and customers range from multinational companies to not-for-profit organizations.

HELPING TO FIND MALARIA

42 Technology has worked with the Foundation for Innovative New Diagnostics, FIND, for a number of years to develop improved diagnostic devices for diseases such as TB and malaria. The aim is to help develop low cost and more

effective tests that are simple and robust enough to be used in challenging locations and closer to patients.

One of 42 Technology's latest projects with FIND could help to detect individuals with asymptomatic malaria who might otherwise be missed with current testing methods. Identifying those who have malaria but don't show any symptoms is an important step in controlling the spread of the disease.

An existing and proven sample processing method has been re-designed and developed for an established DNA-based amplification text, specifically adapted to screen up to 90 human specimens simultaneously. The new system is simple to use, portable and robust, and could also be used to help diagnose other diseases. It will allow local healthcare workers to screen entire communities more quickly and more easily, and identify asymptomatic malaria patients so that they can be treated. The system is currently undergoing field trials in Zanzibar.

Far left: Health workers in Zanzibar participate in field trials of the new malaria testing system.

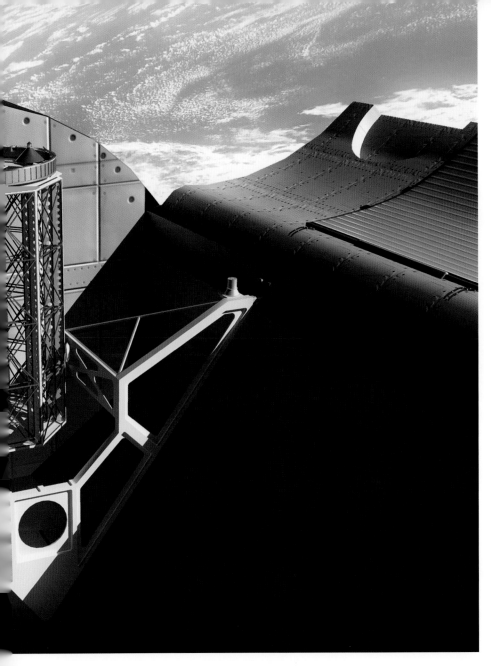

PLEXTEK

Another part of the technology consultancy constellation is Plextek, which specializes in electronics. Founded by former PA employee Colin Smithers along with Ian Murphy and Tim Jackson in 1989, the company includes an illustrious list of top global names among its more than 300 customers, including QinetiQ, Thales, the UK Ministry of Defence, Frontier Silicon, BAE Systems and Rolls-Royce. With over 100 employees, Plextek is one of the largest specialist electronics design consultancies in Europe.

Over the years, Plextek has also invested in, incubated and spun out several related companies where it has built a particular area of expertise. Plextek invested in the early stages of Iceni Mobile, a company formed by several of the developers of the M-Pesa mobile payment platform. Iceni is now the platform for RedCloud Technologies, which has partners across Africa, the Middle East and Asia.

In 2013, the Plextek Group was formed, in order to separate the consultancy side of the offering from two other businesses that had been incubated within and launched from Plextek, Blighter Surveillance Systems and Plextek RF Integration. Blighter Surveillance Systems has a successful track record in supplying ground-based radar systems for surveillance and security. Plextek RF Integration specializes in wireless radio frequency devices for a wide range of applications.

SMART LIGHTING TECHNOLOGY USED FOR PARKING IN CHINA AND RUSSIA

Telensa was spun out of Plextek in 2010, having been incubated within the company for five years, and its ultra narrow band (UNB) telemetry technology for remote monitoring of outdoor lighting is now deployed by many major local authorities in the UK. The most recent is in Doncaster, where 33,000 LED streetlights are to be connected wirelessly and monitored using the PLANet system from Telensa. Doncaster authorities estimate savings of approximately £1.3 million a year, reducing energy consumption by 8.7 million kilowatt hours and carbon emissions by 4,700 tonnes.

Telensa's UNB technology has also recently been applied to smart parking, delivering real-time information to drivers about where there are free parking spaces. The PARKet system has already been deployed in Shenzhen (China), Minsk (Belarus), and St Petersburg, Kazan and Moscow in Russia. In Moscow,

Above: *Skylon, the reusable space plane, is being developed by Reaction Engines. 42 Technology was called in to tackle several mechanical and engineering challenges presented by the project.*

Right: *The Linde EVOS Ci multifunctional gas valve developed with 42 Technology has received two international design awards: an iF Design Award in the product design category in February 2016, and a Red Dot Award: Product Design 2015.*

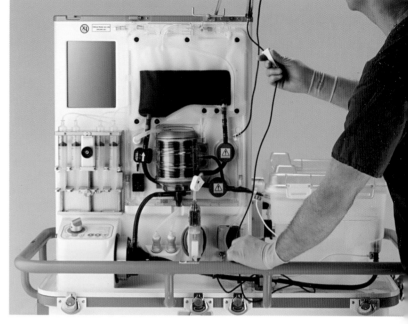

the system is said to have reduced traffic congestion by more than 25%.

Worldwide, nine million Telensa UNB devices have been deployed in 30 countries, including the US and China as well as Russia and the UK.

CAMBRIDGE DESIGN PARTNERSHIP

Cambridge Design Partnership has offices in Silicon Valley and a purpose-built R&D centre near Cambridge, where most of its more than 85 employees are based. It works across several sectors, including healthcare, consumer, energy and industrial equipment. With a track record stretching back 20 years, and a global customer base, Cambridge Design Partnership helps demonstrate the strength and depth of the technology consultancy sector around Cambridge, with plenty of space in the ecosystem for companies of different sizes and specialisms.

TEAM CONSULTING

Team Consulting specializes in the medical sector, with its vision to change lives for the better. Owned by the staff following a buyout, the company has around 75 employees and a group of associates and contractors who are called on when a project requires their particular skill sets.

The client base is mostly from the pharma sector. Team has worked with all top ten pharma companies over time, and generally is working with around six of them at any

one time. Services include device designs, redesigns and making products ready for the regulatory approval process. One of the company's strengths is in its usability and design focus, as technology is no longer the only differentiator for medical products, and ease of use and error-proofing are increasingly important.

But it's not just about big pharma for Team. Work with Dutch start-up ProFibrix led to the development of a new surgical device, Fibrocaps, that uses blood clotting agents fibrinogen and thrombin in a novel dry powder formulation and has been demonstrated in clinical trials to help reduce surgical bleeding. Patents associated with the technology originated in another Cambridge company, Innovata, and were licensed to ProFibrix following Innovata's acquisition by Vectura. Results from the clinical trials led to the acquisition of ProFibrix for $100 million plus a further $140 million in milestone payments as Fibrocaps achieves regulatory approval, with some of those payments returning to Vectura.

Above: *The metra system developed by OrganOx and Team Consulting is able to keep a liver functioning for at least 24 hours.*

Far left: *Hertfordshire highways control room: Will Gibson (left), CEO of Telensa and Cllr. Douris, Hertfordshire County Council, with telecell on luminaire and the PLANet system in the background.*

THE WORLD'S FIRST SUCCESSFUL LIVER TRANSPLANT USING A LIVER KEPT ALIVE OUTSIDE THE BODY

In 2013, when King's College Hospital, London, announced the first successful human liver transplant using a liver kept alive outside the body, the team at Team Consulting were ecstatic – and profoundly moved. Years of work with Oxford University spin-out OrganOx had paid off spectacularly.

Waiting lists for organ transplants are notoriously long, and the problem is compounded when the organ has to be transported to the recipient. The traditional method for transporting a human liver is to keep it cold and then check for viability when it reaches the recipient, but keeping fingers crossed and hoping for the best play far too large a role in the process.

Viability checks rely on the surgeon's knowledge rather than any empirical data obtained about the liver itself, and around a quarter of livers transported are no longer suitable for transplant by the time they reach the operating theatre. With around 30,000 people on the waiting list for a liver transplant in Europe and the US every year, that amounts to a large number of deaths simply because a suitable organ cannot reach the patients in a healthy enough state to be transplanted.

If a method could be found to preserve the liver outside the body for longer, without cooling it, that would not only increase the numbers of livers available for transplant because they could be transported safely, but also improve the quality of livers transplanted because they would be in a better condition when they reached the recipient.

An Oxford University spin-out, OrganOx, had been developing a perfusion system to keep the liver alive by mimicking conditions inside the body, but their set-up filled an entire room – just the pump for circulating the blood was the size of a filing cabinet – and transporting a liver using their method was out of the question.

Team Consulting brought together a multidisciplinary group encompassing electronics, engineering, design, software, fluidics, mechanics, chemistry and more to work on the challenge of shrinking the system from the size of a room down to something that could be picked up and transported, but keeping the functions – of a 'lung', a 'heart', and temperature regulation to 37 degrees Celsius – not only running successfully but also simple and easy to set up and use. The original also involved many metres of tubing, which could take

Left: *Team Consulting worked with ProFibrix to develop Raplixa™ (previously Fibrocaps™), a dry powder fibrin sealant based on a mixture of fibrinogen and thrombin proteins that occur naturally in blood.*

an hour or two to get right when prepping in a normal surgical environment, and these too had to be reduced and simplified.

Despite all the advances in modern medicine, the fundamentals of liver transplantation have not changed in decades. This is why the device is so exciting. If we can introduce technology like this into everyday practice, it could be a real, bona fide game changer for transplantation as we know it.

Nigel Heaton, Consultant Liver Transplant Surgeon and Director of Transplant Surgery at King's College Hospital

The metra system developed by OrganOx and Team Consulting is able to keep a liver functioning for at least 24 hours, can run on batteries for up to two hours during transportation, and has sensors and monitors that provide surgeons with highly useful data on the physiological state of the liver itself. Setting the machine up takes minutes rather than hours, and back-up and redundant systems ensure that the liver is kept alive should a peripheral feature fail.

It was astounding to see an initially cold grey liver flushing with colour once hooked up to our machine and performing as it would within the body. What was even more amazing was to see the same liver transplanted into a patient who is now walking around.

Constantin Coussios, Oxford University Department of Engineering Science and Technical Director of OrganOx

"

There wasn't a dry eye in the house.

Dan Flicos, CEO, Team Consulting

The field of inkjet printing has grown from a small group of spin-outs to a mini-cluster of its own.

INKJET PRINTING

When you receive a magazine through the post, check the sell-by date on a litre of milk in a supermarket, throw out some medication that is no longer usable, or even retile your bathroom, there's a very high chance you're enjoying the benefits of technology from Cambridge.

A group of spin-outs, many of them coming directly or indirectly from Cambridge Consultants, have created a mini-cluster around one technology sector: inkjet printing. The advantages of industrial inkjet printing are many, not least the ability to verify the safety of perishable goods. As a process, it is more cost-effective than traditional printing, prints where other printers cannot go, is flexible enough to allow quick changes and short print runs, and even takes up less space on the production line. And because inkjet printing is non-contact, it can be used to print on brittle and fragile surfaces.

Although not a new technology per se, commercializing inkjet printing and making it work in a variety of industrial settings was down to some firsts from Cambridge, which started with the emergence of Domino Printing Sciences from Cambridge Consultants in 1978. Other companies focusing on different aspects of the sector followed, and the mini-cluster created has had a significant impact not only around Cambridge, but also globally. With the vast majority of revenues for the companies in this sector coming from overseas, and multiple offices and distributors around the world, the Cambridge inkjet cluster is truly international.

But its impact is not just about making money here and abroad – the benefits to society of safer food, safer medicines and reducing the risk of harm from counterfeit products are clear. Consumers also benefit from lower costs of items such as printed ceramic tiles and fabrics, and even lower distribution costs for their magazine subscriptions. While not everyone will appreciate the customization possibilities that inkjet printing brings to marketing and promotions, they do appreciate the level of traceability that the same process brings to the foods they eat and the medicines they rely on.

Development of the industry around Cambridge has also been helped by the founding of the Inkjet Research Centre in the University's Institute for Manufacturing. Initially funded for five years from 2005 by government and companies in the industry, funding was extended in 2010 for a further five years. By doing fundamental research into inkjet technologies at the Centre, researchers developed an understanding of the basic science that the companies involved could then take into their R&D programmes to develop further.

The sector continues to expand and grow. Nowadays, many products have to be labelled in more than one language, so require more sophisticated labelling technology. New research has led to the development of nanosilver inks, which can print circuits to carry electricity, and solar energy technology is starting to explore how to print on to very thin silicon. 3D printing is another area where inkjets can display their versatility. Recent interest has been sparked by the possibility of printing with 'functional fluids' that carry cells and other compounds needed to build a biological structure. The inkjet mini-cluster is only just getting started.

DOMINO PRINTING SCIENCES LEADS THE WAY

When Graeme Minto and a handful of colleagues spun out of Cambridge Consultants with some interesting technology that looked promising for commercializing non-contact printing, they thought there would be a good market for their novel technique in printing wallpapers and fabrics. But they coincidentally put themselves in the perfect position to take advantage of new EU legislation. By mandating that 'sell-by' dates had to be provided on perishable goods, the EU made non-contact printing a necessity for the food production industry. Domino Printing Sciences, the company that Minto formed, was in exactly the right place for the coming revolution in food labelling.

Domino was the first company in the world formed to commercialize continuous inkjet technology, and was followed two years later by Videojet in the US. Its early success was driven by a market opportunity, but also by the fact that the company was ready to take that opportunity.

As EU legislation on the labelling of perishable goods was being drawn up, no one had found a way to print onto moving, three-dimensional objects such as bottles or cans going through a production line. Having to stop the line – which could be going along at a rate of hundreds or even thousands of bottles per minute – could make the process economically impossible.

Non-contact inkjet printing, which uses electric currents to direct minute droplets of ink as they emerge from a nozzle, spraying the ink onto the surface rather than placing it there by contact, was the answer, and it wasn't long before Domino's machines were being used to date label perishable goods from bottles of milk to sacks of potatoes.

But the high-speed printing technology had another benefit in that each print could be different, and the publishers of the *Daily Mirror* newspaper seized the opportunity and created a 'lucky number' competition. Using Domino's technology, *Daily Mirror* newspapers were all printed with a different number on the outside, and a single, winning number on the inside: if the two numbers matched, the lucky reader won a prize. Domino's machines printed the numbers on the newspapers at a rate of 70,000 per hour. Following the introduction of the

Above: *The Domino A-Series printer.*

competition, circulation of the *Daily Mirror* increased by 3%, a not inconsiderable amount in the world of mass circulation newspapers.

The development of systems with multiple printheads meant that more lines of text or numbers could be printed simultaneously, and this method found a market in printing addresses on letters and magazines. *Time* and *Newsweek* used the technology to print subscribers' names directly on to their copy of the magazine, and even to customize advertisements inside.

Domino grew and evolved as the market grew and evolved. Listing on the London Stock Exchange in 1985, the company's shares were 43 times oversubscribed. Domino expanded internationally as more countries brought in legislation around labelling goods and medicines and the new printing revolution took hold. Manufacturing spread to include the UK, the US, Germany, Sweden, China and India,

near to customers and positioned to take advantage of local developments in specific markets.

In the early 2000s, Domino began to move into the digital printing market, and more specifically printing from a computer image file. This meant considerable investment, and started to put Domino up against a different breed of competitor, including companies like Epson and Xerox. While it is a hard market to conquer, the potential for digital printing is huge – despite all the growth in industrial inkjet printing, 97% of the world's printing is still done using the traditional, analogue method, so there is plenty of room for expansion in digital offerings.

In early 2015, the *Financial Times* reported that Domino and its two closest competitors, US companies Danaher and Dover, together covered 85% of the global market in coding and marking equipment, and that Domino was one of the world's biggest makers of barcode printers. Not surprisingly, the company has collected multiple Queen's Awards for Industry and plenty of other accolades over the years. It also had the remarkable track record of revenues growing every year for 33 years up until 2012.

Revenues for 2014 were over £350 million, and Domino reported customers in more than 120 countries, served through a network of 25 offices and over 200 distributors. There were around 2,300 employees worldwide, and sales were spread across multiple sectors, including food and drink, pharmaceuticals, industrial, electronic components and others. Only 7% of Domino's revenues came from the UK, with 23% from the Americas and 27% from the Asia Pacific.

"

I would struggle to name a country where we don't have customers.

Nigel Bond, Domino Printing Sciences Annual Report, 2009

Above: *Domino Research and Development.*

Plans for expansion included new factories in India, the UK and China to meet growing demand, and continued growth in servicing the aftermarket business for the machines. Domino also started work on a new building at its Cambridge site, to bring together departments that were currently housed in separate buildings.

In 2015, Domino was acquired for over £1 billion by Japanese company Brother. The acquisition was part of a growth strategy for Brother, as Domino was in different areas of the market, and Brother intended to keep Domino operating as a stand-alone division within the company, maintaining operations in Cambridge where the story first began.

THE CAMBRIDGE CLUSTER OF INKJET COMPANIES LEADS THE WORLD

Inkjet and Cambridge became almost synonymous in the years following the foundation of Domino, attracting a pool of investment and promoting growth in a technology that was proving a global success.

Following the establishment of Domino, Corby company Willett set up a research and development facility in Cambridge in 1981; this was followed by the founding of Elmjet in 1985. Linx came next, in 1986, and then Xaar in 1990. Domino gave birth to its own spin-out, Xennia, in 1996, and Inca Digital joined the party in 2000.

Far right: *PragmatIC Printing creates integrated circuits that are thinner than a human hair.*

Below right: *Scott White, CEO of PragmatIC.*

Each company had its own particular place in the ecosystem, focusing on different markets with different needs, such as coding and marking, ceramics, or wide-format printing for textiles, wall coverings and outdoor advertising.

The inkjet cluster in Cambridge proved to be a honeypot for US and other international rivals. Danaher acquired Willett and Linx. Videojet acquired Elmjet, but was then itself taken over by Danaher a few years later. TenCate acquired Xennia eight years after it was founded, and Dai Nippon Printing added Inca Digital to its collection in 2005.

Since Brother acquired Domino in 2015, the last of the bigger companies in Cambridge's inkjet mini-cluster 'left standing' is Xaar. But there are plenty of smaller companies targeting specific areas of a complex technological system growing around Cambridge and talking to the world.

Global Inkjet Systems develops the software and electronics that drive the printheads in inkjet printing systems. Their customers include global OEMs such as Fujifilm Dimatix, Konica Minolta, Ricoh, Toshiba Tec and local neighbour Xaar. The GIS Print Manager Board works with a variety of different,

and interchangeable, GIS Head Interface Boards, allowing for flexibility and the ability to upgrade easily to the latest printing technology. With offices in China and Japan, the company has already received a Queen's Award for Enterprise in International Trade, despite being only a few years old at the time. In 2012, 89% of sales were international, up from 47% in 2010, and the company continues to expand.

PragmatIC Printing is making waves in the area of ultra low-cost electronics, with technology that prints integrated circuits that are thinner than a human hair – thinner and more flexible than the chips currently found in items such as passports.

Much cheaper than conventional silicon chips, extremely thin and flexible, the technology from PragmatIC is being touted as a game changer in the Internet of Things because it can be applied to so many everyday objects without affecting their size or shape. Customers already include multinationals in consumer goods, packaging, security printing and mainstream electronics. Using the technology, wireless security labels have been developed for De La Rue, the world's largest producer of banknotes and passports, and printed electronic greetings cards created for a subsidiary of Hallmark.

A recent round of investment from ARM and Cambridge Innovation Capital is driving research in Cambridge and helping to increase production capacity to 100 million flexible integrated circuits annually at PragmatIC's facility at the National Centre for Printable Electronics at Sedgefield.

143

XAAR IS THE CAMBRIDGE STAR AT THE 2012 'MAKE IT IN GREAT BRITAIN' EXHIBITION

Xaar was one of the first companies to promote the commercialization of drop-on-demand (DoD) printing. Today, more than 95% of Xaar's sales are outside the UK, with over 50% of its sales coming from Asia. China is the largest market for Xaar, but the market in India is growing.

The evolution from continuous inkjet printing using single nozzles to DoD was a step change. The piezoelectric printheads developed for DoD could have multiple nozzles and so multiple droplets of ink could be deposited simultaneously. In addition, the size of the droplets could be decreased. More nozzles meant faster and more cost-effective printing with a greater variety of inks, and smaller droplets meant greater accuracy. But reliability and dependability were a problem in the early days, and Xaar was set up to create robust printhead systems that would make DoD attractive to industry.

Founded in 1990, the company was initially based on a model of licensing its ink and printhead technology, and early licensees included IBM, Minolta, Seiko Instruments and Toshiba Tec. The relationships involved more than just licensing, however, and the partnerships with other companies helped to develop the technology further.

Following a successful listing on the London Stock Exchange in 1997, Xaar moved into manufacturing in 1999 by buying back the licence from MIT in Sweden and acquiring the company's manufacturing facilities in Järfälla, Sweden. Xaar set up operations in India in 2004. In 2006, Xaar invested £6 million in a new manufacturing plant near Cambridge, and in 2010 a further £22 million went into expanding production in the UK to meet increasing demand for the Xaar 1001 printhead. By this time, Xaar had rejected two offers from Danaher to buy the company.

The rise in popularity of the Xaar 1001 resulted in part from the adoption of inkjet printing by the ceramic tile industry, and with getting on for half of the ceramic tiles in the world being produced in China to serve the building boom there, growth in this market was rapid. Another growth market has been India, where over 21 million printhead nozzles were delivered within seven years of setting up operations there in 2004.

Another sector that has seen growth for Xaar is wide-format printing – for instance, for outdoor advertising materials such as billboards and banners – but there is still a huge untapped market where manufacturers have yet to make the switch to digital. However, as the ceramics and wide-format sectors demonstrated, once a few manufacturers have taken up digital, many more will follow. There are clear advantages in flexibility and customization with digital printing over traditional methods, and other sectors will no doubt make the move to digital in the future.

Left: *The Xaar 1001 GS12 printhead, developed for the ceramic tile industry, was introduced in 2012.*

Right: *The 'Direct Print Powered by KHS™' system with Xaar 1002 printheads in production at Martens Brouwerij. The digitally decorated Dagschotel PET beer bottles 'talk' to you and each other using a smartphone app.*

Maria Thankachan, winner of
the RCUK Best Use of Research
Prize (right) and Dr Sarah Elderkin,
a group leader in the Nuclear
Dynamics programme at the
Babraham Institute, examining
their Western blot during Maria's
visit on 29 July. The Babraham
Institute is a world-class research
institution, situated at the heart
of the Babraham Research
Campus. The Institute's mission
is to be an international leader
in research, focusing on basic
cell and molecular biology with
an emphasis on healthy ageing
through the human lifecyle.

RESEARCH INSTITUTES

There is no doubt that research leads to impact, but it can take upwards of 20 years for the pay-off to be felt. Nevertheless, there is an increased emphasis today on the importance of commercializing research to ensure that the benefits reach society, particularly when the research is funded by public money.

Cambridge is home not just to the groundbreaking research that goes on within the University, which itself leads to impressive results in a number of ways, but also to a collection of associated and independent research organizations that also develop innovative technologies and contribute to the wider ecosystem of the Cambridge Phenomenon.

There is a highly productive, symbiotic relationship between the University and the various research institutes set up around Cambridge. There is an equally productive relationship between the research institutes and a number of companies that have been founded to commercialize the fruits of particular projects.

Research plays a central role in the impact of the Cambridge Phenomenon, and, while some of the most significant breakthroughs to date are mentioned elsewhere, it is important to recognize here some of the research-based organizations that contribute so much to the national and international reputation of Cambridge and its technology cluster.

BABRAHAM RESEARCH CAMPUS

The Babraham Research Campus houses the Babraham Institute and over 60 early stage and growing life science companies, and is managed and developed by Babraham Bioscience Technologies Ltd (BBT). The impact of the Institute derives principally from groundbreaking scientific research, while that of BBT is demonstrated in the expanding success of the bioincubator facilities and services it provides to bioscience start-ups.

Being in the top ten worldwide for epigenetics research, as assessed by Thomson Reuters' service ScienceWatch. com, puts the Babraham Institute in the same league as such illustrious universities as Johns Hopkins, Harvard and MIT. Research at the Institute focuses on basic cellular and molecular biology, and core funding comes from the UK Government's Biotechnology and Biological Sciences Research Council (BBSRC), with additional funding from the Wellcome Trust, the European Union, the UK Medical Research Council and others.

The Babraham Institute began life as the Institute of Animal Physiology in 1948, set up after World War II to increase food production in the UK. It became the Institute of Animal Physiology and Genetics Research in 1986 following a merger with two research institutes based in Roslin, Scotland. In 1993, the Babraham Institute separated from the Roslin operations as a discrete entity, and by 1998 had ceased working on agricultural research altogether.

Liposomes were discovered at the Babraham Institute by the so-called 'father of liposomes', Alec Bangham, who published the first paper characterizing liposomes in 1965. The discovery launched not only a range of applications from the medical to the industrial, but also a new branch of research with its own journal and an international society. Globally recognized cosmetics companies such as Dior, Lancôme

and Elizabeth Arden adopted liposomes to use in innovative skincare products, while Bangham himself worked on using liposomes to create artificial lung surfactants for the treatment of babies with respiratory problems.

> **"**
>
> *The Babraham Institute produces a very high standard of fundamental research with high and increasing impact. Its epigenetics research has been categorized in the top 10 worldwide.*

Alacrita LLP, *Capturing the Economic Impact* of the Babraham Institute, 2013

Left: *The Babraham Research Campus.*

Far right: *David Willetts, former Minister for Universities and Science, opening the Jonas Webb Building on the Babraham Research Campus in 2013.*

Below: *Babraham Institute.*

Subsequent work at Babraham on lipid signalling led to the characterization of the PI3 kinase enzymes in the 1990s. These enzymes play important roles in the regulation of cell proliferation and migration, and are also central to the regulation of the immune response. Mutations of P13 kinase are frequently detected in human cancers, and thus inhibitors of this kinase are now a major focus for many pharmaceutical companies as they have potential applications not only as anti-cancer therapeutics but also in the treatment of immunological diseases.

The Babraham Institute was also involved in early antibody research in Cambridge, collaborating with César Milstein and colleagues at the Laboratory of Molecular Biology to produce some of the first 'useful' antibodies in the late 1970s. Work was also carried out on obtaining therapeutic antibodies from genetically modified rodents, and the processes developed are a source of royalty revenue for the Institute.

Today, the Babraham Institute focuses on four strategic programme areas associated with health and wellbeing:

epigenetics, nuclear dynamics and function, lymphocyte signalling and development, and signalling. The aim is to further understanding of how cells and organs maintain function and change with age, but much of the work is also highly relevant to various aspects of disease, and hence the Institute has a number of collaborations with pharmaceutical companies such as AstraZeneca, GSK and CellCentric, and life sciences start-ups.

Babraham Bioscience Technologies Ltd (BBT) creates its own impact by helping bioscience start-ups get off the ground, and by attracting funders and international companies to locate on the Babraham Campus. BBT was set up in 1996 as a wholly owned trading subsidiary (in 2013 BBSRC took a 25% equity stake in BBT) to support new companies and facilitate the commercialization of biomedical research. To do this, one of its tasks was to help new bioscience companies get access to the facilities and equipment they needed without having to spend

all their start-up funding on accommodation and expensive machinery. The idea of a bioincubator was to provide not only flexible office space for such companies, but also shared laboratory facilities where they could use the latest equipment without the financial outlay.

The first bioincubator at Babraham was opened in 1998 in an existing building on the site, Building 405, and by 2001 it was full, as was another building on the site, the Daly Laboratories. The model proved so popular that a new building, named Minerva, was purpose-built and opened in 2005. Meditrina followed in 2007 and Maia in 2010, the latter being fully let before it was completed. In the 2011 budget, the Chancellor announced a £44 million investment for the campus to develop additional facilities to support early stage life science companies. Using this funding, the Moneta building was officially opened in 2012, and the Jonas Webb chemistry laboratory was opened in 2013. Finally the Bennet building was opened in September 2014, and it, too, was fully let before construction was completed – to Kymab and Eagle Genomics.

The expansion continues, with additional funding supporting the construction of the Eddeva building, which will be fully occupied in January 2016, and a new conference, restaurant and meeting facility to accommodate the needs of the growing campus community due for completion at the end of 2016.

In February 2015, Imperial College London announced plans to build a 49,000 square-foot facility at the Campus to house life science spin-outs from the College. The first tenant will be Abzena, expected to move in by the end of 2016.

In total, including the Imperial College building, Babraham in 2016 will have close to 200,000 square feet of space available for life science companies, but at present this is insufficient and there is a waiting list of potential new tenants hoping to join some 60 companies already operating on the Campus. The growth continues – BBT has obtained planning consent for an additional 18,000 square feet of development on the Campus.

Around three-quarters of the companies on the Campus interact in some way with the research and resources at the Babraham Institute, which reflects the activities of the knowledge exchange and commercialization team within the Institute, the need for companies on the Campus to be working in life science R&D, and the policy of BBT to prioritize tenants that have healthcare or pharmaceutical aims that could have potential synergies with the work of the Institute.

In 2013, it was reported that 69 companies had 'graduated' from the bioincubator at Babraham, having between them raised more than £360 million in investment funding. The bioincubator has also attracted other organizations – with Imperial Innovations setting up its first office outside London at Babraham, and Cancer Research Technologies leasing half the Jonas Webb building to house around 30 researchers working in cancer therapeutics. Particular companies of note that started at the Campus include CAT (acquired by MedImmune, Arakis (acquired by Sosei), Horizon Discovery, XO1 (acquired by Johnson & Johnson) and Kymab (Wellcome Trust).

THE CAVENDISH LABORATORY, UNIVERSITY OF CAMBRIDGE

The Cavendish Laboratory is perhaps most famous in terms of impact for the breadth and depth of the discoveries in physics that have emerged from it over the years, leading to more than 20 Nobel Prizes in fields ranging from subatomic physics to radio astronomy.

But it has also had an important impact on the growth of the Cambridge technology cluster, with discoveries and innovations that have since become the driving force behind technology companies all over the world, and its very presence attracting researchers to Cambridge who have gone on to found companies and commercialize new technologies.

The Cavendish Laboratory was designed by James Clerk Maxwell, first Cavendish Professor of Experimental Physics, and

Above: *The Cambridge Centre for the Physics of Medicine, Cavendish Laboratory, University of Cambridge.*

Above right: *left to right:JJ Thomson, discoverer of the electron. Ernest Rutherford, who first split the atom. Charles Wilson, who invented the cloud chamber for tracking subatomic particles. Lawrence Bragg, who won the Nobel Prize in Physics for his work in X-ray crystallography.*

Right: *Richard Friend, Cavendish Professor of Physics.*

was one of the UK's first purpose-built laboratories for teaching and research when it opened in 1874. It was named for William Cavendish, seventh Duke of Devonshire and Chancellor of the University, who gave £6,300 to build the laboratory.

Since its inception, the Cavendish has been associated with many illustrious names and numerous Nobel Prize winners in Physics, including JJ Thomson, who discovered the electron, the first known subatomic particle; Ernest Rutherford, who first split the atom; and Charles Wilson, who invented the cloud chamber for tracking subatomic particles. Lawrence Bragg, another Nobel Laureate, developed X-ray crystallography at the Cavendish, which was to play a crucial role in the determination of the structure of DNA. Indeed, it is perhaps Crick and Watson's identification of the structure of DNA that has led to the greatest number of company formations and therapeutic breakthroughs of any scientific discovery (see pages 20–23).

The Laboratory's illustrious pedigree attracted many extremely bright researchers to Cambridge over the years, some of whom went on to play important roles in the technology cluster. Michael Cole not only co-founded Metals Research, a highly successful Cambridge company in the 1960s and 1970s, but also invented the 'Cole vacuum principle', which enabled uniform evaporation of solvents from multiple samples, won his fifth Queen's Award for Innovation and is still used worldwide. Colin Fisher moonlighted from his PhD studies at the Cavendish in the 1960s to help Metals Research develop the first commercial image analyser, the Quantimet A, which was recognized globally as an important tool in research, particularly in haematology. Malcolm Boston helped found several highly specialized engineering companies in Cambridge to commercialize his inventions in electron beam welding and high vacuum furnaces.

More recently, the current Cavendish Professor of Physics, Richard Friend, has co-founded two spin-out companies to

commercialize technology developed in the Laboratory in the new area of organic thin film transistors, or plastic electronics. Cambridge Display Technology was set up in 1992 to develop polymer organic light-emitting diode (P-OLED) technology, and was acquired by Sumitomo Chemical in 2007. Plastic Logic was founded in 2000 to commercialize organic thin film transistors, or plastic electronics. In 2015, Plastic Logic was separated into two entities. Plastic Logic Germany, based in Dresden, continues to manufacture thin, flexible electronic displays, and the renamed FlexEnable, in Cambridge, develops technology for organic thin film transistors.

In 2015, the impact of the Cavendish Laboratory was recognized by the UK Government in its announcement of a £75 million grant towards building new facilities.

THE INSTITUTE FOR MANUFACTURING, DEPARTMENT OF ENGINEERING, UNIVERSITY OF CAMBRIDGE

The Institute for Manufacturing (IfM) is helping address some of the most profound challenges facing manufacturing firms and governments today through research into management, technology and policy. Its work in innovation and technology management, for example, has helped hundreds of companies around the world turn R&D into successful products, processes and services. Research into global operations networks has supported some of the world's largest companies as they redesign their production and supply networks to reach new markets and cut costs. And work from the IfM was instrumental in developing the UK Technology Strategy Board's High Value Manufacturing Catapult strategy and making the case for funding Catapult Centres around the UK to promote collaboration between businesses, engineers and scientists in driving economic growth.

The IfM also conducts research into a number of areas where new technologies are transforming the manufacturing landscape, including inkjet and 3D printing, industrial photonics and nanomanufacturing. The University of Cambridge received more grants for research into manufacturing from the EPSRC than any other UK university in 2015, and manufacturing research received more funding across the University than any other subject.

'Manufacturing is not just about what goes on in factories, important though that is. It's about designing radical new business models, providing services as well as products, understanding and exploiting new technologies – and creating the policy conditions in which they can flourish. At the IfM it's our job to help businesses and policymakers find more efficient and resilient ways to create economic wealth – while preserving our planet's resources for future generations.'

Andy Neely, Head, IfM

2015 saw the 50th anniversary of the first students arriving to take what was originally known as the Advanced Course in Production Methods and Management. Now the MPhil in Industrial Systems, Manufacture and Management, the course is regularly five times oversubscribed and its graduates are

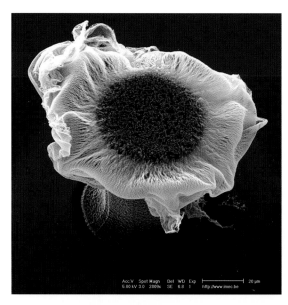

Left: *Microstructure made out of carbon nanowires.*

Below: *The Institute for Manufacturing.*

Above: *Mike Gregory, Head of IfM from 1998 to 2015.*

Above right: *Andy Neely, Head of IfM from 2015.*

Below: *Ultrafast laser processing of glass in the IfM's Centre for Industrial Photonics.*

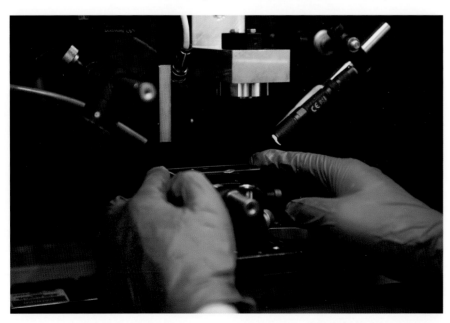

programmes run by IfM Education and Consultancy Services (IfM ECS), a company owned by the University of Cambridge,. The international digital services giant, Atos, with 93,000 staff worldwide and £11 billion in annual revenues, selected IfM ECS from a global shortlist to work with a partner university, Paderborn in Germany, to deliver a high-level training course for the company's IT specialists.

As well as offering executive and professional development, IfM ECS also provides consultancy based on IfM research. Working with IfM ECS has helped more than 50 household names in automotive, white goods, pharmaceuticals and other sectors to optimise their global supply chains, release savings of hundreds of millions of pounds and boost revenues by equally significant amounts. One engineering company reported that it had invested some £250 million in improvements to its supply chain which were expected to result in a £750 million boost in tangible value. Another, in the pharmaceuticals sector, invested £50 million and expected this investment to drive revenues from new products of around £500 million.

For SMEs, IfM ECS developed and delivered a three-year PrISMS (Practical & Innovative Solutions for Manufacturing Sustainability) programme, funded by the European Regional Development Fund, the EPSRC Centre for Innovative Manufacturing in Industrial Sustainability and others, and completed in June 2015.

The PrISMS programme worked with 120 companies over its three-year duration, and aimed to help companies not only grow revenues, but also improve the sustainability of their products and operations. With 126 new jobs created and cumulative turnover for 60 of the companies increasing by £18.8 million during the first year, the programme demonstrated the benefit of providing active support to help small companies grow.

IfM ECS also supports the development of government policy through a framework developed for roadmapping technology and innovation management. Over 250 projects have been conducted by IfM ECS in 26 countries, and the roadmapping framework has been tailored and applied to a variety of situations, from the UK's synthetic biology sector to the Australian automotive industry. A new landscaping project is underway to identify priorities and opportunities for UK manufacturing as far ahead as 2030. IfM ECS gifts any profits it makes back to the University to fund future research.

in high demand. Students graduating from the Manufacturing Engineering Tripos are equally sought after, having spent the last two years of their engineering degree learning how to combine theory with practice in order to solve real industrial problems. The IfM also has more than 75 students doing PhDs or research MPhils across the spectrum of management, technology and policy.

People working in industry and government can also learn about the new ideas and insights emerging from the IfM through the executive and professional development

THE MEDICAL RESEARCH COUNCIL
LABORATORY OF MOLECULAR BIOLOGY

The Nobel Prize 'factory' that is the Medical Research Council Laboratory of Molecular Biology, the MRC LMB, is world-renowned and has been the origin of numerous scientific breakthroughs, many of which have been recognized with the world's most famous international award.

Ten Nobel Prizes have been awarded to scientists for their work at the LMB, seven in Chemistry and three in the category of Physiology or Medicine. Fred Sanger, one of very few people in the world to have won two Nobels, and even fewer to have won two in the same subject, received both his awards while working at the LMB. In 1962, the LMB collected two in the same year: the Nobels were awarded to John Kendrew and Max Perutz for Chemistry (in their work on the structure of globular proteins and developing protein crystallography), and to Crick and Watson in Physiology or Medicine, for discovering the structure of DNA (carried out when they were working in the predecessor to the LMB, the MRC Unit for Research on the Molecular Structure of Biological Systems housed in the Cavendish Laboratory).

But the most important impact of the LMB has been the science behind the Nobels. The DNA story is well known (see Life Sciences and Healthcare section starting on Page 19), and as a result of the discoveries made and techniques developed at the LMB, the human genome has been sequenced and hundreds, if not thousands, of companies have been set up to exploit this knowledge in some way, from tracing ancestors to fighting disease.

Above and right: *The Laboratory of Molecular Biology.*

Above: *Greg Winter, Master of Trinity College, Cambridge.*

Monoclonal antibodies, also described elsewhere (see pages 38–43), and subsequently humanized monoclonal antibodies, have revolutionized medicine, with around a third of all new treatments reaching patients being based on monoclonal antibodies. The technique to humanize mouse monoclonal antibodies developed by Greg Winter and colleagues was licensed to around 50 companies, and royalties from the therapeutics that have been derived as a result have provided a major source of income for the LMB.

The technique for isolating fully human antibodies led to the setting up of Cambridge Antibody Technology and the eventual approval of Humira, the biggest selling therapeutic drug in the world. And more recently an alternative technique for obtaining fully human monoclonal antibodies from mice developed by the late Michael Neuberger has begun to be exploited to develop new therapeutics.

The growth in antibody therapeutics was helped initially by the LMB's strategy of non-exclusive licences (except for that agreed with Celltech), which promoted widespread use of the techniques and arguably helped things grow faster than if usage had been restricted by exclusive licences.

Companies that have been set up to commercialize work at the LMB include Cambridge Antibody Technology (Greg Winter), Domantis (Winter and Ian Tomlinson, 2006, purchased by GSK for £230 million), Heptares Therapeutics (2007, moved to Welwyn Garden City), Bicycle Therapeutics (2009), and Mesolens (2009, exploiting a new type of microscopy developed by Brad Amos at the LMB that can look deeper into tissues). A new potential asthma treatment, the Anti-IL-25 antibody, has been licensed to Janssen Biotech Inc in the US, a subsidiary of Johnson & Johnson, for development.

TWI

NASA, Boeing, Airbus, Ford, Toyota – if you've been to space recently, or in a plane, car or train, a process invented at TWI in the early 1990s, friction stir welding (FSW) will have been involved in constructing your mode of transport.

We live in a joined-up world, and it is not just large machines made of metal that require complex and reliable methods to fix them together. Clothing of all sorts, from waterproof outer layers to lingerie, is joined by means other than stitching. Medical devices with cameras attached to them, mobile phones, crisp packets – all require joins that must not fail and must not interfere with the item's use or operation, often fixing one type of material to a completely different material. And many of the technologies to create these

"

TWI has been delivering an international impact for decades. We have on average eight technical enquiries every hour, and more than 15,000 visitors every year from around the world.

Christoph Wiesner, CEO, TWI

Examination of fatigue test specimen.

Right: *Friction stir welding.*

Below: *Placement of carbon fibre-reinforced plastic sample inside three-dimensional X-ray microscope.*

joints have been developed at TWI, along with innovations in materials testing, fatigue and fracture research, cutting, surfacing and other manufacturing processes.

Having begun life as the partly government-funded British Welding Research Association in 1946, TWI became independent of direct government support in the 1970s, and now operates on membership fees, research grants from a wide range of sources including the EU, and projects undertaken for clients in diverse industries such as aerospace, defence and power. It also works with more than 20 universities in providing postgraduate training and research.

Not only is TWI behind the most critical welding and joining technologies used every day worldwide, but it also trains and certifies around 25,000 welders and inspectors every year and works with over 1,800 industrial member companies in 70 countries. TWI has five facilities in the UK and a further 13 around the world. The associated professional association, The Welding Institute, is a membership body for the welding and joining industry, and has around 6,000 individual members worldwide. TWI also hosts the largest collection of reference materials on joining and welding in the world, a resource that continues to demonstrate its worth.

The new National Structural Integrity Research Centre (NSIRC) was opened on the TWI campus in 2015 to provide facilities and leadership in postgraduate engineering research. An initiative of TWI and Brunel University, the NSIRC is jointly funded by the UK government and industry, with the founding sponsors being the Lloyd's Register Foundation, BP and TWI. In addition to Brunel, academic partners now number over 20 leading universities. The research undertaken at NSIRC is driven entirely by industry needs, and, for example, in November 2015 NSIRC invited applications from around the world for ten PhDs funded by the Lloyd's Register Foundation in structural integrity and systems performance.

Understanding fractures is one of the most important aspects of designing and the safe operation of fabricated structures for applications such as pipelines, nuclear reactors and chemical plants. TWI is associated with a number of innovative developments in fracture research that have become standard test methods used worldwide. Crack tip opening displacement, CTOD, as a concept for measuring resistance to fracture was first described by TWI's Alan Wells in the early 1960s. His next contribution was the Wells wide plate test, which identifies conditions under which parent material or joints fail.

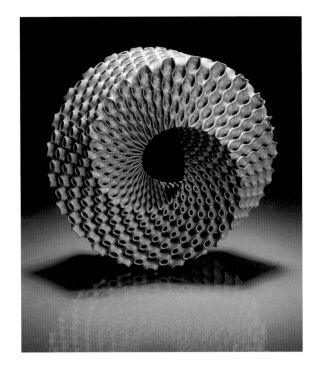

Left: *Titanium Mobius Ring created using Selective Laser Melting.*

Right: *High-power laser cutting for nuclear decommissioning.*

The use of high-powered CO_2 lasers for cutting metals, and subsequently non-metals, also emerged from TWI. An initial experiment by Peter Houldcroft when he was Deputy Scientific Director at TWI in 1967 demonstrated how lasers could cut accurately and precisely, using a laser cutting nozzle that he had designed. The technique went on to be widely adopted in industry, and cutting is probably the most common use of high-power lasers in materials processing today, with lasers being used not only to cut metals but also other materials such as fabrics for the mass production of clothes and other items.

A new use for laser cutting developed by TWI received an innovation award from the UK's Nuclear Decommissioning Authority. TWI's remote laser cutting technique will make a dramatic difference to the costs of decommissioning the metal containers used to store and transport nuclear waste. These containers are radioactive and thus require special storage, but the contaminated portion only amounts to the first 1.5mm from the metal's surface. Since a major cost of storing nuclear waste is related to its volume, TWI came up with a technique to cut the containers into five sections and then remove the radioactive layer of metal, resulting in only 50kg of material having to go into storage, rather than the entire container at 450kg.

Right: *Welding with chocolate demonstrated to HRH The Princess Royal by children from Great Abington Primary School.*

“

We were breaking new ground. Testing the plates required compact 600 tonne capacity equipment….none of us will forget the first successful fracture test. About half a tonne of equipment flew out of the end of the hut.

Alan Wells, speaking about the development of the Wells wide plate test, twi-global.com

THE WELLCOME TRUST SANGER INSTITUTE

The largest single contribution to the Human Genome Project,
the gene sequencing methods used worldwide in research,
drug discovery and the development of personalized medicine,
and a growing repository of genomics data that is made
available to the global scientific community, are just some of

Below: *The Wellcome Trust Sanger Institute.*

Above: *The Biodata Innovation Centre.*

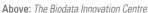

the ways that the Wellcome Trust Sanger Institute is impacting on all our lives.

Opened as the Sanger Centre, the Institute had fewer than 50 employees when double Nobel Laureate Fred Sanger declared it officially open in October 1993. Today, there are more than 1,000 people employed directly by the Institute, and roughly another 1,000 working on the Wellcome Genome Campus, either at one of its partner organizations or in spin-out companies or associated projects.

The Campus hosts the European Bioinformatics Institute, part of the European Molecular Biology Laboratory, EMBL-EBI, which is funded by EU member states and has around 570 employees. It is also the location for a number of other collaborations and joint projects, including the ELIXIR Technical Hub (a pan-European, data-sharing organization), funded by EU member states; the 100,000 Genomes Project, a UK-wide project focusing on individuals with rare diseases or cancer and managed by Genomics England, part of the Department of Health; the Centre for Genomic Pathogen Surveillance in association with Imperial College London; and the Centre for Therapeutic Target Validation, which is a project with international pharmaceutical company GSK.

A further collaboration with the Drug Discovery Unit at Cancer Research UK is screening for inhibitors of a novel oncogene discovered at the Institute that is associated with basal-like breast cancer (BLBC), responsible for 15% of breast cancer deaths.

The Institute established a Translation Office in 2011 to promote relationships with industry and researchers, and to identify potential commercial and scientific collaborations. One of the most recent spin-outs based on Wellcome Trust Sanger Institute technologies is Congenica (see Page 31). The new Biodata Innovation Centre, due to open in 2016, will house more start-up companies seeking to exploit genomics technologies and data in the public health arena.

The Institute increases its global impact through a commitment to sharing data and ensuring open access. This is carried out in various ways, including distributing materials in the form of whole genome human and mouse gRNA libraries, and making its database of somatic cancer mutations available to licensees. A screening collaboration with AstraZeneca combines the genome-editing expertise of the Institute with compounds and cell lines developed by AstraZeneca, and the findings of this collaboration are intended to be shared with the scientific community.

With over 24,000 visitors each year coming to the Wellcome Trust Sanger Institute from around the globe, the Institute remains at the heart of, and drives, genomics research worldwide.

FOUR OTHER SECTORS THAT ADD VARIETY TO THE CAMBRIDGE MIX

Left to right: *The Marshall Group are the UK's largest independent aerospace and defence company; Cambridge has a rich legacy of global impact in the agritech sector; Meridian Audio has played a unique role in the development of better audio technology; the Cambridge Satchel Company is just one of Cambridge's many successful direct-to-consumer businesses.*

AEROSPACE

> "
> *The droop nose…is a 23 ft variable geometry nose fairing with a retractable glazed visor. The visor retracts into the nose fairing and the hinged nose fairing is lowered to provide cockpit visibility for take-off, approach and landing. The visor was designed to fit glove-tight to the aircraft in the raised position to meet aerodynamic requirements and reduce cockpit noise levels. Operating times were specified as six seconds for retracting the visor, 12 seconds for lowering the nose and 19 seconds for raising the nose and visor. The droop nose is a large moving component within the full air flow of the aircraft. This was an exciting challenge…*

Arthur Marshall, *The Marshall Story*

THE MARSHALL GROUP

Supersonic flight, satellite launchers, world records, rescuing Hercules planes from the deserts of Arizona: the Marshall Group has a track record of delivering extraordinary and one-of-a-kind projects. As Cambridge's largest private company, with over 4,000 employees operating out of 54 locations worldwide and an annual turnover exceeding £1 billion, Marshall has seen a lot in its more than 100 years in automotive, engineering and aerospace. The Marshall Aerospace and Defence Group is the UK's largest independent company in this sector, and Marshall's largest division, with more than 2,000 employees. The Aerospace and Defence Group has been the driving force behind many of the company's most memorable challenges.

MARSHALL PLAYED A CRUCIAL ROLE IN GETTING CONCORDE OFF THE GROUND

The only UK company apart from the British Aircraft Corporation (BAC) with authority to work on the Concorde's airframe structure design, Marshall had to step in when Concorde's distinctive droop nose looked like it might be impossible to engineer after all. Concorde was a joint project between BAC and French company Aérospatiale.

The 23-foot-long droop nose and retractable visor were novel engineering challenges, but essential to provide the correct aerodynamic profile for supersonic flight along with the ability for the pilots to see when landing or taxiing on the ground. The challenge was actually even greater, because Concorde was to be the first aircraft built out of machined components, rather than the riveted 'bent tin' method that had been used for aircraft manufacture until then. This very dramatic change in aircraft engineering helped remove weight constraints that had previously hindered aircraft design, but brought new problems, such as the need for long bed machining capabilities, which Marshall had to develop alongside its design work on the nose.

The design and build of the droop nose had thwarted BAC, and a phone call from the general manager of BAC to then-manager Arthur Marshall put his company on the case.

The prototype Concorde, with Marshall nose, took off from Toulouse Airport in 1969. Several years of flight tests and modifications followed, and the first Concorde in commercial service flew on 21 January 1976. The aircraft flew for British Airways and Air France for almost 30 years, retiring from service in 2003.

THE HEAVIEST ITEM TO BE RELEASED FROM AN AIRCRAFT

Pegasus was the first rocket launched from an aircraft to place satellites in orbit, and Marshall converted the aircraft, a Lockheed L-1011 former airliner, to cope with the heaviest Pegasus rocket, the XL.

The most expensive part of launching a satellite into orbit is the first stage: getting it off the ground and through the Earth's atmosphere. An economic way round this problem is to use a modified plane to fly the satellite and its launching

rocket as high as possible and then release them, with the launcher taking the satellite the rest of the distance to 160km and more above the planet.

The Pegasus XL satellite launcher is one such device, designed to be dropped from an aircraft flying in the stratosphere, 40,000 feet above the Earth. It is the heaviest item ever to be released from an aircraft under gravity, and the technological and engineering challenges of take-off and launch at altitude are considerable.

Marshall was tasked with converting a Lockheed L-1011 to carry the Pegasus rocket into the stratosphere in the early 1990s, and the aircraft, christened the 'Stargazer', launched the first Pegasus XL in 1994. Since then, 42 launches of Pegasus rockets have successfully placed more than 80 satellites into low Earth orbit, most using the Lockheed L-1011 converted by Marshall.

Left: *A Marshall technician working on an aircraft.*

Below: *A technician working in one of Marshall's Autoclave Ovens at its Advanced Composites business.*

RESCUING HERCULES FROM THE DESERT

Marshall keeps planes flying for more than ten air forces around the world, and in 2006 'rescued' two Hercules aircraft from the desert near Tucson, Arizona, upgraded them and got them back into service for the Royal Netherlands Air Force.

Many air forces around the world rely on the Lockheed C-130, better known as the Hercules, for a variety of roles, including troop transport, cargo and search and rescue. Military aircraft are designed to have very long service lives, but that long service requires regular servicing and upgrades to keep the aircraft airworthy and capable of performing the variety of functions it is used for.

Working with partners Lockheed Martin and Rolls-Royce, Marshall leads the maintenance and technical support in a novel arrangement first agreed with the UK's Ministry of Defence in 2006. The Integrated Operational Support agreement places the onus on Marshall and its partners to maximize the availability of the aircraft in whatever way it deems necessary, rather than relying on a contracting body within the MoD telling it what to do. The model has proved so successful that it has already been rolled out for five other air forces. The complex challenge of upgrading Hercules' cockpits from analogue to digital is just one of the operations that Marshall provides under this arrangement.

Above: *A selection of C-130 Aircraft in Marshall Aerospace and Defence Group's Hangar 16.*

Left: *A C130J Hercules aircraft from 47 Squadron RAF Brize Norton.*

A QUEEN'S AWARD FOR GETTING SENSITIVE MEDICAL EQUIPMENT TO THE FRONT LINE

Getting emergency medical and laboratory equipment to inhospitable locations, whether they be conflict zones or areas that have suffered a natural disaster, is another challenge that Marshall has tackled, and it is the only company that has succeeded in putting a full CT scanner into a containerized system that can be transported over rough terrain.

In 2013, Marshall Land Systems, a division of Marshall Aerospace and Defence, received a Queen's Award for Enterprise Innovation for its work addressing the problems of placing and operating sensitive and costly equipment in unfavourable conditions. The award was given for the company's development of a deployable, containerized system that could be used to deliver CT scanning and forensic laboratory facilities to remote areas.

Working with Philips Healthcare and its Ingenuity Elite 128-slice CT scanner, which is designed to cope with the need for speed and accuracy in emergency medical situations, Marshall designed and built a containerized unit for the scanner that can be transported by land, sea or air and yet can be ready for operation within four hours of arrival at its final destination. By developing an ingenious method of ensuring that the scanner itself does not move in transit, the equipment does not need to be recalibrated before it can be used in situ.

The UK, France and Norway are among the countries whose military medical services use the Marshall CT scanner.

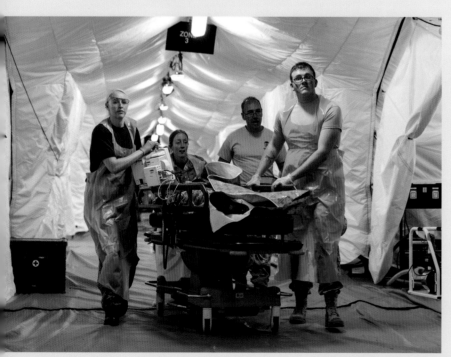

Above: *Marshall proving ground – deployment of Modular Role 3 hospital.*

Above: *The new Airbus A350 XWB.*

HEXCEL GETS COMPOSITES IN THE AIR

Composite materials that are found in the Eurofighter Typhoon, helicopters, space launchers, satellites and the new Airbus A350 XWB, among others, owe their origins to the early days of aviation in Cambridge – and a major new £6 million research and technology facility being built by Hexcel will continue that tradition.

Hexcel, with its global HQ and development facilities in Duxford, has more aerospace qualified composite products than any other company in the world, and the new facility will add to the company's capacity for research and development along with production methods for composite materials.

The company traces its history back to one of Arthur Marshall's first flying pupils, Norman de Bruyne, and his innovative synthetic adhesives and novel honeycomb designs for construction materials. What began life as de Bruyne's company Aero Research Ltd in 1934 and later became part of Ciba-Geigy, is now part of a global organization that supplies critical materials to not only the aerospace industry, but also the renewable energy and sports equipment sectors.

Composites are increasingly being used to replace metals because they are not only strong, but also light. The constant search to create lighter, more fuel-efficient planes means that Hexcel's major customers are Boeing and Airbus. Both the Boeing 787 airframe and the new Airbus A350 are made up of more than 50% composite materials, and Hexcel supplies both. All of the primary structure prepreg for the Airbus A350 XWB comes from Hexcel, and the wings are almost entirely composite. The first Airbus A350 XWB went into service for Qatar Airways in December 2014.

Each Eurofighter Typhoon contains over one ton of composite material developed and supplied by Hexcel, and the Eurocopter and Sikorsky helicopters have composite rotor blades.

Above: *Hexcel products are found in the blades of wind turbines.*

Right: *The single-seater e-Go plane.*

While aerospace accounts for some 80% of Hexcel's business, its products have also found their way into wind turbine blades (enabling the blades to be much bigger than those made out of metal) and sports goods such as tennis racquets, racing bicycles and snowboards. Although Hexcel no longer manufactures its own range of skis, its materials are found in many leading brands. New opportunities are emerging in areas such as the automotive industry, where fuel efficiency requirements, new regulations, and electric cars all point towards a greater need for materials that are light but strong.

THE E-GO

Cambridge is home to the latest in personalized flying machines – after the gyrocopter and the microlight, the next development in this field could be the e-Go.

The single-seater e-Go plane has been a project of Chief Designer Giotto Castelli for some years. Now backed by a number of Cambridge entrepreneurs

and funds, including Cambridge Angels, Cambridge Capital Group and Martlet, the corporate angel fund for the Marshall Group, the project also has support from a wide group of researchers and companies involved in cutting-edge aeronautical technology.

Just like James Bond's Acrostar mini-jet in the opening sequence of *Octopussy*, the plane can be refuelled at a petrol station. But while it might be considered by some as an expensive toy, the novel features of the e-Go and the use of composite materials may have other, unforeseen applications in the future.

AGRITECH

> **" **
>
> *Strong research plus productive land plus experience in growing technology companies is a very good set of ingredients for the future of agritech.*

Belinda Clarke, CEO, Agri-Tech East

Cambridge has a rich legacy of global impact in the agritech sector, most notably perhaps in plant breeding, originating in the former Plant Breeding Institute (PBI). While PBI has long ceased to exist, a closely associated organization also set up in Cambridge, the National Institute of Agricultural Botany (NIAB) has evolved into a key player in the agritech sector and is poised to help drive the next wave of innovation in the sector.

Other associations with agritech – such as the Animal Research Institute (a previous occupant of what is now the Babraham Institute) and the National Seed Development Organisation, have long been disbanded or sold off, but their legacies may be revived as food security rises up the agenda.

THE ONLY POTATO WITH A QUEEN'S AWARD FOR INDUSTRY CAME FROM THE PBI

When you pick up a bag of Maris Piper potatoes in the supermarket, you're selecting a variety with a Queen's Award for Industry. In fact, four of the PBI's new varieties achieved this award in the 1970s and 1980s, two types of wheat and a kale being the other champion crops.

You may drink beer made using Maris Otter winter barley, or buy bread made with Yeoman wheat, just two more of the improved varieties that came out of the PBI and found their way onto tables in the UK and beyond. The Maris varieties – there are several more – are named for Maris Lane in Trumpington on the outskirts of Cambridge, where the PBI was based.

Left: *Maris Piper potatoes.*

Right: *NIAB farmland.*

The PBI was founded in 1912, and was originally part of the Department of Agriculture in the University of Cambridge. It became a separate institute under the UK Government's Agricultural Research Council in 1948 and was then broken up in the late 1980s, with part being sold to Unilever and part relocated to the John Innes Institute in Norwich. Plant Breeding International Cambridge, the operation retained by Unilever in Cambridge, delivered Consort wheat, which also became a major export. The operation was sold to Monsanto in 1998, and gradually wound down.

Speaking at an event to celebrate the centenary of the founding of PBI in June 2012, one of the PBI staff who transferred to Norwich, John Snape, commented that 'You can hardly go to an institution in the UK, Europe or even the world which hasn't been influenced by the PBI.'

NIAB'S ROLE EVOLVES, BUT IT IS STILL THE LARGEST FIELD-TRIAL OPERATOR IN THE UK

The National Institute of Agricultural Botany, NIAB, was founded as a government-funded institution in 1919 and worked closely with the nearby Plant Breeding Institute. NIAB was set up to test seed quality, trial new varieties of crops and improve agricultural practices, all activities that it still pursues. Privatized and becoming a not-for-profit organization in 1996, NIAB continues to conduct seed testing for government and is the largest field-trial operator in the UK.

With no core government funding, NIAB operates primarily as a member organization, with around 2,300 farmer members, along with a further approximately 1,300 individual and corporate members. It also secures grant funding from the Biotechnology and Biological Sciences Research Council (BBSRC), but this must be won against competition and is not guaranteed.

Things are changing for NIAB, though, as various factors have recently come into play. One of these was the announcement in 2013 of the UK Government's new National Strategy for Agricultural Technologies, the first time in 30 years

that agritech had been included as part of the UK's industrial strategy. Along with this was the launch of a £70 million fund for an 'Agri-Tech Catalyst' and £90 million in funding for Centres for Agricultural Innovation.

The launch of Agri-Tech East, the UK's first agritech network, seems destined to follow the success of other groups, such as Cambridge Network, set up to bring people and technologies together and promote entrepreneurship.

Alongside the new impetus from the government, Cambridge itself has started to wake up to what is on its doorstep. The East Anglia region has 40% of the UK's best arable land, but Cambridge is also home to companies that could find novel applications for their technologies in agriculture. Companies not traditionally in the agritech space, such as ARM, are starting to participate in Agri-Tech East special interest groups to identify if their technologies might have a role to play. Microsoft Research's interest stems not only from the food security agenda, but also as an adjunct to thinking about the smart cities of the future and how to feed the people who live in them.

Unlike other sectors, such as computing or telecommunications, there aren't many big agritech players in Cambridge. There's some activity from Bayer and Monsanto, but Cambridge is no longer a hub for agritech as it was in the past, but it may well be again in the future.

One possible example of a future direction for agritech is **KisanHub**. Based at NIAB and in India, and supported by funding from the Cambridge Judge Business School and others, KisanHub is developing software that aggregates multiple data sources – such as weather patterns, pest populations and soil conditions – for farmers and agronomists. Highlighted by the *Financial Times* as an innovation to watch, the aim of KisanHub (*kisan* meaning 'farmer' in Hindi) is to provide better and more easily understood data to help farmers improve their crop management practices, including spraying, irrigation and harvesting. Already revenue generating and going into 2,000 UK farms, the technology is tested on the experimental farm at NIAB.

AUDIO

Hi-fi aficionados will recognize names such as Arcam, Meridian, Mission and Quad, all companies that grew up in and around Cambridge in the heyday of high fidelity. Mission and Quad are now part of the Chinese IAG Group, and while Quad maintains a research and development facility in Cambridge, manufacturing is carried out in China. Two that are still going strong and manufacturing in Cambridge are Arcam and Meridian Audio.

Arcam started life in 1976 as Amplification and Recording Cambridge, and has grown into a hi-fi and home cinema audio company that has won many awards. Three Arcam products were singled out at the *What Hi-Fi?* Sound & Vision Awards 2014, the 'Oscars' of the hi-fi and audio visual industry. The Arcam FMJ A19 won amplifier of the year in its price range for the second year running, and the company's miniBlink Bluetooth digital music converter took the top award of Product of the Year in the accessories category. In 2015, the miniBlink won again, being named best Bluetooth receiver.

Arcam's Alpha 10 was the first domestic DAB tuner, and the company also launched the first add-on digital to analogue converter, or DAC, for consumers. The launch of the iconic rCube iPod dock in 2010 has been expanded into a range including a personal audio converter and a digital dock for iPads and iPhones.

In 2015, Ketan Bharadia of *What Hi-Fi?* magazine compared the classic Arcam A60 from 1976 with Arcam's latest FMJ A19 and, although acknowledging that the technology had come a long way in 40 years, gave a nod

> "
> *This level of sound quality doesn't come easily to products like this, which makes the miniBlink's abilities all the more special.*

Joe Cox, Digital Editor, *What Hi-Fi?* magazine April 2014.

Above: *The Arcam MiniBlink.*

Below: *Ray Dolby studied for his PhD in Cambridge and left a legacy of £35 million to his college, Pembroke, in recognition of the crucial role Pembroke, and Cambridge University, played in his life.*

Above: *Co-founders of Meridian Audio, Allen Boothroyd (left) and Bob Stuart.*

to the A60 being at the top of the game for its time, since 'we found ourselves returning to the older amp time and time again. There's just something addictive about its expressive, entertaining delivery.'

Meridian Audio was founded by Bob Stuart and Allen Boothroyd in 1977. Having won getting on for 200 awards over the course of its history, Meridian has played a unique role in the continual development of better audio technology.

In almost 40 years of attending audio press events, only rarely have I come away feeling that I was present at the birth of a new world.... in early December [2014], at Meridian's New York offices, I heard Bob Stuart describe the UK company's MQA technology, followed by a demonstration that blew my socks off.

John Atkinson, Editor, *Stereophile* magazine

The Lecson amplifier, designed by Boothroyd and Stuart in the early 1970s, has the distinction of being included in the permanent collections of the Museum of Modern Art in New York and the Victoria & Albert Museum in London. In 2012, the Lecson was included in an exhibition of the best of British design to mark the Golden Jubilee of Queen Elizabeth II and the London Olympics, alongside other iconic designs such as the Mini and Concorde.

Meridian produced the world's first audiophile quality compact disc player in the 1980s, and the world's first digital surround processor in the same decade. More recently, Meridian Lossless Packing, the proprietary system developed by Meridian for compressing audio data, has become the standard for DVD-Audio. It is also part of Dolby TrueHD, the standard for Blu-ray and HD DVD, which Meridian developed with Dolby Laboratories.

Meridian products appear regularly in movies, associated with characters being portrayed as rich and sophisticated, from Tony Stark in *The Avengers* to the Cullen family of vampires in the *Twilight* saga.

Years of development have also led to Meridian loudspeaker systems being launched in several luxury automobile brands. The Range Rover Evoque had the Meridian Signature Reference System installed, the world's first in-car 3D surround sound, when it was unveiled at the 2010 Paris Motor Show. Jaguar and McLaren Automotive also offer Meridian sound systems in their vehicles.

Over the last few years, Meridian has opened boutiques in Thailand, China, India, the US, Kuwait, Mexico, Korea and elsewhere around the world, and along with an extensive network of dealers and partners, these promote growing worldwide sales.

1Ltd (now Cambridge Mechatronics) developed the first digital sound projector, or sound bar, to create virtual surround sound from a single speaker. Launched in Pioneer systems in 2003, the technology was also licensed for flat screen TVs from major brands such as Mitsubishi and Loewe, with the IP eventually being acquired by Yamaha in 2013.

More recently, Cambridge companies working with sound have branched out from delivering the best sound systems possible. CEDAR's post-production audio technology is so well-respected in the film industry that the company has won a 'Sci-Tech Oscar' from the Academy of Motion Picture Arts and Sciences, and Bob & Barn's music and sounds for video games, film and TV has received a BAFTA nomination. Audio Analytic offers software that detects and analyses multiple types of sound for security and domestic warning applications.

CONSUMER

A G7th capo.

"

Hard to say anything other than in its second generation, the [G7th] Performance is probably the best capo there is.

Music Radar

Direct-to-consumer businesses are rather unusual in the Cambridge Phenomenon, as the vast majority of Cambridge start-ups develop technologies that sit inside products with more familiar brand names on the outside. Some point to the first pocket calculators from Sinclair Research as heralding the new era of handheld devices, and it is not disputed that Acorn and Sinclair kick-started the UK's home computer sector, but Cambridge rarely throws up a direct consumer play.

There are, however, a few exceptions.

G7th Ltd was founded by Nick Campling, one of the co-founders of technology consultancy 42 Technology, to develop his innovative guitar capo. The G7th is used by internationally renowned names from the music industry such as Eric Clapton, Richard Thompson, KT Tunstall, Marcus Mumford and Bryan Adams. The company has won a Queen's Award for Enterprise and its capos have won multiple industry awards.

The Cambridge Satchel Company was famously founded at Julie Deane's kitchen table with the help of her mother Freda Thomas and a budget of £600. Within three years, they were selling 3,000 satchels a week, had opened their own factory in Leicester and their products had featured on US TV show *Gossip Girl*. The Cambridge Satchel Company was also one of those chosen to be filmed for a series of Google Chrome TV adverts, and the episode has been viewed millions of times on YouTube.

Julie Deane, founder of the Cambridge Satchel Company.

Hotel Chocolat founders Peter Harris and Angus Thirlwell.

The Cambridge Satchel Company opened its first store in London's Covent Garden in 2013 and moved to larger manufacturing premises. In the same year, the company won a Queen's Award for International Trade, with their satchels now sold in 86 countries, including in China via the country's biggest online trading site, Tmall. Sales have been boosted by the satchels' popularity with celebrities such as Taylor Swift, Sophie Ellis-Bextor and Alexa Chung, and the company has also collaborated on new ranges with major designers such as Rei Kawakubo (founder of fashion label Comme des Garçons) and Vivienne Westwood.

Hotel Chocolat is the only British brand to rank in the UK's top ten 'most advocated' brands – those most likely to be recommended by customers to their friends – according to analysts Bain. They share the accolade with international brands like Rolex, Apple and Mercedes, remarkable for a company with around 1,000 employees and a turnover of approximately £80 million.

Peter Harris and Angus Thirlwell, co-founders of Hotel Chocolat, were among the early Cambridge computer entrepreneurs, but switched to mint and then chocolate in the late 1980s. The Hotel Chocolat brand was born in 2003, after a customer, a hotel company, had requested a branded, miniature box of four chocolates.

All products are made at the company's Huntingdon facility, a few miles from Cambridge. The first manufacturing line cost £750,000, and paid for itself in nine months, and the company has now invested a total of over £7 million in chocolate-making, to good effect.

> *Making our own chocolate is an important part of our strategy. We know from our shops what is selling well, and can adjust quickly to ramp up production. If we imported our chocolates, we wouldn't be nearly as responsive to demand.*
>
> Peter Harris

Hotel Chocolat sells its products – which now include a cocoa-based line of beauty products, Cocoa Juvenate – online and through around 85 branded shops in the UK, Europe, and the US. Hotel Chocolat products are also distributed through various partner retailers in the UK and David Jones stores in Australia. Shop turnover has risen from around £400,000 to £16 million in three years.

Many companies claim that they listen to customers, but Hotel Chocolat has taken that strategy further than most. It is Hotel Chocolat customers, and most notably members of the company's 100,000-strong Chocolate Tasting Club, that have been behind the purchase and renovation of the Rabot Estate sugar plantation in St Lucia and a highly successful and innovative exercise in crowdfunding.

> *We started the Chocolate Tasting Club in 1998 and it has always been a fundamental part of our growth – not just because it helps even out cash flow in the quieter months, but also because it's a great way of engaging with our customers.*
>
> Peter Harris

> **"**
>
> *Our original chocolate brand, Chocolate Express, spoke about speed; the new brand, Hotel Chocolat, demonstrated our commitment to quality.*
>
> **Peter Harris, co-founder, Hotel Chocolat**

A member of the Tasting Club sent Angus Thirlwell a book, a 1920 edition of *Cocoa and Chocolate: Their History from Plantation to Consumer*, and the idea to take the company back to its roots and grow its own cocoa was born. A search in the West Indies led Thirlwell and Harris to St Lucia and the Rabot Estate, the oldest cocoa plantation on the island, which they purchased in 2006. Since the company was privately owned, the two co-founders could take this perhaps risky step without having to obtain permission from shareholders or investors. But as they worked to restore the plantation and set up the Engaged Ethics Cocoa Programme on the island to promote production elsewhere on St Lucia, it became clear that more investment would be needed to realize their dream of sharing the Rabot Estate with customers.

Hence the innovative 'Chocolate Bond', which was offered to members of the Tasting Club and private investors in 2010. The bond raised over £4 million to fund a three-year expansion plan, including the development of a boutique hotel and restaurant, Boucan, and a spa, Cocoa Juvenate, at the Rabot Estate. Investors receive no cash interest payments – instead, their investment returns are 'paid' in chocolate.

Fuelled by a second successful chocolate bond offering, Hotel Chocolat continues to expand its hospitality offering into cafes and restaurants around the UK and overseas, with the newest cafe opening in Hotel Chocolat's Cambridge home in 2015.

MODELS, MONEY, MAGNETISM AND MENTORS

There's a well-known saying, 'it takes a village to raise a child', and in Cambridge, you could say 'it takes a cluster to raise a company'. The impact of the Cambridge Phenomenon is therefore not only about the companies themselves, it is about everything else around them – the examples of innovative business models, sophisticated funding, the buzz of being where the innovation is happening, and access to inspirational and successful entrepreneurs.

Fauna & Flora International: sustainable harvesting of fynbos in Flower Valley, South Africa.

Left: *As part of the April 2016 opening of the building named in his honour, David Attenborough abseiled down the building's 13-metre-high living wall. The David Attenborough Building houses the Cambridge Conservation Initiative's conservation campus, which provides a collaborative working environment for over 500 biodiversity conservation practitioners and researchers from the Initiative's 10 partner organizations.*

The Cambridge Phenomenon benefits enormously from what can only be described as a thriving entrepreneurial ecosystem. No entrepreneur setting up in Cambridge is short of examples of how to start and grow a business, in myriad formats and ways – from garden shed to global HQ, and from bootstrapping to the London Stock Exchange. And no entrepreneur setting up in Cambridge is more than two phone calls away from advice and help.

MANY MODELS

We've already seen numerous examples of different, and successful, business models in the Cambridge Phenomenon. ARM grew on the back of licensing revenues and royalties, RealVNC took to merchandising to help fund its early growth, the technology consultancies grew by taking an entirely new approach to supporting industry, and other companies used IPOs to get to the next level.

But the Cambridge Phenomenon is nothing if not generous, and many of its companies play active roles in supporting social causes locally and globally. The impact of ARM's work

with UNICEF and other projects is described elsewhere in this book (see page 74), and the Raspberry Pi Foundation was set up to drive a step change in computer science education supported by sales of the Raspberry Pi computer. Many other companies are involved in making a difference in a variety of ways, but Cambridge is also home to not only the world's oldest conservation organization, Fauna & Flora International, but also one of the world's most innovative education charities, Camfed, which has been entrepreneurial from the start.

FAUNA & FLORA INTERNATIONAL IS THE WORLD'S OLDEST CONSERVATION ORGANIZATION

Headquartered in Cambridge, Fauna & Flora International (FFI) is one of the world's leading wildlife conservation charities with a work programme now comprising more than 100 projects in over 40 countries. Its global reach extends into some of the most remote and threatened ecosystems on the planet, including conflict and disaster zones where many counterparts fear to tread.

the leading lights in the organisation were closely involved in setting up the International Union for Conservation of Nature (IUCN) and, later, the World Wide Fund for Nature (WWF). The Red Data Books, a comprehensive register of the status and distribution of all endangered species (and the precursor of the IUCN Red List), were the brainchild of the Society's then chairman, Peter Scott, and provided the framework for the Convention on International Trade in Endangered Species of Wild Fauna and Flora (CITES).

The innovative approach that characterises FFI today has been evident throughout the organisation's history. Operation Oryx, launched in 1962, was an ambitious plan to rescue the Arabian oryx from extinction by capturing some of the last surviving individuals and setting up a captive breeding programme. It culminated, almost 20 years later, in the first successful reintroduction of a species into the wild.

In 1979 the world's largest great ape was on the brink of extinction due to a combination of poaching and habitat destruction. Following a direct appeal from David Attenborough, FFI set up the Mountain Gorilla Project. Known today as the International Gorilla Conservation Programme, it is a renowned example of a partnership that transcends political boundaries. Since mountain gorillas do not recognise international borders, it is vital to coordinate conservation efforts across the Democratic Republic of Congo, Rwanda and Uganda. FFI and its partners have played a central role in creating one of the world's most successful transboundary conservation initiatives, and in securing a groundbreaking

FFI began life in 1903 as the Society for the Preservation of the Wild Fauna of the Empire, which was set up by a prescient group of big game hunters who realised that wildlife populations in Sudan and elsewhere in Africa were in need of greater protection. FFI's pioneering founders paved the way for much of today's sophisticated global conservation network.

The Society played a pivotal role in the so-called London Convention of 1933, which provided a blueprint for future wildlife conservation agreements throughout the world. FFI was also instrumental in the establishment of Africa's first national parks, including Kruger and Serengeti, while some of

Above: *Following a direct appeal from David Attenborough, FFI set up the International Gorilla Conservation Programme.*

Right: *The toad* Bufo valliceps, *photographed near Calera camp in Bladen Nature Reserve.*

tripartite agreement between the three countries. Success also hinges on helping the impoverished local communities who live cheek by jowl with the mountain gorillas to find sustainable alternatives to forest exploitation, hence the development of enterprise linked to tourism. As a result of these efforts, mountain gorilla numbers have virtually doubled since the programme began, with a current population estimated at 880 individuals.

Nurturing local talent to help communities become effective custodians of their own natural heritage is a central tenet of FFI's approach. The 6,000-hectare Golden Stream Corridor Preserve in Belize harbours a rich diversity of wildlife, including all five wild cat species native to Central America, and forms a vital ecological link between the Maya Mountains and the mangrove forests and coral reefs of Belize's southern coast. Golden Stream is owned and managed by FFI's local partner, Ya'axché Conservation Trust. Ya'axché began as a handful of local enthusiasts, but with FFI support has blossomed into a nationally recognised leader in conservation and sustainable development. The one-time head of Ya'axché, Lisel Alamilla – who cut her teeth as country director of FFI's Belize programme – went on to serve as Minister of Fisheries, Forestry and Sustainable Development from 2012 to 2015, putting nature conservation at the heart of the country's development plans.

The Golden Stream is one of the many species-rich ecosystems that FFI has safeguarded through its Halcyon Land & Sea fund. Established in 1998 thanks to the vision and generosity of Lisbet Rausing, this was originally conceived as a land purchase mechanism. With support from additional benefactors, it has evolved into a broader tool for securing the long-term protection of critical habitat across the globe. Since its launch, Halcyon has leveraged an additional $120 million in funding from other sources, secured over 9.5 million hectares of vital habitat, and contributed directly to the conservation of over 55.7 million hectares, an area almost as large as Kenya. In 2011, a substantial new grant from Arcadia enabled FFI to intensify its focus on marine conservation.

At a time when it was fashionable for conservation organizations to view big business as the 'enemy', FFI took the bold step of actively engaging with leading companies in the very industries (mining, extractive, oil & gas) perceived to have potentially the most detrimental impact on biodiversity. In 1999, FFI organized the first international business and biodiversity conference, at London's Chatham House, and went on to establish partnerships with a select group of global companies programme, working with them to strengthen their business practices in relation to biodiversity and to develop the concepts of 'no net loss' and 'net positive impact'. In 2007, an Environmental Markets programme was added to harness the potential of commercial markets to protect threatened habitats and provide tangible benefits to the local communities who depend on them.

FFI's partnerships with the business sector take many forms. A groundbreaking collaboration with ARM that began in 2013 resulted in FFI and its United for Wildlife partners joining forces with Google.org in 2015 to launch WILDLABS. NET. This new online platform enables conservationists and technologists to share ideas, information and resources to tackle the illegal wildlife trade and other pressing environmental challenges. Such collaborations hold the key to developing new solutions to biodiversity loss.

FFI was a driving force in the establishment of the Cambridge Conservation Initiative. This visionary partnership between the University of Cambridge and a cluster of leading biodiversity conservation organizations is now based at the intellectual heart of the city, on a new campus named in honour of FFI's vice-president, David Attenborough, and is expected to be home to innovative collaborations that will change the future of conservation.

FFI has worked with Ya'axché Conservation Trust since 1998; since that time it has become a recognized leader in conservation and sustainable development.

Camfed founder Ann Cotton in Tanzania.

to support more girls. There are now over 5,270 partner school communities working with Camfed in five countries. Camfed has increased its own support from cake enthusiasts to governments, NGOs, charitable foundations, trusts and corporate donors as well as individual donations, and is recognized globally.

Camfed's education and associated social assistance programs succeed because Camfed gives communities the power and responsibility to run the programs. It is this opportunity which enables communities to become capable, over the long term, of better supporting their children and themselves, through the practice of good governance.

Accounting to the Girl, Report on the governance of Camfed, Linklaters, 2010

CAMFED GOES FROM CAKES IN KITCHENS TO THE UNITED NATIONS

The education of over one million girls in the sub-Saharan countries of Ghana, Malawi, Tanzania, Zambia and Zimbabwe has been supported directly by Cambridge charitable organization Camfed, and a further 3.5 million children have benefited from the knock-on effects of an improved environment for education in their communities.

But Camfed is no ordinary charity helping to fund education – it works on a unique model that drives systemic change in poor rural communities, where the biggest barrier to a girl's education is not culture but poverty. In a world that knows that educating girls is the biggest indicator of better outcomes in health, gender equality, community improvement and many other factors, Camfed is showing how an innovative, data-driven model can make a difference.

Twice the *Financial Times'* seasonal appeal charity, Camfed was started by Ann Cotton following a trip to Zimbabwe in 1991 to determine the factors behind the low enrolment of girls in school. While many Cambridge businesses start in spare bedrooms and garden sheds, Cotton's enterprise started in kitchens, as cake sales raised funds to send the first group of 32 girls to school.

Camfed was formally launched in 1993, and, with the model proving successful as the first girls completed their education, fundraising gradually expanded to enable Camfed

With the help of partner organizations such as the The MasterCard Foundation and Salesforce Foundation, Camfed is able to demonstrate the power of data in innovating not only in targeted funding support, but also in education in general. Typically, organizations in the charitable sector measure their progress in increasing income, but Camfed measures its own progress on the impact of what it does: the numbers of girls, schools and communities supported, and the clear evidence of development.

Near-real-time data is obtained via handheld devices operated by trained staff who track school attendance and associated factors such as exam results to ensure that Camfed's support is effective. And that data is returned to the communities to promote engagement and help the community to identify ways to improve the programme for their particular situation.

Camfed's alumnae association, CAMA, is unique in the world. Its membership of over 33,000 women who have completed their education thanks to the support of Camfed is the largest network of its kind in Africa, and is behind a number of further initiatives that grow the women's home communities. Many have gone on to further education and the professions, and many return to their communities as teachers or entrepreneurs, setting up businesses that help drive economic improvement.

The maturity of the programme means that some Camfed alumnae have now reached global platforms and received international awards.

Former Camfed student Abigail Kaindu was one of ten young people from around the world selected to join the UN's Youth Advocacy Group and advise UN Secretary General Ban Ki-moon on his Global Education First Initiative.

Another CAMA member, Ruka Yaro De-Liman from Ghana, was selected as one of 500 Mandela Washington Fellows from 50,000 applicants, and was one of only 36 to receive an award at the Washington Fellowship for Young African Leaders' Summit in 2014. Yaro De-Liman was awarded $25,000 in recognition of her entrepreneurship and leadership, and originally started her business with a Camfed Innovation Bursary as part of a project with The MasterCard Foundation.

After completing her education, Penelope Machipi has gone on to help set up and run the Samfya Resource Centre, which provides internet access and ICT services in her home community in northern Zambia. Machipi received a Goldman Sachs-Fortune Global Women Leaders Award in 2009.

Camfed has been recognized by the OECD as a model of best practice in taking innovation to scale, and founder Ann Cotton has been recognized internationally, most recently receiving the WISE (World Innovation Summit for Education) Prize.

Penelope Machipi received a Goldman Sachs-Fortune Global Women Leaders Award in 2009.

Ruka Yaro De-Liman, Mandela Washington Fellow, started her business with a Camfed Innovation Bursary.

> **"**
> *Just imagine one million girls in Africa, all of whom are from a background of rural poverty; all of whom understand the anxiety and the frustrations of poverty. Just imagine them working in the education and health systems, in politics, in journalism, in law, in engineering, in science – just imagine the power of what they can do to transform our world.*

Ann Cotton, accepting the 2014 WISE Prize

"

Cambridge has a secret weapon to see its high-tech and scientific businesses through times of economic hardship: the 'super-angel'.

Financial Times, 4 November 2012

Hermann Hauser, founder of Acorn Computers.

Victor Christou, Chief Executive of Cambridge Innovation Capital.

GROWING FUNDING TO GROW IMPACT

New companies need money. As the Cambridge Phenomenon has grown, so too has the funding ecosystem in and around Cambridge to support that growth, and the impact of many of the Cambridge Phenomenon companies is due at least in part to the availability of funds, and in many cases the advice that comes along with those funds. But the vibrant, and international, funding ecosystem that supports Cambridge today had to evolve against a background of disbelief, bursting bubbles and changing investment trends.

In the early days, it was the vision of Matthew Bullock and Walter Herriot at Barclays Bank in Cambridge that kept the novel young technology companies going in the face of uncertainty over the prospects of the innovations they were pursuing. One of the most notable of these was Acorn Computers, which Barclays 'rescued' when the company urgently needed a large loan to fulfil higher than expected orders for the BBC Micro.

As successes mounted, some of Cambridge's entrepreneurs began to support the companies that came after them. The **Cambridge Angels**, sometimes described as a dining club with an investment problem, at other times as an investment club with a dining problem, marry technical knowhow with business acumen. Members have all been involved in successful companies, and many invest the proceeds of their previous successes into the start-ups that survive the rigorous Cambridge Angel investment selection procedure. Around a quarter of the Cambridge Angels are not based in Cambridge and some pitching sessions are held in London to extend the reach and remit of the group's investments, but the focus is always on excellence.

> *Whilst we consider the financial performance of our portfolio to be an important measure of our success as Angel investors, we also invest because we want to give good people with good ideas the chance to create successful new businesses.*
>
> Cambridge Angels website

Although the Cambridge Angels typically provide seed funding of between £50,000 and £1 million, some investments have accumulated higher totals over several funding rounds. Established in 2001, to date the Cambridge Angels have invested some £20 million in total in around 50 companies. Exits have included Bango, listed on AIM; AlertMe.com, sold to British Gas; Neul, acquired by Huawei; and Ubisense, also listed on AIM. The current portfolio of around 47 companies represents multiple sectors, including Phico Therapeutics and Eagle Genomics in life sciences, CRFS in telecoms, PsychologyOnline in healthcare, Undo Software in computing and even the art market, with online art sales portal Artfinder.

Amadeus Capital Partners was co-founded in 1997 by successful Cambridge entrepreneur Hermann Hauser, founder of Acorn Computers, Cambridge Network Ltd and Virata, among others; Anne Glover, a technology entrepreneur and former venture capital investor with Apax Partners; and Peter Wynn. The intention was to plug the funding gap between early start-up investments in the tens of thousands and Series A funding in the millions.

In 2000, the Amadeus III fund, which had closed above target at over $310 million, was one of the largest venture funds raised in Europe at the time, and included 70 investors from outside the UK. Amadeus was reported to have over £470 million under management in 2011, and in 2014, the first close for its Amadeus IV Digital Prosperity Fund came in at $76.5 million.

In 18 years, Amadeus has invested in more than 90 start-up companies, and its 30 exits have included lastminute.com, CSR, Solexa and Velocix. Amadeus first invested in CSR when it was spun out of Cambridge Consultants, and participated in follow-on rounds until the company listed on the LSE in 2004 with a valuation of £240 million. Amadeus sold its last shares in the company in 2005, by which time CSR had already joined the FTSE 250.

Amadeus expands the impact of Cambridge investing beyond the UK, and has a number of overseas companies in its current portfolio, including companies in Brazil, Italy and Israel. Amadeus itself has offices in Cambridge and London in the UK, San Francisco in the US and Stockholm in Sweden.

A relatively new arrival, **Cambridge Innovation Capital** (CIC) launched in 2013 with an initial fund of £50 million, which it is using to support technology companies that demonstrate potential for high growth. With Cambridge supplying its own seed and follow-on funding, the attention is now turning to longer term investments that seek to grow companies rather than find the best exit after a relatively short period of time, and CIC intends to help companies grow through the so-called 'valley of death', where companies often fail due to lack of sufficient funding.

Supported locally by the University of Cambridge Endowment Fund and ARM Holdings, and with Invesco Perpetual and Lansdowne Partners as lead investors, the aim for CIC is to provide long-term and follow-on funding to its portfolio. CIC has a team of directors and advisors that have more than 300 years of experience in technology entrepreneurship between them.

The first three investments for CIC were Cambridge Imaging Systems (now Imagen), Jukedeck, and Origami Energy. Jukedeck, one of *Wired* magazine's '100 Hottest European Startups', uses artificial intelligence to compose music. The company has since gone on to raise another £2 million in a follow-on round and launched its first product, Jukedeck MAKE, in December 2015 at TechCrunch Disrupt London. At the same event, Jukedeck also won the £30,000 Startup Battlefield award, knocking the opposition for six with a one-minute rap that perfectly summed up their proposition – original, royalty-free music for videos 'written' by computer.

CIC's portfolio now also includes Abcodia, Audio Analytics, Congenica, GeoSpock, Iceni Therapeutics, Inivata, Morphogen-IX, PragmatIC Printing and Undo Software. Following the initial CIS seed investment, Congenica went on to receive a £2 million Genomics England SBIR Phase II grant, and completed a £2.2 million Series A round.

MAGNIFYING IMPACT THROUGH THE POWER OF ATTRACTION

When asked why he robbed banks, famous criminal Willie Sutton reportedly replied, 'because that's where the money is'. Given the numbers of international companies, foundations, funders and institutions that have been attracted to Cambridge, their response to a similar question might be, 'because that's where the innovation is'.

Below: Jukedeck won the £30,000 Startup Battlefield award at TechCrunch Disrupt London in 2015.

Above: *The offices of Microsoft Research Cambridge.*

AstraZeneca, Broadcom, Huawei, Illumina, Mundipharma, Qualcomm and Schlumberger are just a few of the global companies that have bought into, invested into or simply moved into Cambridge – the list is long and getting ever longer. The most recent new arrival is rumoured to be Apple, which has reportedly acquired speech recognition start-up VocalIQ. In addition to acquisitions and relocations, many other international organizations have partnerships with Cambridge companies.

The important thing for Cambridge is that many of the international corporations that acquire Cambridge companies maintain, and often grow, operations in the city. Alcatel-Lucent's acquisition of Velocix resulted in a tripling of head-count and the co-location of a Bell Labs dedicated research facility in Cambridge, and MedImmune has gone from strength to strength on Granta Park.

Other organizations also choose Cambridge as the location for their research base. Microsoft Research set up its first operation outside the US in Cambridge in 1997, and in 2013 moved to purpose-built facilities near the railway station, to take advantage of fast train travel to London. Olivetti, AT&T, Philips and many more have had or continue to have a presence in Cambridge.

With all this activity, Cambridge also attracts funders from outside Cambridge who want a piece of the action. Numerous UK funds have invested in Cambridge companies, and they have been joined by Silicon Valley and European venture capital funds such as Index Ventures, Oak Investment Partners, Sequoia Capital, Silver Lake. Imperial Innovations having already invested in several Cambridge businesses, established an office on the Babraham Research Campus and relocated one of its portfolio companies, Abzena, to the Campus. *MISSION* Therapeutics and Crescendo Biologics, two other Imperial Innovations investees, are also on the Babraham Campus.

"

It's another great example of computer giants looking to Cambridge for solutions.

Andy Harter, CEO of RealVNC, on the company's relationship with Google, reported in the *Cambridge News*

THE ROLE OF THE UNIVERSITY

Cambridge University contributes to the impact of the Cambridge Phenomenon in many ways, not least because, as one of the top five universities in the world, it attracts the brightest students and academics.

This cohort of people in turn attracts funding that promotes and expands research. Recent major donations have included £8 million from the James Dyson Foundation to fund new state-of-the-art laboratories and the Dyson Engineering Design Centre in the University's Engineering Department. The Sainsbury Laboratory Cambridge University is funded by the Gatsby Charitable Foundation to undertake research into plant growth to contribute to food security and the sustainability of plants as natural resources. The Bill & Melinda Gates Foundation set up a $210 million endowment trust in 2000 to fund one of the largest university scholarship programmes in the world, the Gates Cambridge Scholars, and also provided half the costs of the William Gates Building, which houses the Computer Science Department of the University.

It used to be said that the University's greatest contribution to technology transfer was its graduates, but there are two particular strands of activity that have grown steadily over the years and now form a significant part of the University's

> "
> *More than 80% of Cambridge Enterprise's income comes from intellectual property that is at least ten years old. It's a luxury for us to be able to take a long-term view on our investments, and better for the companies, too.*

Tony Raven, CEO, Cambridge Enterprise

Above: *Following a Cambridge tradition, Tom Dyson pours a bottle of locally brewed beer in a 'topping out' ceremony for the James Dyson Building (right) at the University of Cambridge, November 2015.*

Left: *Breathing Buildings, a spin-out from the Cambridge University BP Institute, was one of Bloomberg New Energy Finance's ten New Energy Pioneers in 2014, selected from entries from all around the world. Breathing Building's natural ventilation technology can reduce the energy consumption of buildings by up to 50%. Shown is the Mushroom r-Series.*

Right: *Tony Raven, CEO, Cambridge Enterprise.*

role in growing the technology cluster. These are Cambridge Enterprise and the Cambridge Judge Business School.

Cambridge Enterprise was named the University Venturing Unit of the Year in 2013 by Global University Venturing. Since 1995 it has invested in and supported over 100 companies, which have themselves gone on to raise over £1.2 billion in funding.

Cambridge Enterprise also helps University academics to license their innovations where a spin-out is not deemed appropriate or desirable, and develops consultancy services with academics to tackle challenges that require their particular expertise, an activity that saw a 9% increase in 2013–14 over 2012–13. In 2014, 130 licences were signed, and operating income for Cambridge Enterprise from licensing and consultancy was £10.7 million.

Cambridge Enterprise evolved from the Wolfson Cambridge Industrial Unit, which was set up in the 1970s to promote links between industry and the University's Engineering Department. It underwent several restructurings until Cambridge Enterprise was separated from the University administration structure as a wholly owned subsidiary in 2006. Cambridge Enterprise operates on behalf of, and returns profits to, the University.

The emphasis for Cambridge Enterprise is to have an impact by benefiting society rather than necessarily making money, although its investments since 1995 have returned a multiple of 2.4. One early investment was Solexa, which achieved a successful return when it was acquired by Illumina for $600 million, but the impact of the technology – faster and more accurate gene sequencing – has been felt around the world, in the Human Genome Project and the steady advance of personalized medicine. Another Cambridge Enterprise portfolio company, BlueGnome, was also acquired by Illumina.

Consultancy services similarly may have a much larger societal than financial impact. For instance, a Cambridge academic was called on to advise when the Hammersmith flyover in London was closed in late 2011 due to structural problems. Just seven months before London was due to host the 2012 Olympics, and with the Hammersmith flyover being on a key route into London from Heathrow Airport, getting it repaired and opened again was a matter of extreme urgency, with the potential for severe economic repercussions being extremely high. It is not just the sciences that are represented in such contracts. The University's Law Department, for instance, has a consultancy arrangement with Trinidad and Tobago focusing on effective policing to tackle very high crime rates, and the Divinity Department provides advice on radicalization among youths.

Cambridge Enterprise also has an International Outreach Programme which helps universities around the world to improve knowledge transfer activities and increase the commercialization of their research. Projects have been undertaken in numerous countries, including Brazil, Chile, Kazakhstan, Mexico, Thailand and Saudi Arabia.

Cambridge Judge Business School, CJBS, has evolved in many ways since its establishment in 1990, especially in the teaching and nurturing of entrepreneurship. While it continues to provide the level of business education that keeps it ranked among the top business schools in the world, its programmes for entrepreneurs are beginning to show impressive results.

The CJBS Entrepreneurship Centre now incorporates the Centre for Entrepreneurial Learning, Accelerate Cambridge, the SME Growth Club, Ignite, and other programmes tailored to particular groups of entrepreneurs, such as students (ETECH Projects) and women in science and technology (EnterpriseWISE). CJBS is also a partner in delivering the new online course for entrepreneurs, Digital Business Academy, which it developed with University College London, Founder Centric and Tech City UK. Over 14,000 people had signed up to the Digital Business Academy within six months of its launch in late 2014.

The Centre for Entrepreneurial Learning, CfEL, was launched ten years ago and has itself been entrepreneurial in developing courses and programmes for entrepreneurs at the early stages of the business journey. With the recently launched SME Growth Club, it is now offering skills development for SMEs (small and medium-sized enterprises), where managerial capability might be the main barrier to growth.

Accelerate Cambridge is an incubator programme for early stage ventures, and to date has helped more than 80 ventures which have between them raised over £10 million in start-up funding and have a reported combined value of more than £150 million. Ignite is an intensive week-long summer school for entrepreneurs that has now been run for 16 years and has had around 750 participants from 26 countries. Around 170 businesses have been created on the back of the Ignite programme. A 2013 survey of alumni from the Ignite programme found that ventures created by Ignite participants between 2011 and 2013 had raised more than £120 million between them and created around 2,500 jobs.

Collaborative blogging site Niume took advantage of two of the programmes at the Entrepreneurship Centre to help grow its novel blogging platform quickly.

Niume was launched in July 2014, and the co-founders Francesco Facca and Daniel Gennaoui both enrolled on the Postgraduate Diploma in Entrepreneurship in September of that year. They also entered Niume for the Accelerate Cambridge programme, and were successful in getting accepted.

The team then launched a fundraising round on SyndicateRoom, itself set up by two Cambridge Judge MBAs, Gonçalo de Vasconselos and Tom Britton, and reached their £100,000 target in less than a week. They eventually went on to raise £170,000.

Niume is a social network driven by users' interests, rather than their relationships, and consists of a number of themed communities. By August 2015, just over a year after launching, the site had half a million users, and, with a growth rate of 20% per month, the founders were expecting to reach one million users by the end of 2015. With the BBC and Lonely Planet having already shared content from Niume, the site is attracting the kind of interest that will help it grow.

A slightly different route was taken by SimPrints, a company that has developed a fingerprint scanner that is being introduced in Bangladesh to access patient records. The

Above: The Cambridge Judge Business School.

Below: *SimPrints has developed a fingerprint scanner (right) that is being introduced to access patient records.*

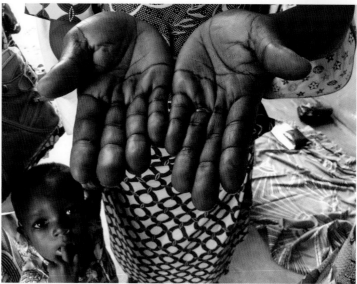

Right: *Hanadi Jabado, Accelerate Cambridge.*

founders of SimPrints first went through the ETECH Project while they were still undergraduates at the University, and then moved into the Accelerate Cambridge programme.

In August 2014, SimPrints won a $250,000 grant from the Saving Lives at Birth Grand Challenge, funded by the Bill & Melinda Gates Foundation, and this award unlocked $180,000 in funding from Cambridge company ARM Holdings. The company has also received additional funding from USAID, UKAID, the Norwegian Ministry of Foreign Affairs and Grand Challenges Canada.

In 2015, SimPrints was awarded £250,000 by the UK Government's Department for International Development (DFID) to initiate a project in Bangladesh that will cover around 22,000 expectant mothers and their babies in an area where births are often not registered and matching patients with their health records is extremely challenging. Using SimPrints' low-cost and easy-to-use fingerprint scanners, community health workers will be able to track their patients' health and make sure that infants and children receive all the vaccinations they need.

POD Point was founded in 2009 by Peter Hiscocks, a Senior Faculty Member of CJBS, and Erik Fairbairn, an alumnus of Ignite.

The company supplies charging points for electric cars, expected sales of £6.5 million in 2015, and employs 50 people. POD Point has seen average growth of 46% between 2012 and 2015, which puts it into *The Sunday Times* Tech Track 100 in 2015, a ranking of the fastest growing private technology companies in the UK.

POD Point raised £1.5 million through crowdfunding in 2014, believed to be the second largest fundraising for a private company in the UK at the time. In 2015, the company launched a second crowdfunding campaign, through Crowdcube, seeking to raise a further £1.5 million in equity funding to continue growing the main business of supplying charging points to individuals and companies, and £250,000 in bond funding to expand its network of public Open Charge points. Both targets were exceeded well before the investment deadline.

While some might quibble that entrepreneurs are born and not made, the variety of programmes provided by the CJBS Entrepreneurship Centre, and the successes that have come out of them, suggest that even natural entrepreneurs benefit from opportunities to learn new skills and refine their ideas.

The **Cambridge University Entrepreneurs**, better known locally as CUE, has been promoting entrepreneurship and running business creation competitions since 1999. In that time, more than 40 start-up companies have won over £500,000 to help them build their businesses, and companies that have emerged from CUE have gone on to secure over £100 million in investment. Microsensor experts Owlstone Nanotech and recycling technology company Enval are just two CUE alumni companies that continue to grow, while another CUE winner, Rapportive, was acquired by LinkedIn in 2012.

THE INTANGIBLE IMPACT OF NETWORKING

Any discussion of the entrepreneurial ecosystem in Cambridge has to acknowledge the role that networking has played in the overall impact of the technology cluster, even though it is a factor that is very hard to quantify.

Networking is of course a well-known aspect of modern business life, but Cambridge has been perfecting its networking ecosystem for hundreds of years. Students and academics at the University are constantly meeting within their colleges, where they are exposed to many different disciplines, and in their subject Faculties and Departments, where they meet those with the same interests. The combination of a multidisciplinary environment and one where there is a distinct focus enables links to be made that otherwise might never happen.

The Cambridge Phenomenon, too, has its own ways of creating opportunities for serendipity and fortuitous meetings. The small size of Cambridge — even Greater Cambridge has a smaller total population than the number of people working in IT in Silicon Valley — means that people interact frequently in many different ways. The collegiate atmosphere of the University inevitably leaks out into the companies situated around it, not least because many of them hire Cambridge graduates or are founded by members of the University.

With the **Cambridge Network**, and the many smaller networking organizations that have grown up around it, the city also has a formal way of encouraging introductions across disciplines and sectors. The Cambridge Network in particular, with its diverse membership, is a key locus for generating the kinds of ideas and thinking that can only happen at the intersections between disciplines and sectors.

Above: Winners of the Cambridge University Entrepreneurs 2015 C R Lowe Carpe Diem Enterprise awards (left to right): Tim Guilliams, founder and CEO of Healx (Life Science Business of the Year), Philip Grayeski (Life Science Young Entrepreneur of the Year), Darrin Disley, CEO of Horizon Discovery, Simon Engelke (Technology Innovation, Social Media and Social Enterprise Young Entrepreneur of the Year), David Holden-White (Life Science Young Entrepreneur of the Year), Luana Bulat, CUE President 2014–2015.

Left: The POD Point.

Various reports and academic studies have explored the importance of these networks in the growth of the Cambridge Phenomenon, and all point to the number of encounters and links between people being key to building the kind of trust that enables people to go on and set up, or invest in, companies together. The Cambridge Network has been facilitating these connections since it was founded in 1998, organizing events, training, special interest groups and recruitment resources.

Many regard [the Cambridge Network] as having brought an unprecedented degree of interactivity and cohesiveness to the Phenomenon…The sort of initiative and involvement that the Cambridge Network represents is an indication of the Phenomenon's growing support structure and also the ways in which the need for more collaborative interaction is being addressed.

Rob Koepp, *Clusters of Creativity: Enduring Lessons on Innovation and Entrepreneurship from Silicon Valley and Europe's Silicon Fen*

There are over 1,000 corporate members of Cambridge Network, and they come from every sector, from materials to biotech and from cleantech to academe. Corporate members are also any size, from very small start-ups to global companies. The professional service organizations are well represented, too, a useful reminder to entrepreneurs that businesses need more than just good technology innovations.

Below: *Clare Ruskin, CEO of Cambridge Network.*

Below right: *Harriet Fear, CEO of One Nucleus.*

Networking in Cambridge is very good. We have a few people who participate in Cambridge Network's Learning Collaboration peer learning groups…I belong to its Cambridge Leaders Academy and that has been a great experience. The willingness of companies to share information and best practice is refreshing. Not many of us have competitors locally, so that enables us to share a lot of ideas.

Paul Larbey, CEO, Velocix, and President of Video Business, Alcatel-Lucent, *Cambridge Business* May 2015

One Nucleus is Europe's biggest private, not-for-profit membership organization for life sciences and healthcare. Around 60% of all UK biotech is located in the Cambridge–London corridor, and in the first ten months of 2014, this region received 40% of all investment in life sciences in the UK, so it is hardly surprising that One Nucleus, formed from the merger of the Eastern Region Biotechnology Initiative and the London Biotechnology Network, is such a success.

But members of One Nucleus are not limited to the Cambridge–London corridor, nor indeed to the UK, and membership is global, reflecting the desire of many outside the UK to access the sector here. And One Nucleus reaches out, too, collaborating with four top life science member organizations in the US, MassBio, MassMEDIC, Biocom and BayBio. Memoranda of Understanding with each of these organizations give One Nucleus' members access to a number of benefits in the US, and vice versa, and has already resulted in a number of events and exchanges. One Nucleus is also a member of the Council of European BioRegions and strategic partner in a European consortium to develop e-learning training tools for promoting international trade, e-learning for Life Science Internationalisation, eLSi.

One Nucleus runs the UK's largest group purchasing scheme, saving its members some £4 million a year, an important benefit for start-ups who want to use every penny on growing their business proposition.

Andy Harter, Chairman of the Cambridge Network and co-founder and CEO of RealVNC, identified that, while there may supposedly be six degrees of separation between two individuals, in Cambridge, the networking ecosystem is so efficient that there are only two steps between anyone with a good idea and the person who can help them make that idea happen.

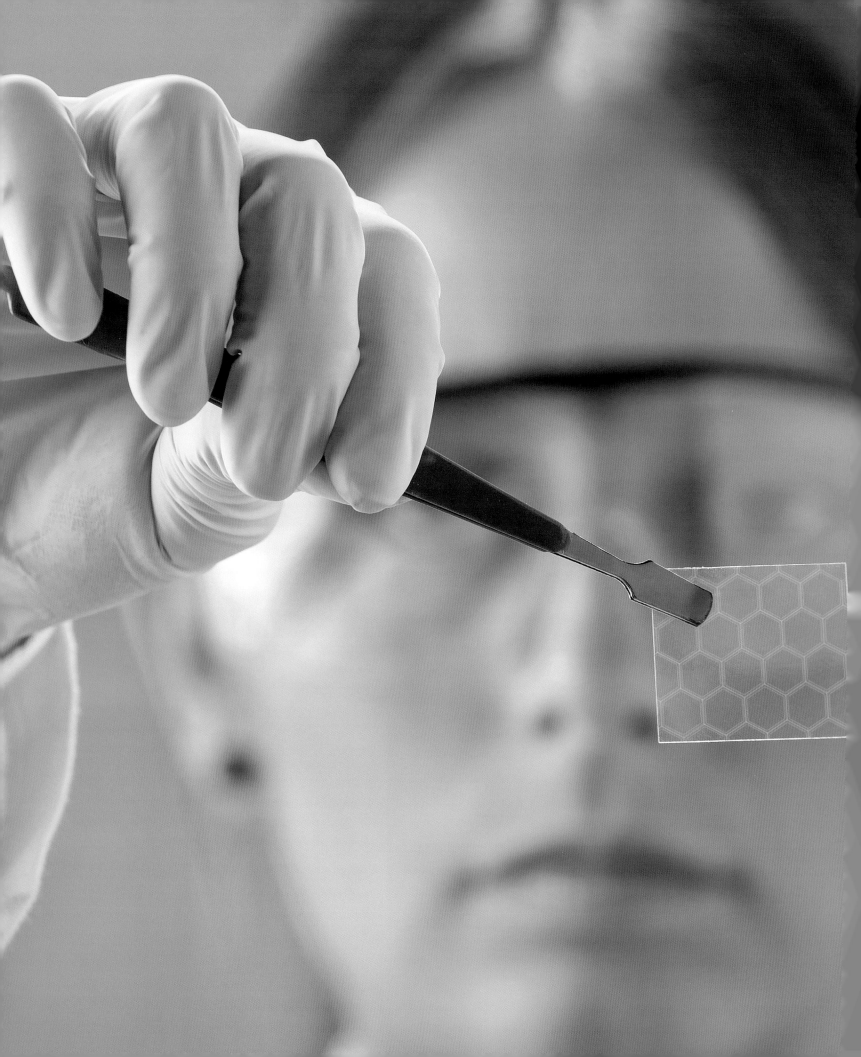

TRANSFORMING THE FUTURE

We've already seen in this book how many Cambridge companies and institutions have embarked on innovations and research that have transformed our lives – from the first computers to smartphones, from gene sequencing to personalised medicines, and from Bluetooth to satellite communications. But things are by no means slowing down in Cambridge. If anything, they're speeding up as more fields open up to the entrepreneurs, scientists and companies who thrive in this hotbed of innovation. With waves of exciting new developments taking place in Cambridge, we will see a continuing contribution to advances helping individuals and societies around the world to enjoy healthier, safer, more productive and stimulating lives. Without raising any hostages to fortune, here are a few areas where Cambridge is at the forefront of the new technologies and leading the way into the future.

Graphene is just one of the transformative technologies currently being developed in the Cambridge Cluster.

LIFE SCIENCES AND HEALTHCARE

Over hundreds of years, medical breakthroughs have resulted in treatments, palliatives and occasionally cures for many, but by no means all, common diseases and health problems. Since the start of this millennium, efforts have intensified to address the health needs of people around the world, but until recently, the result has been a lottery in which the remedies available may work for some people but are ineffective for others. Today, there is an increasing chance that there is a solution for more people across an ever-widening range of defined medical needs. It is realistic to believe that round the corner is the solution that will work for each individual, regardless of their health needs, whoever they may be, whatever their age, and wherever they may live.

In Cambridge, huge strides are expected in the fields of digital healthcare, gene therapy, stem and other cell-based therapies, gene editing, epigenetics, liquid biopsies, monoclonal antibodies, immuno-oncology and rare diseases, which will deliver benefits for a significant proportion of the population.

Digital healthcare combines medicine with advances in computing, big data analytics, mobile communications and sensors. It creates the rich ongoing longitudinal profile of data on an individual that will be the baseline against which all future medical diagnoses and interventions are made, and will be the backdrop for the personalization of medicine. The major investment into the EPIC e-hospital system at Addenbrooke's Hospital positions Cambridge in the vanguard in this space in the UK.

Chronic conditions such as heart disease, diabetes, neuropsychiatric and neurodegenerative disorders, obesity and lifestyle challenges such as cessation of smoking can very often be better managed, with technology such as remote patient monitoring, telehealth and apps that encourage lifestyle modification, helping to make early diagnosis, treatment and prevention widely accessible at a fraction of current costs. Owlstone, Congenica, Ieso Digital Health and Cambridge Cognition are just some of the Cambridge companies already making an impact in digital healthcare.

Genetic engineering continues to advance. The latest significant development is a new technology called CRISPR (Clustered Regularly Interspaced Short Palindromic Repeats) which provides an easy, cheap, and very precise way to 'edit'

Above: *Huge strides are expected in the field of digital healthcare in Cambridge in the coming years.*

Right: *Evonetix intends to do for DNA synthesis what Solexa (now Illumina) did for DNA sequencing.*

the DNA of living cells. Early applications include genetically modified mosquitos that not only resist malaria, but spread this resistance to other mosquitos. In a few years, assuming the ethical questions can be resolved, we will see this technique applied to plants, animals and humans. In humans, it has the potential to address rare genetic disorders such as haemophilia, sickle cell anaemia and other inborn errors of metabolism. Horizon Discovery is one of the Cambridge-based companies leading initiatives in this area.

Epigenetics involves the understanding and exploitation of biological mechanisms that switch genes on and off, and particularly changes to the genome that do not affect the primary nucleotide base sequence. Cambridge Epigenetix, co-founded by Shankar Balasubramanian (a founder of gene sequencing company Solexa), is one of the early providers of epigenetic tools that are easy to use and will assist the spread and application of this fast-moving area of molecular biology.

Liquid biopsy is a less invasive way of detecting cancer than tissue biopsy, and uses a simple blood, or other body fluid, test. It promises early detection and also classifies patients so that their likely response to a particular treatment can be determined. Inivata, a spin-out from the Rosenfield Lab at Cancer Research UK's Cambridge centre, is pioneering the use of circulating tumour DNA analysis to improve personalized healthcare in oncology.

Human monoclonal antibodies, which resulted from scientific breakthroughs in Cambridge, account for one third of all new treatments. These now include therapeutic products for breast cancer, leukemia, asthma, arthritis, psoriasis and transplant rejection, and dozens more that are in late-stage clinical trials which address a current global market of $75 billion. One of the most exciting new companies in this space is Kymab, which received $90 million in funding in 2015 and has the ambition and potential to be another Cambridge world-leader.

The application of human monoclonal antibodies and biologics therapies in immuno-oncology is another key area with the potential to deliver very significant patient benefits. This approach recognizes that the immune system has a key role in controlling cancer, and increasingly immunotherapies can unleash the immune system to kill tumours. It has been described as the ultimate in personalized medicine, and current applications address skin, lung, liver and blood cancers. Medimmune, part of AstraZeneca, is one of the leading companies in this rapidly evolving field.

The Cambridge Rare Disease Network was established in 2015 and the Wellcome Genome Campus ran its tenth annual meeting on this subject in 2016. Rare diseases are defined as those affecting fewer than five people in 10,000. Although individually rare, there are more than 7,000 such diseases and together it is estimated that 350 million people worldwide are affected. Rare diseases are an underfunded field of research but sufferers, 75% of whom are children, deserve the attention of more healthcare specialists to improve their survival, quality of life and the prospect of cures. Healx employs data analytics, machine learning and modern computational biology techniques to identify novel drug applications and candidates in the area of rare diseases.

Richard Feynman said: 'What I cannot create, I do not understand.' Synthetic biology is trying to do this for biology, and Cambridge companies like Evonetix, a spin-out from Cambridge Consultants, is intending to do for DNA synthesis what Solexa (now Illumina) did for DNA sequencing. This will open a new chapter in our understanding of life as we start to produce and use biological building blocks to see how it works. Synthetic biology could create a global market of over $35 billion by 2020.

COMPUTING AND TELECOMMUNICATIONS

We are approaching the limits of Moore's Law – the rate of advance in computing power and speed – as the features on silicon semiconductors are becoming so small that quantum effects are coming into play. One solution is to use these quantum effects to design a new class of computers, which have the potential to be orders of magnitude faster than today's supercomputers. Cambridge Quantum Computing is one of the entrants in this new technology.

Machine learning is iterative and allows computers to find hidden insights without being explicitly programmed where to look, producing reliable, repeatable decisions and results. It is not a new science – but is one that's gaining fresh momentum, particularly with the expansion of interest in big data. Fields as different as genomics, cyber security, banking, health and retail all produce vast amounts of data, and understanding that data is critical. Microsoft Research in Cambridge collaborates with the University of Cambridge Machine Learning Group to advance machine learning and our understanding – and use – of big data.

Machine learning is also an important enabler of the latest method for data entry in computing devices – voice recognition. Data entry has evolved from paper tape, punch cards and keyboards to voice control, and we can expect voice control to become much more widespread in the future for tasks such as ordering tickets and retail items on line, controlling the home environment, operating televisions, etc. Apple's rumoured acquisition of VocalIQ is an indicator of the attraction of Cambridge technology in this field. Evi, a Cambridge company that was acquired by Amazon last year, contributed to the development of the Amazon Echo, one of the most talked-about new products. It uses beam-forming microphones to pick up the user's voice from across the room, and the software enables it to answer questions or obey commands. Voice is fast becoming the ubiquitous interface to the Internet of Things.

According to ARM, one of the leaders in the rapidly evolving Internet of Things (IoT), devices and services delivering end-to-end solutions will be the key functions of IoT. The potential is enormous, and it is interoperability between nodes and cloud services across market segments that will unleash the full potential of the IoT. Although the IoT market is made up of many vertical segments, most applications that can make use of internet-connected devices have a common foundation. For example, smart cities, wearables and smart home devices require basic operating system functionality such as drivers, device security and provisioning support. And while network connectivity varies from application to application, in general the IP networking, security, application layer and device management needs are all common, whether over wired or wireless connections. More controversially, a parallel Internet of People (IoP) linking wearable sensors and healthcare management systems is beginning to appear on the horizon.

Our daily lives, the economy, and national security depend on stable, safe and resilient cyber security, which will only become more important as more devices become connected to the internet and IoT grows. Darktrace, a fast-growing cyber defence company, is backed by Mike Lynch's Invoke Capital. Lynch was the co-founder of one of Cambridge's most successful companies, Autonomy, which was acquired by HP in 2011, and his involvement represents how experienced entrepreneurs maintain a forward focus.

Another area where computing is playing an important role in innovation is in the funding of private companies. Funding has seen rapid changes recently as traditional venture capital has retreated to 'safer' later stage investing and an increasing share of early stage funding is now coming from private individuals. Angel investing and crowdfunding, supported by tax incentives, have taken on a major role. Financial technology, or FinTech, companies use technology to make financial services more efficient. Many of these companies are start-ups founded with the purpose of disrupting incumbent financial systems and corporations that rely less on software. Crowdfunding company Syndicate Room recently became a member of the London Stock Exchange, taking its disruption of the funding model one step further as it now offers small investors access to IPOs that are more normally the preserve of large and institutional investors.

The Amazon Echo includes voice recognition technology from Cambridge company Evi.

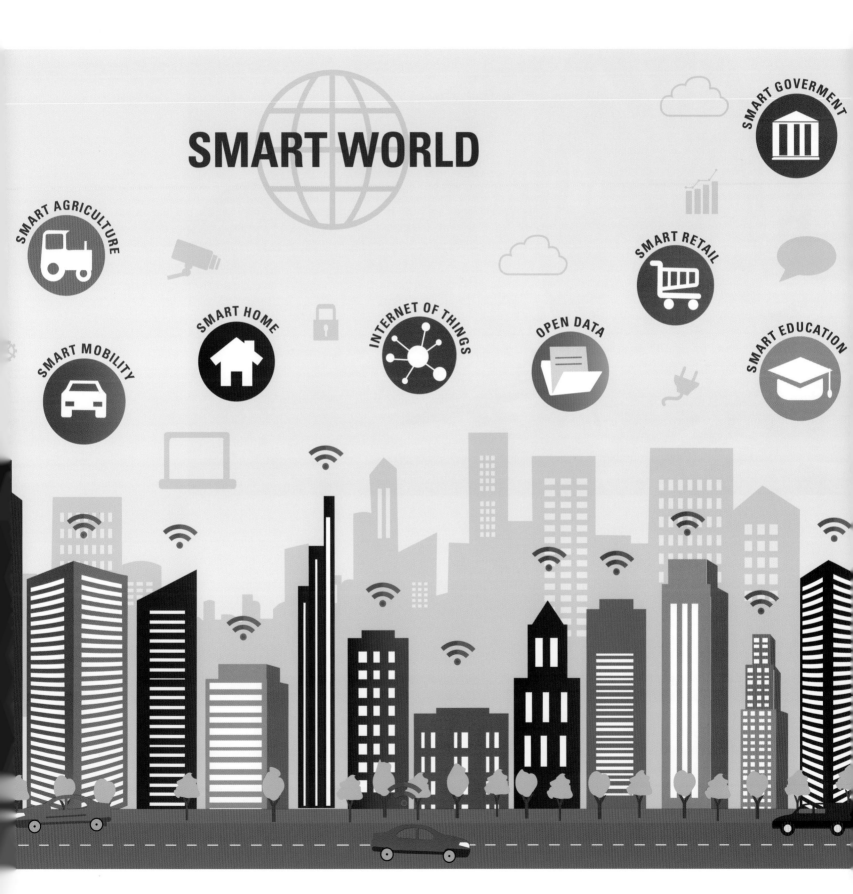

Left: JDR Cables develops subsea power cables for the offshore energy industry.

OTHER TECHNOLOGIES

Innovative welding techniques and novel adhesives are two key areas of expertise in the Cambridge Phenomenon that will continue to advance as new materials are developed and new requirements to join them emerge. TWI, originally The Welding Institute and founded in 1923, is the leading international organization for welding and joining professionals. It continues to pioneer ways of joining metals and non-metals.

Cambridge has been a leader in synthetic adhesives and composites since Norman de Bruyne founded Aero Research in 1934 to research their use for aircraft construction. Now Hexcel, the original Duxford site is still the home of breakthroughs in composites technology that benefit the world of aerospace and other high performance industries, including automotive and wind energy. Composites have revolutionized the way that aircraft like the Airbus and Boeing Dreamliner are designed and built, and there is ample promise of more to come from Hexcel.

JDR Cables is a very different company in the joining business. It designs, develops, manufactures, deploys

and manages subsea umbilicals and power cables for the offshore energy industry. Future supplies of oil, gas and electrical power will depend on their innovations.

Graphene is an extremely exciting new material and is receiving a lot of attention around the world for its strength and electrical properties. The Cambridge Graphene Centre is engaged in research, and Cambridge Nanosystems is supplying high volumes of ultra-high-quality graphene products which will benefit companies around the world.

Precision agriculture is beginning to parallel precision medicine and has the ability to improve the efficiency and sustainability of agricultural practices. As we saw on pages 162–3, there is a long tradition of agricultural research in Cambridge, and while the sector is relatively small at the moment, NIAB, Agri-Tech East, KisanHub and others are part of a growing resurgence in this important area.

STUDENT ENTREPRENEURSHIP

The vitality of the Cambridge University Entrepreneurs (CUE) business plan competition, and the range of prizes, gives a good indication of the continued and growing enthusiasm for entrepreneurship among the next generation in Cambridge. The 2015 top prize-winners were Sinclair Fire (Science and Technology), Madanyu (Social Enterprise), Converge (Software). Healx (CR Lowe Carpe Diem Enterprise 'Life Science Business of the Year') and Cambridge Cardiology (CUE Angel Prize). The range of winners, from a novel fire detector for the home to a computer education extension programme in India and drug repurposing for rare diseases, demonstrate the breadth and depth of what is bubbling under in Cambridge.

The next generation is also working actively to extend the reach of Cambridge's entrepreneurial and collaborative mindset.

The Innovation Forum, co-founded by a group of Cambridge doctoral students in 2012, aims at making things happen across the intersections between academia, industry and government policy, and also across national boundaries. The Innovation Forum network has already grown to over 10,000 individuals and has 14 branches in nine countries, including China, Japan, Spain and the USA. The popularity of the two Innovation Leaders Conferences organized by the Forum to date suggest that it is an idea whose time has come.

These are just some of the areas and ways in which the Cambridge Phenomenon is continuing to supply the world with innovations that have the potential to change lives for the better. Transforming the future is the modus operandi for Cambridge.

Below: *Innovation Forum at the Cambridge Judge Business School.*

*A photograph of the aurora shared by ESA astronaut Tim Peake,
taken from the International Space Station in January 2016.*

PLATINUM

ARM
Astex Pharmaceuticals
AstraZeneca
Barclays
Cambridge Consultants
Cambridge Enterprise
Cambridge Innovation Capital
Cambridge Judge Business School
Cambridge Network
Cantab Capital Partners LLP
Domino Printing Sciences plc
Greater Cambridge Greater Peterborough
    Enterprise Partnership (LEP)
Horizon Discovery Group
Innovation Forum
Johnson & Johnson Innovation
Marshall of Cambridge
MedImmune
Mundipharma International Limited
Oak Investment Partners
PA Consulting
RealVNC
S-Tech
St John's Innovation Centre
TTP Group

GOLD

Adder Technology
Arecor Ltd
Babraham Research Campus
Bailey Fisher Executive Search
Berenberg
Bidwells
Cambridge Business Travel
Cambridge Wireless
Congenica
Grosvenor Developments Ltd
Illumina
IP Group
Kleinwort Benson
Kymab
Mills & Reeve LLP
MISSION Therapeutics Ltd
Money Mover
Parkwalk Advisors
PwC
Qatalyst Partners
Qualcomm
Schlumberger
SQW
SyndicateRoom
Taylor Wessing
TWI Ltd
Virata

Kleinwort Benson

pwc

TaylorWessing

kymab

MILLS & REEVE

Virata

Schlumberger

M NEY
M VER

SQW

SILVER

Abcam
Dr. Andy Richards CBE
Audio Analytic
Bango
Birketts
Brookgate
Cambridge Ahead
MPhil in Bioscience Enterprise (MBE)
Cambridge Capital Group
Cofinitive
Cognidox
Deloitte
DisplayLink
Fauna & Flora International
Global Inkjet Systems
Hexcel Composites Ltd
Howard Group
Imperial Innovations
KisanHub
One Nucleus
Owlstone
RAND Europe
Savills
Ubisense

LIST OF SUBSCRIBERS

Robert Alston

Argon Design Ltd

Gary Atkinson

John Biggs

Roz Bird

Jonathan Brech

Rhys Bury

CAM Trade Marks & IP Services, Cambridge

Charles Chadwyck-Healey

Charlotte Cooper

Ann Cotton

Claire Cotton

Gareth Cotton

Helen Cotton

James Cotton

Peter Cowley

Pierre-Arnoul de Marneffe

Michael A. Elliott

Marshall Evans

Roderick Evans

Stuart Evans

Thelma Evans

Shaun Fitzgerald, Breathing Buildings

Adam Jollans

Dr Soraya Jones

Dr J.W. King

Vinay Kishore

Henk Koopmans

Bridget Langridge

Guido F. Mengelkamp

Marilyn Morris

Roberts Paeglis

Pete Paglia

Debajyoti Pal

Prima Electronics

Clem Robertson

Chris Shore

John Souter

David Thomas

Dr Walter Tuttlebee OBE

John Vandore

Miranda Weston-Smith

David Wong

INDEX

Italics denotes an illustration

ACKNOWLEDGEMENTS

This book has been a massive collective effort, from the good folks at Mills & Reeve hosting our early morning Advisory Board meetings, to our patient spouses who lived and breathed this project almost as much as we did.

Our Advisory Board (listed on page 10) have been exemplary at challenging and probing what is and what isn't impact, and what is and what isn't Cambridge. They have pointed us in a few directions where we might not have thought to look, and pointed out why not everything that comes out of Cambridge is world-beating, however much we would like it to be. Their rigour has been welcome, but we must confirm that any residual errors or omissions are entirely our own.

Cambridge is a very supportive place for technology businesses, and also a very supportive place for slightly off-the-wall projects such as this, so in addition to our Advisory Board, we have had help and advice from numerous others involved in a variety of ways with the Cambridge Phenomenon. Too numerous to mention, as always, but Catherine Condie of TWI supplied more wonderful photos than we could use, Rowena Gardner of MedImmune had some very helpful comments, and Sarah Fell of the Institute of Manufacturing also provided some useful pointers. Phil O'Donovan, co-founder of CSR, had so many ideas that he has sown the seeds of another book, and Alan Davidson has filled a few gaps with his – as always – wonderful photography. We are also very grateful to James Cotton and his team at Onespacemedia for their concepts and original ideas for the website which supports the book.

There isn't space to list all the Cambridge entrepreneurs, academics and CEOs we interviewed as the book developed, but over 100 of them were generous with their time and ideas, and we are immensely grateful to them.

The team at Third Millennium, now part of Profile Books, have once again been wonderful to work with, and wonderfully patient as the project has evolved. It has been a pleasure to see *The Cambridge Phenomenon: Global Impact* taking shape under their watchful eyes, and the end result is a fitting celebration of what Cambridge does best.

Kate Kirk and Charles Cotton

PICTURE CREDITS

Every effort has been made to contact the copyright holders of all images featured in this book. In the case of an inadvertent omission, please contact the publisher.

114–115 from l–r Cambridge Consultants, PA Consulting, TTP, Sagentia
116–117, 118, 120 both Cambridge Consultants
117 Iridium Communications Inc.
119 Sun Pharmaceuticals
121tr Hoppier
121br InstantWild
123t Drayson Technologies
123b Ora
124b PA Consulting
124–125 © Land Rover BAR/Mark Lloyd
125b Unilever
126–127 all Sagentia
128 Scalextric
129t Sagentia/Mars Drinks
129b Aqualisa
130–131, 132 TTP
133 TTP/Tonejet
134l 42 Technology
134–135 Reaction Engines/42 Technology
135b Linde Group/4 Technology
136l Telensa
136b ProFibrix/Team Consulting
136r OrganOx/Team Consulting
15b, 138–139, 140, 141, 142 Domino
143 both PragmatIC Printing
144 Xaar

144–145 Martens Brouwerij/Xaar
146–149 Babraham Institute
149 both Max Alexander
150–151 BDP
151tr Science & Society Picture Library/SSPL/Getty Images
151b Cavendish Laboratory
152–153 Institute for Manufacturing
154 both The Laboratory of Molecular Biology
156–159 TWI
160–161
161 Biodata Innovation Centre
162–163 from l–r Marshall Group, Michel de Nijs/iStock, Meridian Audio, Cambridge Satchel Company
14l, 165–167, 168b Marshall Group (contains public sector information licensed under the Open Government License v3.0)
169t © Vestas Wind Systems A/S
169b e-Go
170b Agri-Tech East
171 NIAB
172 Arcam
173r Meridian Audio
174l G7th Ltd
174r Cambridge Satchel Company
175 Hotel Chocolat

176–177 Flower Valley Conservation Trust/Slingshot Media
178l Toby Smith/CCI
178–179 Sir Cam @camdiary/CCI
179t Robert Acaster
179t Juan Pablo Moreiras/FFI
179b Erik Hammar/FFI
180 Jeremy Holden/FFI
181–182 Camfed
183t Bryn Colton/Getty Images
183b Cambridge Innovation Capital
184–185 TechCrunch Disrupt 2015
185t © Diane Auckland/Fotohaus
186t, 186–187 Breathing Buildings
186b James Dyson Building
187t Cambridge Enterprise
12–13, 188–189, 199 both Innovation Forum
189t SimPrints
189b Accelerate Cambridge
190b POD Point
190–191 CUE
191l Cambridge Network
191r One Nucleus
192–193 BONNINSTUDIO/Shutterstock
195 Cambridge Antibodies Technologies
198 JDR Cables
221 Jo Anthony Photography

 ADDER

 Bailey Fisher
Executive Search

 Cambridge Innovation Capital

DEFINING THE FUTURE | GREATER CAMBRIDGE GREATER PETERBOROUGH ENTERPRISE PARTNERSHIP

 MISS Therapeu

 Arecor

 BARCLAYS

 UNIVERSITY OF CAMBRIDGE
Judge Business School

 GROSVENOR

 Johnson & Johnson
INNOVATION

 M M

 ARM

 BERENBERG
PARTNERSHIP SINCE 1590

 Cambridge Network

 horizon

 Kleinwort Bens

 astex
pharmaceuticals

 BIDWELLS

 CW CAMBRIDGE WIRELESS

illumina

kymab

mund

AstraZeneca

 CBT
Business Travel

 CANTAB
CAPITAL PARTNERS

 Innovation.
FORUM

 Marshall

 OA INVE PART

 Cambridge Consultants

 CONGENICA
GENOME BASED MEDICINE

 MedImmune
A member of the AstraZeneca Group

 Babraham Research Campus

UNIVERSITY OF CAMBRIDGE
enterprise

DOMINO

 ipgroup

 MILLS & REEVE

CON TECH INN